Michael Palumbo's previous books, *The Palestinian Catastrophe* and *The Waldheim Files*, have both attracted widespread attention and debate, establishing him as one of the most meticulous and balanced of contemporary historians. *Imperial Israel* is his most important book yet.

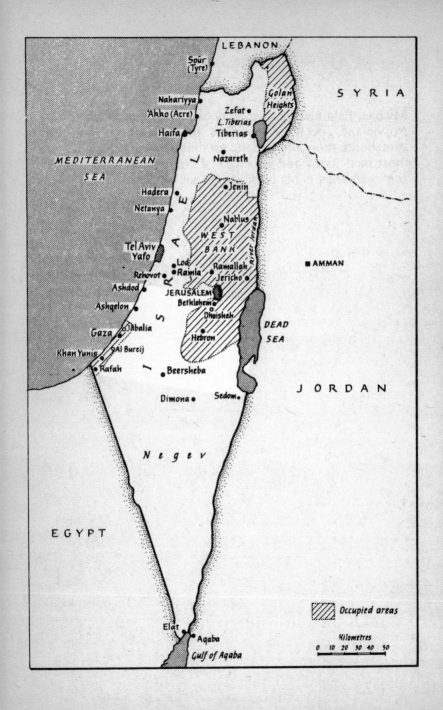

LEBANON

Sour
(Tyre)

Nahariyya
'Akko (Acre)
Haifa

MEDITERRANEAN
SEA

Zefat
L. Tiberias
Tiberias

Golan
Heights

SYRIA

Nazareth

Hadera
Netanya

Jenin

Nablus

WEST
BANK

River Jordan

Tel Aviv
Yafo
Lod
Rehovot   Ramla
Ashdod
Ashqelon

JERUSALEM
Bethlehem

Ramallah
Jericho

AMMAN

Dheisheh

DEAD
SEA

Gaza   Jabalia
Khan Yunis   Al Bureij
Rafah

Hebron

Beersheba

Dimona

Sedom

JORDAN

N e g e v

EGYPT

Occupied areas

Kilometres
0 10 20 30 40 50

Elat
Aqaba
Gulf of Aqaba

Imperial Israel

The History of the Occupation of the West Bank and Gaza

Michael Palumbo

BLOOMSBURY

To Helene

May there be peace in the Middle East
when you are old enough to read this book.

First published in Great Britain 1990
This revised paperback edition first published 1992
Copyright © Michael Palumbo 1990, 1992

The moral right of the author has been asserted

Bloomsbury Publishing Ltd, 2 Soho Square, London W1V 5DE

A CIP catalogue record for this book
is available from the British Library

ISBN 0 7475 0101 7

Phototypeset by Falcon Typographic Art Ltd
Edinburgh
Printed in Great Britain
by Cox & Wyman Ltd, Reading, Berkshire

Contents

Acknowledgements

Thanks go to Marilla B. Guptil, deputy director of the UN Archives; Rima Bordcosh, reference director of the UN Library; Martin Elzy, of the Carter Center in Atlanta, Georgia; the staff of the Lehman Library at Columbia University; the Jewish Division of the New York Public Library; and Saleh A. Fawaz of the Palestine Aid Society.

The author received no subsidy or financial assistance from any source during the preparation and research for this book.

PROLOGUE

I stood gazing in amazement at the Tel Aviv shop window. In New York I had seen Jewish New Year cards before, but this one was well beyond my experience and indeed my imagination. On the front was a picture of Moshe Dayan, the hero of the 1967 war which had been fought three years earlier. Flanking him on one side was a tank and on the other a jet fighter. Both weapons of war were belching fire, which was coloured red. Could it be possible, I thought to myself, that this is the way Israelis greet each other during their most solemn holy season?

Such was my impression of Israel in that autumn of 1970. I was visiting the country as a tourist, but my stay there was to be one of the major educational experiences of my life. Like most Americans in those days, I accepted the image of Israel as a country founded by determined Holocaust survivors who were bravely attempting to build a nation despite being surrounded by sinister and treacherous Arabs. As things turned out, little of what I saw reflected the image portrayed by the American media.

A visitor to Israel is constantly seeing reminders that he is in a garrison state; evidence of the military is everywhere. On a local bus I sat next to a soldier who was carrying an automatic rifle. I could not help noticing that he held the weapon in such a position that the muzzle pointed directly at the base of my skull – this was particularly disturbing since the bus kept bouncing up and down. Traffic mishaps are common in Israel, which has one of the highest accident rates in the world; I kept thinking that with one jolt my

1

neighbour's gun could go off and bring my visit to a sudden halt. I mentioned my concern to the young soldier. He smiled and pulled a lever on his rifle. 'Oh, don't worry,' he said, 'the safety catch is on now.'

Before coming to Israel I had always thought of Jews as being reasonable, restrained people who tended to avoid violent confrontation. But the personal aggressiveness of the Israelis often shocked me. There was also much else about the Jewish state that I found surprising.

The attitude of Israelis toward foreign Jews was quite different from what I had expected. Because of my New York accent as well as my name (which is of Italian origin but is also common among Sephardic Jews) I was invariably taken for an American Jew, a class of people about whom, I soon learned, Israelis have intensely mixed feelings. Particularly disliked are American Jews who display a great deal of wealth. No one, of course, likes the rich relative on whom one is dependent. Besides, many Israelis believe that foreign Jews are 'Hebrews second class' because the true place for all Jews is the Zionist homeland.

Young foreign Jewish men are resented, since many Israelis feel that they should be in the IDF (Israeli Defence Force) helping to defend the Jewish state. Most Israeli youth consider American Jews their own age to be effete, bookish, money-grubbing and therefore worthy of contempt. Everywhere I went in Israel in 1970 I encountered hostility from young Israeli men who thought I was an American Jew. At the hotel where I was staying I noticed that the young Israeli staff treated the other guests, who were almost all Scandinavian, with considerable courtesy. There was, however, more than a little hostility directed against me. I had made friends with a tour guide from Scandinavia, a German Jew named David who had fled to Sweden during the Holocaust; he was a frequent visitor to Israel and knew the hotel staff well. I told him of my problem and he noticed the antagonism towards me. One evening, David called over several of the staff who had treated me with discourtesy. He told them: 'Mike is an American but he is not Jewish. His family came from Italy.' They shook my hand, and to my amazement were friendly

2

to me after that. To this day I find it ironic that American Jews contribute so generously to a country where they are so cordially disliked.

But despite their resentment Israelis clearly feel a kinship with foreign Jews, whom they regard as potential immigrants to their country. It is of course towards the Palestinians that Israelis direct their real hatred. Before my trip, I had met a Jewish American woman who had lived in Israel for some time. She spoke of a social system in which Sabras (Jews born in Israel) ranked highest, followed by American Jews, European Jews, Middle Eastern Jews and North African Jews in descending order of status. I asked about the Arabs. 'Oh, they don't count for anything,' she replied. As the woman was somewhat arrogant and not particularly bright, I did not take her remarks too seriously. But once in Israel, I realized that she had not exaggerated in the least.

My most memorable experience on that trip (aside from the antics of some of the young Scandinavians in my hotel, which is part of another story) was a tour of Jerusalem and the West Bank that I took along with a bus full of English-speaking tourists, most of whom were American Jews. As an experienced traveller I usually avoid guided tours, but there really is so much to see in Israel that I assumed the unaccustomed role of tourist. Our guide, Yossi, was an Israeli veteran of the 1948 'War of Independence' whose blunt and highly opinionated style frequently offended the sensibilities of many people in the group, and typified the attitude of so many of his countrymen towards the Palestinians.

The tour began at the Wailing Wall, an important site for Jews who observe their faith. Yossi criticized the people whom we found renting the sacred objects required for the ritual prayers. Indeed all over the Holy Land there are numerous examples of the cheap commercialization of Jewish, Moslem and Christian holy places. No one could really disagree with our guide's outspoken remarks about the hawkers and vendors who degraded the most sacred spot in the Jewish world. But while respectful of Jewish holy places, Yossi displayed an obvious lack of consideration for Islamic sites.

At the Dome on the Rock, the major Moslem shrine which stands above the Wailing Wall, our guide was reproached by an Arab guard who admonished him for his boisterous and disrespectful remarks. The American tourists were surprised by Yossi's contemptuous attitude. One American told the guide that it was simply good manners to respect holy places of all religions. Yossi replied that during the 1948 war Arab troops had fired at Jews from the Dome on the Rock, and that therefore it was no holy place to him. Besides, he said, this was his country and he didn't have to take orders from an Arab.

Without expressing an opinion on the American's remarks, I jokingly told Yossi in private that it wasn't wise to argue with a customer.

'Oh, him,' he said. 'He doesn't know what he's talking about. He isn't a Jew and shouldn't interfere in what doesn't concern him.'

Were there any other non-Jews in the tour group? I asked.

Yossi turned to me. 'No, he is the only one,' he said. 'I can always tell a Jew.'

I recalled the scene in the movie *Exodus*, where Paul Newman, playing an Israeli disguised as a British officer, is assured by an anti-Semitic British officer (Peter Lawford) that he can always recognize a Jew.

After our morning tour of Jerusalem our group spent the afternoon visiting the West Bank, which had been occupied by Israel in the 1967 war. We drove for what seemed like hours to some desolate location so that Yossi could point out what we were told were Jewish ruins that proved that the West Bank had been continuously inhabited by Jews. Unlike some of the other tourists, I was not impressed, but I lacked the courage to ask how many Christian and Moslem artifacts could be found in the same area.

More noteworthy than the questionable archaeological dig was the dramatic scenery. As a non-believer I found no religious significance in the numerous ruins and artifacts, but their historical value was obvious. Here Phoenicians, Romans and Babylonians, to name only a few, had lived, fought and died. But it was hard for me to believe that in the late twentieth

century people would lay claim to a country on the evidence of
a two-thousand-year-old vase or an inscription which only a
handful of scholars could read. Surely this was not sufficient
reason to displace an indigenous population that had lived
on this land for centuries?

On our tour of the West Bank we saw very few of the
local inhabitants. We visited no Arab towns, nor were the
Palestinians ever mentioned. I was just beginning to wonder
if there really were Arabs in the occupied territories when our
bus overtook a local bus crowded with Palestinians. The contrast between our modern vehicle and the dilapidated Arab
bus was remarkable. I glanced at the faces of the Arab passengers as they passed by my window, and wondered what they
thought of us who were making a selective tour of their country in such comfort. My unspoken question was answered by
an old man seated in the rear of the Arab bus. As he passed,
he gave us an internationally recognized hand signal which
made it obvious that the Palestinians did not appreciate the
benefits of 'history's most humane occupation'.

That first trip to Israel in 1970 planted in me seeds of doubt
about the wisdom of America's unquestioned support of
Israel. Some years later I began a study of the exodus of the
Palestinians during the 1948 war from what became the State
of Israel.[1] In the UN Archives in New York I found reports
by neutral observers which clearly indicated that many of the
Palestinians had been expelled from their homes in 1948 at
the point of a gun. It was in order to check Israeli archives
for that book that in 1986 I made my second trip to Israel.

Although my purpose was to conduct historical research, I
could not help noticing the contemporary situation in Israel.
On the El-Al plane, along with the in-flight movie we were
shown a documentary describing life in Israel. One of the epi-
sodes dealt with IDF veterans who, because of the economic
situation, were forced to take menial jobs 'usually reserved
for Arabs'. The clear implication was that Arabs in Israel, like
blacks in South Africa, were considered inferior creatures fit
only to do unclean work that was too degrading for Israelis.
The only sympathy in the film was for the unlucky Jews,

who had been reduced to the level of a race destined to be 'hewers of wood and drafters of water for the House of our Lord'. In America many blacks and Hispanics work in menial jobs, but there are government programmes that encourage minorities to move into middle-class employment. I wondered how many Americans, if they knew the facts, would approve giving $3 billion a year to a government that enforced a kind of apartheid.

But when I arrived in the country I also noticed many features of Israeli life that were obviously praiseworthy. There was certainly a thriving free press serving a highly literate public. As a foreign scholar, I was treated with considerable respect by both fellow professionals and the general population. Of course I was careful not to be too specific as to the subject of my research. Everyone seemed pleased that I was writing a book on the 1948 'War of Independence', but I doubted that they would have appreciated a study of the expulsion of the Palestinians from their homes during that conflict.

In the course of my research I had a chance once again to visit the West Bank, including Hebron, a town well known as the epicentre of the conflict between the extremist 'settlers' and the indigenous population. One had only to glance at the faces of the Arabs in Hebron to see that foreigners were not welcome. As I walked through the streets, the tension was thick enough to cut with a knife. Hebron was a convenient stopover on my way back to Jerusalem from Sede Boqer in the Negev Desert, where I had done research at the Ben-Gurion archives. I had been told that the Hebron area was a good place to buy souvenirs that would be cheaper than in Jerusalem; but the attitude of the local population made it clear that Hebron was no resort.

The principal reason for Palestinian resentment was not too difficult to spot. On the outskirts of the town, Zionist 'settlers' had built an enclave they called Kiryat Arba. Under the leadership of Rabbi Moshe Levinger the Jewish zealots had penetrated into the heart of Arab Hebron, forcing a confrontation in a town known for its devotion to Islam and antipathy towards Jews. Indeed there had been a brutal massacre of Jews there in 1929.

As we drove through the town I saw Hadassah House, which had been occupied by Rabbi Levinger's followers; the building defiantly flew an Israeli flag, throwing down the gauntlet to the Arab population of the town. Even more alarming was the sight of a Jewish school surrounded by barbed wire and armed guards. In order to provoke the Hebronites, the settlers bussed their children from Kiryat Arba to attend school in the heart of a town seething with hatred for Israelis. What kind of people were these, I thought, who would use their children as pawns, indeed as possible targets, in the quest to 'Judaize' the West Bank?

With an Israeli friend I visited a shop set up by the settlers to sell souvenirs to tourists. Most of the articles were of surprisingly poor workmanship, overpriced and commemorating exclusively Jewish themes. Clearly these items were designed to appeal to visitors who shared the goals of 'Eretz Yisrael' (Greater Israel).

Even more depressing than Hebron was the sight of the refugee camps in the West Bank. The workers returning to their hovels from their jobs in Israel reminded me of South African blacks coming home to their dingy 'townships' after a long day of menial labour in the white cities. How infuriating it must be for these Palestinians to see Jews living in comfort in former Arab homes in Jaffa, Haifa, Lydda and so many other towns and villages in Israel from which they or their parents had been expelled at gunpoint in 1948.

In the course of my research I found a constantly recurring social pattern which virtually amounted to a caste system. The administrators and historians in most archives were often Jews of European descent, while the clerks were usually Jews of Middle Eastern origin. Custodial help was frequently composed of 'Israeli Arabs', the descendants of the Palestinian minority who for various reasons were not expelled from the State of Israel in 1948. At the bottom were the workers from the West Bank and Gaza who carried out the rubbish or performed similar tasks. Few Israelis seemed to be particularly concerned with the social structure of their country. Indeed, when they did express an opinion it sounded a lot different from the moderate, humane sentiments typically attributed to them by the American media.

Most memorable was my encounter with a Jewish convert to Christianity who occupied his time attempting to spread the word of Jesus to his former co-religionists in Jerusalem. Like everyone else, he automatically assumed that I was a Jew and therefore believed I required his particular brand of 'Jews for Jesus' redemption. I usually ignore street corner prophets, but this fellow had provided me with excellent directions so I felt obliged to listen.

I soon became bored with his clap-trap (he hated Roman Catholics – especially, for some reason, Mother Theresa) and I changed the subject to politics. This Jewish-Christian zealot rationalized the expulsions of 1948 and the eventual removal of the Arabs from the West Bank on the grounds that, since the Jews developed the land, they had a right to push out the indigenous Arabs, who were lazy and stupid. When I told him his attitude was un-Christian he replied that his position was supported by both the Old and New Testaments. That he believed this did not surprise me, since every injustice in history – including black slavery, numerous wars and even the Holocaust – has been justified by not a few people on religious grounds. His attitude reflected the prejudice not only of many Jews but of many American fundamentalist Christians as well.

Of course not all Israelis exhibit racist attitudes. During my visit I was privileged to meet Dr Israel Shahak, a man who has spent many years campaigning for the human rights of all Palestinians living under Israeli rule. I also came across other Israelis who published books and magazines that attempted to inform the public about conditions on the West Bank and in Gaza. But unfortunately these opponents of Zionist militarism and colonialism who uphold the finest humanistic traditions of the Jewish people are in a minority.

During that trip I avoided Orthodox Jews, since it was well known that most of them believed they had a divine right to Judaea and Samaria (their name for the West Bank). But on my way back I found myself going to the airport in a *Sherut* (a long-distance taxi) with a group of American Orthodox Jews. They were offended when I asked them if they were returning home. Jerusalem was their home, they answered in perfect New York English, which was their native dialect as well as mine.

Assuming, like everyone else had, that I was Jewish, they spoke quite freely to me. When I told them I was writing a book on 1948, they gave me chapter and verse of their own version of recent Middle Eastern history. Like most right-wing Zionists, they claimed that the Palestinians had not been expelled from their homes in 1948, since they were largely the descendants of Arabs who had emigrated into Palestine during the period of British rule before 1948. When I told them that this theory had been refuted by almost every reputable historian, including many Jewish scholars, my fellow passengers labelled the latter 'anti-Semites' and 'self-hating Jews'. Their heroes were the 'pioneers' who were now settling the West Bank, which would eventually be cleansed of the Arab intruders. But out of respect for my status as a scholar and because of the presence of certain other tourists who found my remarks interesting, my Orthodox companions held back the full intensity of their indignation.

I left Israel in 1986 feeling that the situation had become explosive. Why were the Palestinians still so quiet? I wondered. Were they really accepting such a subordinate status in their own homeland without resistance? Few people in Israel, even among those who opposed the occupation of the West Bank and Gaza, expected a Palestinian revolt. Indeed a well-informed book published in 1983 stated that 'the probability of a widespread and sustained uprising is quite low'.[2] I found this conventional wisdom hard to believe, and I was therefore not surprised when in December 1987 a 'widespread and sustained uprising' broke out in Israel's occupied territories.

Like millions of others I watched with great admiration the discipline and courage of the men, women and especially children of the occupied territories fighting their David and

Goliath battle of stones against steel. But how many people viewing TV news coverage of the *intifada* demonstrations in Gaza and the West Bank knew why the people were protesting and what they had suffered for over two decades? My previous book had dealt with the expulsion of the Palestinians in 1948, when the State of Israel had been founded. It was clear to me that it now needed to be complemented by a new book telling the story of the conquest of Gaza and the West Bank by Israel in 1967, and of the occupation of those areas since that date.

News reports in America gave the impression that Israeli atrocities against Palestinian civilians in the occupied territories had begun in December 1987 with the outbreak of the uprising. But from the very outset of the occupation, in 1967, the Palestinians on the West Bank and in Gaza had suffered relentless beatings, torture, deportations, shootings, seizure of land, closing of schools and every other conceivable form of abuse from the Israeli forces.

It is impossible to understand recent events in this region without looking at the history of the occupation. For two decades, tensions had been building up. With every act of repression the forces of resistance had gained new converts, many of them young people who burn with a yearning to end the occupation which has lasted as long as they can remember. The principal cause of the uprising was the lack of a negotiated settlement of the occupation.

Over the years many diplomatic efforts have been made to end Israel's imperial rule in the occupied territories. At first, Arab intransigence appeared to be the chief stumbling block. But there has been a gradual evolution in the Palestinian leadership's position from the original rejectionist stance of the PLO to a more moderate policy in which the State of Israel has been recognized and other substantial concessions have been made. Unfortunately the Israelis have evolved an increasingly hardline position, making it obvious that the ruling Likud party will accept nothing less than annexation of the territories. A study of how and why the positions of the two sides have altered over the past two decades is an essential element in the story of a region that has become one of the major areas of conflict in our time.

Complicating the problem has been the tendency of many to see this issue within a religious context. To the devout Jew, Christian and Moslem the Holy Land is special, since that is where Moses walked, Jesus preached and Mohammed ascended into Heaven. A majority of religious Jews and fundamentalist Christians regard the Zionist right to all of Palestine as the unquestionable will of God, while Moslems, many Catholics and mainstream Protestants question whether Jews have a sole claim to a land regarded as holy by so many (the West Bank in particular has many sites that are sacred to all three religions).

Clearly, religious justifications have been used far too often in the Zionist–Palestinian dispute by politicians and diplomats who cynically wish to manipulate the religious passions of people whose convictions they frequently do not share. As in Northern Ireland, the Indian sub-continent, Lebanon and various other areas of the world, religion has provided a convenient rationale for man to murder his fellow men.

Nonetheless, no serious study of the occupation of the West Bank and Gaza can ignore the importance of religion. Islamic fundamentalism is spreading from its Gaza stronghold into the West Bank. Unlike the PLO, Islamic fundamentalists reject any political accommodations with Israel, which they consider to be Satanic. Many of the settlers in 'Judaea and Samaria' are associated with Gush Emunim ('Block of the Faithful') and practise a type of Judaism which mixes religion with what can only be called racism. This creed regards Palestinians in the occupied territories as usurpers and views territorial compromise as the highest form of heresy. Even more than Islamic fundamentalism, Jewish religious extremism has been a major barrier to a resolution of the situation in the occupied territories.

But at the heart of the problem lies not religion but nationalism, in particular the difficulty of satisfying the national aspirations of both Israelis and Palestinians in such a small strip of territory. Almost 80 per cent of Palestine was conquered by the Zionists and formed into the State of Israel in 1948. It would seem only fair that at the very least the Israelis should allow the Palestinians to keep the remaining 20 per cent to form into a mini-state that might satisfy their national aspirations. But such is the logic of history that few conquerors have ever shown a magnanimous attitude towards their victims. It is only natural to fear and to attempt the elimination of those we have wronged. The European settlers of North America were not satisfied until they had occupied the entire continent, pushing the indigenous Indians to the verge of extinction. Some white South Africans are still loath to make concessions to blacks, whose vengeance they fear. The hardline attitude of Israelis is not without parallel.

Many who write about the Israeli–Palestinian conflict feel compelled to avoid making a judgment on the rights and wrongs of the dispute. Certainly the Israelis, particularly those who seek an end to the occupation, are not devils, and Palestinians, especially those who commit insane acts of terror, are less than angels. But it is difficult to believe that anyone could study the problem for many years without feeling that the justice of the case bears in one direction or the other. If one puts religion or political ideologies aside, it becomes immediately obvious that there are striking parallels between the events in Israel and the occupied territories on the one hand, and what has taken place in South Africa and the tribal homelands (Bantustans) on the other. It is indeed difficult to see how any American or European can oppose South African apartheid and at the same time support the Zionist suppression of the Palestinians' self-determination in their own nation-state.

Most objective students of the Zionist–Palestinian conflict, including many experts in Israel, have now concluded that the only sane resolution of the problem is a two-state arrangement that would result in a Palestinian state comprising the West Bank and Gaza, possibly linked to Jordan, co-existing with an Israeli state roughly confined to the 1967 borders. It is certainly time for Israel to make a conciliatory gesture to strengthen the moderates within the PLO before the Palestinian extremists re-emerge and set the Middle East ablaze, which would cost more innocent lives and perpetuate the conflict for another generation.

How did this impasse come about? Was a solution possible at the outset in 1967, or after the 1973 war, or at Camp David in 1978, or during the diplomatic manoeuvring in the 1980s? Has Palestinian terrorism seriously exacerbated Israeli–Palestinian tensions? Have the roughly one hundred thousand Israeli settlers in the West Bank made a resolution of the conflict impossible? Would a mini-state in the West Bank and Gaza satisfy Palestinian national aspirations? Have all factions within the PLO accepted Arafat's abandonment of terrorism and recognition of the State of Israel? Has the PLO shown the capacity to govern a state? How has the Gulf crisis affected the Zionist–Palestinian conflict? These are thorny questions which must be examined before a way can be found to end Israel's imperialistic rule over the West Bank and Gaza.

1
THE SIX-DAY CONQUEST

There was none of the usual joy, dancing or merriment as the students and supporters of Rabbi Tzvi Yehuda Kook assembled at the Merkaz HaRav Talmudic Academy in Jerusalem on 14 May 1967 for their annual Israeli Independence Eve celebration.[1] All of the guests were anxious to hear the words of Rabbi Kook, who in past Independence Day addresses had offered his followers an inspiring message of hope and optimism. But the rising tensions between Israel and her Arab neighbours cast a shadow on the gathering.

The Syrian–Israeli border in particular was electric with danger because of the Damascus government's support of Palestinian guerilla raids into Israel. On 11 May, on Israeli State Radio, Army Chief of Staff Yitzak Rabin declared: 'The moment has come when we will march on Damascus to overthrow the Syrian government, because it seems that only military operations can discourage plans for a people's war with which they threaten us.'[2] Two days later, Prime Minister Levi Eshkol told the nation that he would take a tough line with provocations from the Arab countries: 'We do not recognize the limitations they endeavour to impose on our acts of response.'[3] Such threats were widely interpreted as implying that Israel planned not just a raid on Syria but an invasion to overthrow the pro-Communist Damascus regime. It was expected that Jordan, Egypt and other Arab states would come to Syria's defence.

Some of those waiting to hear Rabbi Tzvi Yehuda were not despondent over the news of impending war; they included a group of his most devoted disciples who called themselves

14

Gahelet (embers). Many of these men, especially the young rabbis Moshe Levinger and Eleazar Waldman, had for years studied Tzvi Yehuda's romantic interpretation of religious Zionism, which saw the expansion of the modern State of Israel as setting the stage for the fulfilment of Messianism and the redemption of the Jewish people. To the followers of Rabbi Tzvi Yehuda, war and the conquest of new territory was a necessary part of the redemptive process.

Rabbi Tzvi Yehuda was the son of Abraham Isaac Kook, the first Ashkenazi Chief Rabbi of Palestine during the British Mandate.[4] Rabbi Kook the elder played a key role in reconciling Judaism with secular Zionism, which until World War II were seen as mutually exclusive by most religious Jews. Rabbi Tzvi Yehuda expanded on his father's teachings by emphasizing the critical importance of Jewish settlement and control over all parts of the land promised to the Jewish people by God.

About the West Bank, which was the portion of Palestine incorporated into Jordan after the 1948 war, Rabbi Tzvi Yehuda would later write: 'All this land is ours, absolutely belonging to all of us, non-transferable to others even in part.' He added: 'It is clear that there are no "Arab territories" or "Arab lands" here but only the lands of Israel, the eternal heritage of our forefathers to which others have come, upon which they have built without our permission and in our absence.'[5]

In his annual Independence Eve speech Rabbi Tzvi Yehuda had always avoided any mention of Judaea and Samaria; but it soon became apparent that his 1967 speech would be different. It would not be delivered in his usual elliptical manner, filled with rabbinical references which even his closest disciples could not always follow. Though he was generally a quiet man, Tzvi Yehuda's voice reached a crescendo as he berated the crowd for accepting the 1948 partition of Eretz Yisrael:

Nineteen years ago, on the very night that the decision of the United Nations to create the State of Israel was handed down, as the entire people rejoiced . . . , I was unable to join in their happiness. I sat alone – quiet and depressed.

In those very first hours I was not able to accept what had been done, that terrible news that indeed 'my land they have divided' had occurred! Yes, where is our Hebron – have we forgotten it? And where is our Schechem and our Jericho, where – will we forget them?! And all of Transjordan – it is all ours, every single clod of earth, each little bit, every part of the land is part of the land of God – is it in our own power to surrender even one millimetre of it?![6]

not an inch

The impact of his address on the audience was overwhelming, and the Independence Eve celebration became a gathering of mourners. One former student recalled: 'We were taken aback by the choice of that time for reproach and rebuke.' There was an atmosphere of apprehension in the country because of a very severe economic recession as well as a crisis in foreign relations; no one expected the Rabbi to exhort the crowd to conquest during the period of tension between Israelis and their Arab neighbours. When another student asked Tzvi Yehuda if it was permissible to watch the military parade that would be held on Independence Day, he replied: 'Of course. Know that this is the Army of Israel that will liberate Eretz Yisrael.'[7]

marching

The next day, the military parade he spoke of was held in Jerusalem, despite the protests of the Arab governments who claimed that it was a violation of the 1948 armistice agreement and a bid by Israel to gain recognition for Jerusalem as the capital of the Jewish state. A statement issued by the UN observer mission expressed concern that the Israeli military display in Jerusalem would 'intensify the already dangerous tensions'.[8] Indeed, as he reviewed the troops the IDF Chief of Staff, Yitzak Rabin, received word that President Nasser of Egypt had sent two armoured divisions into the Sinai Desert so that they could be deployed against Israel in the event of an attack against Syria. So began a chain of events that culminated in the Israeli attack on Egypt on 5 June 1967, which soon involved Syria and Jordan. In the course of the fighting the West Bank of the Jordan, the Sinai peninsula, Syria's Golan

Heights and above all East Jerusalem would be occupied by Israeli forces.

Israel's occupation of all of Eretz Yisrael so soon after Rabbi Kook's prophetic speech convinced many of his disciples that he was divinely inspired. Many of the graduates of the Merkaz HaRav Talmudic Academy played a prominent part in the war as part of the elite paratrooper unit. A few months afterwards, a former student recalled a conversation with Tzvi Yehuda in which the Rabbi proclaimed: 'God has done his part; it is now up to us to do our part.' The student realized: 'Our part was of course settlement.'⁹ Indeed many of the Rabbi's pupils, particularly the Gahelet group, would become leaders of the Gush Emunim extremist movement, which would play a key role in establishing Jewish settlements on the West Bank conquered during the 1967 war.

The eastern portion of Palestine that we now know as the West Bank had not seen large-scale Jewish settlement for almost two thousand years. During the era of Ottoman Turkish rule before World War I, only a handful of early Zionist colonists emigrated to this hilly region. Most of the early settlers tended to purchase land along the sparsely inhabited coastal plain of Palestine, much of which was owned by a small group of absentee landlords who were willing to sell land to Jews if the price was right. Most of the West Bank land was more evenly distributed among individual farmers, clans and villages who were less inclined to sell to outsiders. Furthermore, the Nablus area of the West Bank was the centre of Palestinian nationalism, while Hebron was known for its deeply rooted Moslem character, which made it hostile to the idea of Jewish land purchase.

The Ottoman laws of land ownership were retained in the West Bank by succeeding British and Jordanian rulers and are locally regarded as valid up to the present time. Under these rules, all land belongs to the Sultan or the state acting as a trustee for God. Land is classified into various categories depending on whether it is used communally, individually or is held in trust as state land. Unfortunately, many West Bank transactions were never recorded in the Ottoman government's land register, and ownership was based on presumed title or informal agreements that were not officially documented. This ambiguity of ownership has been used by the present Israeli occupiers to seize most of the West Bank land.

After World War I, Palestine was ruled by Britain as a League of Nations Mandate territory. The virtual colony was divided into the Northern, Southern and Jerusalem districts. Today's West Bank included most of the Jerusalem district and about a third of the Northern district. Throughout the British Mandate, up to 1948, the Jewish population of the West Bank was less than 1 per cent of the total. There was no Jewish population at all in Ramallah, Nablus or Jenin; a small community of non-Zionist religious Jews lived in Hebron.

Industry in the West Bank during this period was very limited; among the few exceptions were the olive oil soap factories in Nablus. Most industry in Palestine was located in the areas settled by Jews, and often Jewish factory or land owners were pressured by Zionist extremists into hiring only Jewish workers, excluding Arabs.

The exclusionary practices of the Zionists and their obvious desire to dominate the indigenous population led to several popular uprisings in British Palestine. One of the worst occurred in 1929 in Hebron, when sixty Jewish men, women and children were murdered and their synagogue desecrated by Palestinian Arabs who were incited by word that Zionist extremists had desecrated Islamic holy places in Jerusalem.[10] The political unsophistication of the Palestinians was reflected by the fact that most of the Hebron victims were non-Zionist religious Jews, while the right-wing Zionists who had provoked the violence in Jerusalem escaped unharmed. Many decades later the 1929 massacre would haunt Arab–Jewish relations on the West Bank, particularly since the disciples of Rabbi Kook would choose Hebron as the site of their major settlement.

The Arab revolt which began in 1936 and lasted for three years was the largest Palestinian uprising. It was headed by the Grand Mufti of Jerusalem, while most of the other leaders came from the West Bank area, especially the Nablus and Tulkarm-Qalgily regions. The revolt was a disaster for the Palestinians since they foolishly dissipated their strength fighting the British while their real enemies built up their forces for the inevitable Arab–Jewish showdown.

After World War II there was great compassion in the West for the Jews. The Zionists cleverly exploited this sympathy, which they channelled into support for their plans for a Jewish state in Palestine. On 29 November 1947 the UN General Assembly voted to partition British Mandate Palestine and to create in its place two states, one Arab and the other Jewish, plus Jerusalem as an internationalized zone under UN supervision. The Zionists accepted this scheme since they hoped to use their state as a base to conquer the whole country. This was understood by all parties to the dispute, including the Palestinians, who rejected the partition plan. Communal violence erupted in which atrocities were committed by both sides, especially the Irgun terrorists led by the future Israeli Prime Minister Menachem Begin and the Stern Gang, which had as one of its leaders another future Prime Minister of Israel, Yitzak Shamir.

During the 1948 war the Jews retained all of the territory assigned to them under the partition plan and also gained large portions of the proposed Arab state and West Jerusalem. Gaza was occupied by Egypt during the fighting. King Abdullah of Trans-Jordan, who sought to expand his sparsely inhabited desert kingdom, occupied the West Bank, which included what was left of the proposed Arab state plus East Jerusalem. On 6 March 1949 Abdullah issued a royal decree replacing military rule in the West Bank with Arab administration, and a year later the West Bank was formally annexed to the Hashemite Kingdom of Jordan.

On 22 September 1948 an 'All Palestine Government' had been formed at Gaza by the Egyptians, who installed the Grand Mufti of Jerusalem as its head. Although by the end of 1949 it was little more than a hollow shell, this Gaza government was recognized by every Arab regime except Jordan.[11] King Abdullah refused to accept the Grand Mufti's authority over the West Bank, which the Hashemite monarch considered an integral part of Jordan.

The Arab League disapproved of Abdullah's action. King Farouk of Egypt in particular was jealous of the extension of Abdullah's kingdom, since as a descendant of the prophet Mohammed the Jordanian sovereign had dreams of ruling over a much larger state, 'Greater Syria', that would include Palestine, Trans-Jordan, Lebanon and Syria. The Arab League, however, had no authority to force Abdullah to evacuate the West Bank. A compromise was reached whereby the West Bank was regarded as a pledge in the hands of Abdullah 'until the liberation of Palestine'. Abdullah was not asked to withdraw, but none of the Arab states formally approved the annexation of the West Bank, which was recognized only by Britain and Pakistan. (The failure of the Arab states to recognize Jordan's sovereignty over the West Bank would later be used by Rabbi Kook's followers to claim that, after 1967, the West Bank was not occupied but 'liberated' territory which had always been part of Eretz Yisrael.)

In 1951 there were about 467,000 Palestinian refugees in Jordan, comprising about two-thirds of the population.[12] These people had left what became the State of Israel. Some of them had crossed the Jordan and settled on the East Bank, but most refugees in 1948 squatted on West Bank land. Refugees who were middle-class fled with some money, property and, most importantly, work skills which enabled them to settle in various West Bank towns where they integrated into the local population. Many others moved into small villages where they obtained menial work as farm workers. The most unfortunate group ended up in refugee camps where they were eventually cared for not by the Jordanian government but by the United Nations Relief and Works Agency, UNRWA.

An UNRWA report of October 1950 gives some idea of the condition of the early refugees:

It would be necessary to visit refugee encampments or improvised quarters such as old mosques, schools or abandoned barracks or other buildings really to appreciate the desperate situation in which these poor unfortunates find themselves. Generally their clothing and the few household articles they are able to bring with them have reached or are beyond the end of their normal life of usage. A condition which was expected to last a few months has entered its third year.[13]

The Jordanian government pursued a two-sided policy towards the refugees. King Abdullah promised that one day they would return to their homes as 'masters and not as slaves'.[14] Meanwhile the refugees, along with the indigenous population of the West Bank, were regarded by King Abdullah as his subjects: 'They enjoy the same rights and suffer the same obligations and duties as Jordanian citizens. They vote, pay taxes and can acquire property.'[15]

But the refugees resisted efforts to be settled permanently in Jordan because they believed that this would make it difficult for them eventually to return to their homes in what had become the State of Israel. The director of UNRWA noted: 'The desire to go back to their homes is general among all classes. It is proclaimed orally at meetings and organized demonstrations and in writing in all letters addressed to the agency.'[16]

Refugees who had lived in the West Bank for many years would not allow trees to be planted in their camps and some opposed the replacement of their tents with more durable huts since they considered these signs of permanence. There was great mistrust of King Abdullah; indeed he was assassinated in 1951 by Palestinian extremists who feared he might compromise with Israel. After the abdication of his son in 1952, Abdullah's grandson became King Hussein of the Hashemite Kingdom of Jordan.

Despite the fact that many of them were refugees, the West Bankers were in numerous ways more advanced than the East Bankers, whom they considered to be Bedouin camel herders. West Bankers had more education, were more urbanized and possessed more mechanical and other skills than native East Bankers. Palestinians were also much more politicized than East Bankers, who were largely apathetic to events outside their immediate experience.

Under Jordanian rule Nablus, as now, was more politically

conscious than the other two West Bank districts, Jerusalem and Hebron. Its people have always had a deep attachment to their district, from which fewer people emigrated than from other parts of the West Bank. Nablus is good farming country because it has the highest rainfall and richest agricultural yields. The town itself had several factories and a quarter of its workforce was engaged in industry during the 1950s. The district was not as advanced economically as the Jerusalem district, but it was significantly ahead of Hebron.

The Hebron district's population was more staunchly Moslem, with a strong aversion to Western ways. It had little industry and lower levels of education than the other two districts. Many people emigrated, especially to the East Bank and oil-rich Kuwait, where they found lucrative employment. Public services in Hebron were very poor; there were fewer doctors, while none of the West Bank institutions for the young or the elderly was located in the district.[17]

The Jerusalem district, which included Ramallah, was the West Bank region with the most industry and the highest number of educated people, many of whom were Christians. Young men from here went to universities in the West. Once established in their chosen profession, the money they sent back to their families boosted the local economy. Almost 70 per cent of the adult male population of the Jerusalem district was employed outside agriculture, especially in the handicrafts.

Under the UN partition plan of 1947 the city of Jerusalem was supposed to have become an international zone, but the western part was annexed by Israel while East Jerusalem was annexed by Jordan. After the war some Palestinians called for the implementation of the UN internationalization scheme, but both Israel and Jordan rejected this appeal. Abdullah claimed that he did not wish to separate the Arabs in Jerusalem from their brothers in the West Bank, but actually the reason why the King sought to retain the city was its religious significance, which gave his state great prestige in the Arab world.

Abdullah did everything possible to prevent Jerusalem from overshadowing his capital, Amman. All important government offices were transferred out of Jerusalem. One commentator notes: 'The only thing they allowed to develop was the tourist industry', since 'they could not transfer Jerusalem to the East Bank'.[18] Indeed the Jordanians had a very deliberate policy of neglecting the development of the entire West Bank while building up Amman and the rest of the East Bank. At the beginning of Jordanian rule the West Bank was more developed than the East, but by 1961 West Bank per capita income was only half that of the East. Government figures indicate that three-quarters of all industry was located east of the River Jordan.[19] Businessmen were often pressured into starting up in the East Bank or even moving their factories there. They usually agreed, since many feared that Israel was casting covetous eyes on the West Bank. Palestinians were outraged that the Amman government refused to develop the Dead Sea potash deposits or to allow the opening of a university in the West Bank despite the educational hunger of the region.

Perhaps the greatest harm done by the Jordanian government to the West Bank economy was its failure to develop the infrastructure of the area. Roads pointed towards what had become Israel rather than towards the new industry east of the Jordan. The old roads led nowhere, since they were truncated by the 1949 Armistice 'Green Line' between the West Bank and Israel. Palestinian merchants lost their natural markets as well as access to the port of Haifa, and many West Bank workers and farm labourers were cut off from their employment by the 'Green Line' with Israel. The Jordanian government failed to compensate the West Bank population by developing new employment. Palestinians bitterly resented the neglect of their region by the Hashemite regime.

The central government had a divide-and-rule policy towards the West Bank. The Nablus district was favoured with what little development was granted to the West Bank, so that it could be set against the Jerusalem and Hebron districts. The town of Nablus was favoured over East Jerusalem, thus making it difficult for East Jerusalem to become the *de facto* capital of the West Bank. The Jordanians particularly feared the demonstration of any Palestinian or Pan-West Bank sentiments: the civilian governor who was appointed for each district was made accountable to the Ministry of the Interior in Amman, an arrangement that discouraged direct political ties among the three West Bank districts.[20]

Amman also tried to influence elections for the local and municipal councils in order to keep opposition groups from challenging its policies. The central government had the right to appoint two members to the municipal councils as well as mayors of local communities. Thus on 18 October 1964, for instance, the Minister of the Interior in Amman appointed a long-time Hashemite supporter, Sheikh Ali Ja'abari, to the Hebron city council and the office of mayor.[21]

On the national level, many Palestinians were appointed to diplomatic, cabinet and other government positions. Although a few supporters of the Grand Mufti and members of his Husaynis clan were bought off by being given a local office, in general the Amman government avoided appointing people from this group, since the Grand Mufti and the Husaynis clan were seen as symbols of militant Palestinian nationalism. Many Palestinians who held office under the Hashemites were members of or associated with the Nashashibi clan, who were the traditional rivals of the Husaynis.

But the West Bank representatives were never allowed to constitute a majority of the cabinet or of either the lower or upper chamber in Parliament. By law, each branch of the legislature had an equal number of members from the East and West Banks, even though the West Bank had a larger population. The really important posts of Prime Minister, deputy Prime Minister, Minister of the Interior and Minister of Information were in the hands of East Bankers.

Discrimination against Palestinians was most notable in the Arab Legion, Jordan's elite military force. Palestinians were usually only allowed to serve in technical support units, while the combat regiments were composed of Bedouins loyal to the Hashemite monarch. The Amman government wanted to make sure that there would be no problem if the Arab Legion had to be used to put down unrest on the West Bank.

*　　*　　*

On 14 July 1958 news reached Nablus that a revolt in Baghdad led by the Pan-Arab Ba'ath party had overthrown the Iraqi monarchy, which had close political and family links to the Jordanian Hashemites. The demonstration was recalled by the Palestinian journalist Raymonda Tawil, who saw thousands of people carrying banners and placards as they chanted 'Down with the traitors!', 'Down with the Hashemites', 'An end to tyranny!' Tawil was impressed by the crowd's 'angry, impassioned expressions'.[22] The Palestinian journalist believed that the outbreaks showed that the people of Nablus 'were sick of the rule of King Hussein'. Many in Nablus who 'took to the streets to cheer the Iraqi revolutionaries and to boo the hated Hashemites' were supporters of the Jordanian Ba'ath party.[23]

The Ba'athists favoured the creation of a unified Arab nation which would have a major voice in international relations, and the party had been created by a number of young Palestinian leaders in 1953. Another group of young intellectuals formed the National Socialist party, which had an extreme nationalist appeal; while a third group joined the leftist National Front. Of the political opponents of the regime only a small group of communists espoused the creation of a Palestinian state on the West Bank. Such a concept would not gain real support until the 1970s.

Most Palestinians granted the Hashemites, at least at the beginning, 'conditional legitimacy', allowing West Bankers to accept affiliation with Jordan until the creation of a large Palestinian state after the defeat of Israel. Some Palestinians who supported Pan-Arabism saw the union of the East and West Banks as a step towards total Arab unity. Although they had deep reservations about the Hashemite regime, Pan-Arabists believed that it served no purpose to dissolve Jordan because, like Palestine, it was destined to be a province in an Arab state that would stretch from North Africa to the Gulf.

The Amman regime did everything possible to counter the Palestinian opposition, since King Hussein's goal was permanent control of the West Bank. There was in fact considerable support for the Hashemites among office holders and other

Palestinian notables who feared both the Israelis and the Grand Mufti. Many ordinary residents of the West Bank believed that if the Arab Legion withdrew, they would soon be at the mercy of the invading Israelis, whose state showed no sign of withering away.

In October 1956, King Hussein held the only free elections in Jordan's history. The anti-regime parties did well: a government was formed by Sulyman al-Nabulsi of the National Socialist party, while the Ba'athists, the Moslem Brotherhood and the communist-supported National Front all won a substantial vote. Nabulsi attempted to sever Jordan's ties with Britain and to further Pan-Arab unity, and as a result Hussein dismissed the cabinet. Some army units then rose in revolt, but were soon crushed by forces loyal to the King. Following the dismissal of Nabulsi and the failed coup, there was a crackdown on all dissident Palestinian elements. As Raymonda Tawil remembers, Jordanian censorship was severe: 'This was a period of intense repression against all dissident elements, Ba'athists, Communists, Nasserists and Palestinian Nationalists. Houses were ransacked to uncover forbidden literature of any variety.'[24]

By 1959, with the appointment of Hazza al-Majali as prime minister, there was a noticeable relaxation of repression. In the 1960s many Palestinians became increasingly reconciled to the Hashemite government for two reasons. First, by 1961 Jordan had an economic growth rate of 23 per cent; some of this was beginning to benefit the West Bank, especially the booming tourist industry. Secondly, West Bankers were also affected by the failure of the United Arab Republic of Syria and Egypt, which broke up in 1961, and the abortive union of Syria, Iraq and Egypt in 1963. Many Palestinians were pleased by King Hussein's choice of prime ministers during the 1960s – liberals who accommodated some of the Palestinian nationalists' demands. The regime even felt secure enough to allow many of Hussein's banished opponents to return, including those who had led the military revolt against the King.

But in that decade not all Palestinian refugees despaired of liberating their homeland. Like Rabbi Kook's supporters who dreamed of conquering 'Judaea and Samaria', many West

Bank Palestinians in these years believed that some day they would return to Jaffa, Haifa and Safed. This feeling was even stronger in Gaza, the other main repository of Palestinian refugees from the 1948 war.

Before the 1967 War few Israelis looked at Gaza with covetous eyes, since it lacked the religious significance, economic potential or strategic value of the West Bank. Under Ottoman and British rule the area had been a backwater which had not attracted Jewish emigrants. There was little industry and there were few small land holdings since large estates predominated, especially those owned by the powerful Shawwa family. The only real economic asset of the region was the port in Gaza City, which mainly exported grain from the Hebron and Beersheva areas. There were at one time twenty thousand Bedouin, but their economy, based on the horse and camel trade, declined with the advent of the automobile. During the period of the British Mandate many Gaza residents left to find work in other parts of the country, especially Haifa and Jaffa.

Under the UN partition plan, the Gaza district including the strategic port was to form a part of the Arab state, but during the 1948 war much of the province was captured by the Israelis. Gaza City, together with one other town, eight farming villages and a few Bedouin encampments forming what came to be called the Gaza Strip, was occupied by the Egyptians. Perhaps as many as two hundred thousand refugees fled into this tiny area, overwhelming UNRWA, which tried to provide basic assistance to the hordes of desperate people. Conditions in Gaza were worse than in the West Bank and remain so to the present day.

The humanitarian relief workers did what they could, but the Gaza Strip could not sustain such a large population since half the land consisted of unproductive sand dunes. With the establishment of Israel, Gaza Port was cut off from the grain-growing areas that supplied food and exports and the Bedouin of the region lost their grazing land on the other side of the 'Green Line'. Because of the terrible economic situation, thousands of skilled people in the Gaza refugee camps left to find work in the Arab world, especially Saudi Arabia.

Since Gaza had been occupied by Egyptian troops in 1948, after the war the region was governed by Cairo through a military administration. Egyptian rule was not benevolent. King Farouk was distrustful of the Palestinians and refused to tolerate any independent political activity in Gaza. In the early 1950s the people of the area thought that their condition would improve with the coming to power in Cairo, via a revolution, of Gamal Abdul Nasser, who had fought against the Israelis during the war. The Palestinians in Gaza believed that he would lead a new *jihad* or holy war that would take them back to their homes in Jaffa and Beersheva and other areas that were now part of Israel.

In 1954, however, the Gaza refugees were bitterly disappointed when they discovered that the Egyptian President was considering a plan to resettle them in the Sinai Desert.[25] For two days Gaza was consumed by rioters who looted and burned Egyptian buildings and vehicles. Even the communists and the Moslem Brotherhood, who had been ideological opponents, joined in the protests, which demanded repatriation to their homes rather than being sent to permanent exile in the Sinai Desert. Because of the uproar, Nasser abandoned this resettlement scheme.

The refugees looked upon their sanctuary in Gaza as temporary, but as the years dragged on, life in the camps settled into a dull grey monotony of idleness and poverty. A refugee named Akram recalled life as a child in Gaza in the early 1950s:

UNRWA began to build the camp in Rafah, so we registered our names and were given a house. All the houses were the same – eight rows in each block – each row twenty houses. Ours had a roof like a fisherman's net; in the winter we used to catch rain in our pans. We had paraffin lamps for lighting and heating and a standpipe in each row for water which we switched on twice a day.[26]

General E. L. M. Burns, chief of the UN Truce Supervision Organization, noted that in Gaza 'the standard ration provided 1600 calories a day, mostly carbohydrates. By western standards 1600 calories is a reducing diet.'[27] Gaza residents, especially the children, were perpetually hungry. Akram remembers that when a health officer came to his school to give special cards for youngsters to get extra meals from a feeding centre, 'he pointed to the boy next to me who looked pretty ill. I got up with him and registered my name with the teacher.' When Akram got the card he 'dashed off to the centre to get a meal – an egg, an apple and a loaf of bread. A week later I lost my card. My father was furious'.[28]

According to another refugee, Hamdi, 'Everyone was always waiting for things, handouts, forms, cast-off clothes, applications and so on. The whole sense of rootlessness created a sort of paralysis. The world saw our cause as refugees as a humanitarian one instead of a political one.'[29] General Burns called Gaza 'a vast concentration camp, shut off by the sea, the border between Palestine and Sinai near Rufah which the Egyptians will not permit them to cross, and the Armistice Demarcation line, which they cross in peril of being shot by Israelis or imprisoned by the Egyptians'.[30] He added: 'They look to the East and see wide fields over Arab land cultivated extensively by a few Israelis with a chain of Kibbutzim guarding the heights and the areas beyond. It is not surprising that they look with hatred upon those who have dispossessed them.'

But, as in the West Bank, many Gaza refugees did cross the 'Green Line' into Israel in order to visit relatives or to get a glimpse of their former home or land which they hoped to repossess in the near future. Some of the Gaza Palestinians engaged in commando raids which they believed would irritate the Israelis into making brutal reprisals. This, they expected, would lead to a war between Israel and the Arab states that would result in the liberation of their homeland.

The Israelis were anxious to disperse the Gaza refugees, whom they considered to be a nest of vipers. Prime Minister David Ben-Gurion was greatly disappointed that Nasser did not follow through his plan to resettle them in Sinai. Only the opposition of moderate elements in the Israeli cabinet prevented Ben-Gurion from delivering an ultimatum to Nasser in the early 1950s demanding that he carry through the plan. Nor would the cabinet approve Ben-Gurion's other suggestion that Gaza be invaded and annexed, with the hapless refugees being pushed into Egypt. But there was one demonstration of Israeli power. On 28 February 1955 the IDF delivered a devastating assault on Gaza, in which thirty-nine people were killed and many others wounded. This attack alerted Nasser to the danger of Israeli expansionism, which he countered with a substantial arms build-up and an acceleration of commando attacks from Gaza. Arab–Israeli tensions reached a new peak of intensity.[31]

After Nasser nationalized the Suez Canal in July 1956, Israel joined Britain and France in an attack on Egypt. In October 1956, Israeli forces over-ran Gaza on their way across Sinai to the Suez Canal. The Suez war was over in a few weeks, since American diplomatic pressure forced the British and French to abandon their abortive invasion of Egypt. The Israelis expected that their occupation of Gaza would be permanent: long-term contracts with local industry were signed, Arabic-speaking Jews were brought in to supervise the educational system, and a Municipal Council of local notables willing to collaborate was set up.

During the occupation in 1956 the Israelis displayed incredible brutality toward the population of the Gaza Strip. Many hundreds of civilians were murdered in an apparent effort to force the refugees to flee. One of the worst massacres occurred on 3 November, when the Israelis occupied the town of Khan Yunis and the adjacent refugee camp. The Israelis claimed that there was resistance, but the refugees stated that all resistance had ceased when the Israelis arrived and that all of the victims were unarmed civilians. A Gaza resident, Abu Talal, recalled the massacre.[32]

At 5am, Israeli troops broke into his home. Speaking English, he showed them his identity card, saying: 'I am a schoolteacher. I am a civilian.' One of the Israeli soldiers shouted in Arabic: 'Stand still.' Abu Talal recalled, 'Then he opened fire on me with his rifle, hitting me in the elbow.'

The soldier fired again and Abu Talal's brother was instantly killed. His other brother was shot in the legs as he tried to climb out of the window. Abu Talal's ordeal was not over. 'A second soldier then came into the room, took one look around and emptied his rifle at random around the room. I was hit again in my leg and chest.'

Many other homes in Khan Yunis were raided at random. Abu Talal was appalled by the sight. 'There were corpses everywhere and because of the curfew no one could go out to bury them.' An UNRWA investigation later found that 275 civilians had been murdered by the Israelis at Khan Yunis and the refugee camp that day.

Another large massacre took place at Rufah refugee camp, where UNRWA ascertained that 111 civilians were killed.[33] There were many other incidents perpetrated by the Israelis during their reign of terror in Gaza. Women were a particular target, for the Israelis were aware of Moslem sensitivity about attacks on their women.

A Palestinian woman, Intissar, who had lived in Gaza as a teenager, remembered the precautions taken by the local Gaza residents to protect young girls from the invaders. 'The families agreed that they would cry out to warn others if Israeli soldiers came to the houses. We were frequently woken up by these cries. In some places where the entrance to several houses was a narrow street, the families used to build barricades with iron.' According to Intissar there was one particularly brutal atrocity: 'We became very anxious and frightened after an incident when one Israeli soldier killed the husband of the woman he wanted to take. Then he killed the woman.'[34]

Abu Ali recalled that the man killed was a schoolteacher friend of his.[35] He notes that during the curfew 'the soldiers would shoot anything they saw moving, even someone walking in front of a window'. Another of his friends was murdered right in his doorway for no apparent reason. Abu Ali called these deeds 'acts of mindless brutality'.

UNRWA protested vigorously about the atrocities, particularly the murder of eight of its employees.[36] But the outrages continued until the end of the Israeli occupation of Gaza in

March 1957, at which time a mass grave was discovered at Khan Yunis containing the bodies of forty Palestinians who had their hands tied and had been shot in the back of the head. These acts of violence were committed by the Israelis in order to terrorize the Palestinians into fleeing from their refugee camps; dispersing the residents of the Gaza Strip would remain an Israeli goal for many decades.

But the Israelis were forced to evacuate Gaza because of pressure from President Eisenhower, who was perhaps the only American president to stand firm against the Zionist lobby in Washington. The people of Gaza chose to return to Egyptian rule rather than accept UN administration. Nasser was pleased at this show of confidence in his ability to govern, and he rewarded the Gazans by allowing them a much greater say in the rule of the territory. Many posts previously held by Egyptians were given to Gazans, especially in the fields of health and education.

There was also an effort to improve the economic status of Gazans. More people from the territory were allowed to work in Egypt, where most soon showed the capacity for hard work which has made the Palestinians successful throughout the Arab world. It was, however, not thought wise to place major industry in Gaza, for fear of Israeli raids. The economy was stimulated by declaring Gaza a tax-free port. Many goods were sold there which were not available or were much more expensive in Cairo, thus attracting numerous Egyptian visitors who went on shopping sprees in the territory. Smuggling from tax-free Gaza into Egypt also became a major industry.

The citrus industry was greatly developed, most of the fruit being sold in eastern Europe in exchange for construction materials and machinery. About half of the labour force was employed in this industry, while others worked for UNRWA or the government. A few people were also employed in carpet weaving, pottery or other light industry. Although salaries were low, Nasser kept the population fed with subsidized imports of basic food commodities from Egypt.

With increased prosperity, Nasser's popularity in Gaza rose throughout the 1960s. The Egyptian leader's administrative reforms as well as his anti-Israeli rhetoric were also greatly appreciated by the Gazans. Privately, however, Nasser did not really believe that he could liberate Palestine, but he felt compelled to make some form of public commitment. In 1964 he set up the Palestine Liberation Organization (PLO), which he hoped would channel and control the radical tendencies in the refugee camps. A PLO office was set up in Gaza headed by the Palestinian Ahmed Shuqairi, a firebrand whose dire threats against Israel became legendary.

Yasser, a Palestinian activist of the period, recalls:

In 1965 when Shuqairi came here, Gaza became the centre of Palestinian activism and people were filled with high hopes. He raised the level of enthusiasm to fever pitch, as though the battle stage was set and everyone was ready for the shoot-out. The more frenzied they became, the more he poured fire on them. It was ridiculous. You'd think he had come to take people back to their villages the next day.[37]

But there were some who were actively waging armed struggle in order to liberate their Palestinian homeland. Fatah, with its leaders Yasser Arafat (*nom de guerre* Abu 'Ammar) and Khalil Wazir (*nom de guerre* Abu Jihad), was organized by the Syrians, who hoped it would be a counterweight to the Egyptian-controlled PLO. The young militants of Fatah resented Ahmed Shuqairi, who represented the Palestinian Old Guard that had been defeated in 1948 and were hopelessly dependent on the Arab states. Fatah believed that the Palestinians themselves must liberate their homeland.

Some of the Fatah leaders opposed the idea of armed struggle against Israel in the mid-1960s. Khaled al-Hassan, an early member of Fatah's Central Committee, later explained why the organization decided to engage in armed struggle: 'We were pushed down the road we did not want to take by the coming into being of the PLO. Because of its existence, and the fact that it was not the genuine article that so many Palestinians were assuming it to be, we decided that the only way to keep the ideal of real struggle alive was to struggle.'[38]

The Fatah attacks were launched from various countries bordering Israel, including Jordan. The attacks were extremely small-scale and involved only a few Israeli casualties, but were a convenient excuse for the Israelis to launch devastating reprisals out of all proportion to the provocation. Thus in November 1966, when three of their soldiers were killed by a Fatah mine, the Israelis raided the village of Sammu in the Hebron district of the West Bank. The local population of five thousand was routed, 125 homes were demolished and a total of eighteen Arab soldiers and civilians were killed. The attack set off numerous demonstrations in the West Bank which turned into anti-Jordanian protests. 'Yesterday it was Sammu, tomorrow it could happen in Tennin or Nablus', was the common West Bank reaction.[39] There was a general fear that the raid was the beginning of an Israeli offensive designed to annex the West Bank.

Though publicly boasting of the prowess of the Arab Legion, privately King Hussein feared that the Israelis were angling to grab the West Bank. The Hashemite monarch discussed his fears of Zionist expansionism with US Ambassador Findley Burns, who informed Washington. On 23 November 1966 President Lyndon Johnson wrote to the King: 'Ambassador Burns has informed me of Your Majesty's concern that Israel's policies have changed and Israel now intends to occupy territory on the West Bank of the Jordan.' Johnson added, 'While I can understand the reason for the concern, we have good reason to believe it highly unlikely that the event you fear will in fact occur.'[40]

There is, however, abundant evidence that Rabbi Tzvi Yehuda Kook and his disciples were not the only Israelis who sought to gain the West Bank. During the latter part of the 1948 war several commanders urged the Prime Minister, Ben-Gurion, to seize the West Bank from Jordan in a lightning attack in which the population would be expelled. Ben-Gurion refused because he feared British and American reaction, but he indicated that the time for such an enterprise might come in the future.[41]

In the planning sessions for the attack on Egypt in 1956, Ben-Gurion proposed to the British and French a scheme in which Israel would seize the West Bank and Sinai and set up a puppet Christian state in Lebanon, but this was rejected by the Western allies. In 1960 Ben-Gurion visited President de Gaulle in Paris. De Gaulle wrote in his memoirs that the Israeli Prime Minister 'spoke to me of his plan to settle four or five million Jews in Israel, but he could not contain them with her present frontiers and revealed to me his intention of extending these frontiers at the earliest opportunity'.[42] De Gaulle refused to assist such aggression and urged Ben-Gurion not to attack his neighbours.

Menachem Begin, leader of the right-wing opposition, was even more outspoken than the ruling Labour party in advocating Israeli expansionism. Begin was greatly disappointed that not all of Palestine had been gained in the 1948 war. During 1966 and early 1967 many Israelis agreed with Begin that a new war could be used to 'liberate' the West Bank. During this period Air Force Chief Ezer Weizman spoke to Amos Horev of the IDF Central Command headquarters staff in Tel Aviv. Horev told Weizman his view of the border tensions: 'This is the great opportunity to do something terrific to the Jordanians. We mustn't miss it.' He made it clear that his aim was to 'liberate Jerusalem and the West Bank'.[43]

The Arabs fully realized that the Israelis' goal was to use the border tensions as an excuse for a war in which they would demolish Arab military potential as well as conquer more territory, especially the West Bank. On 21 November 1966 Jordan's UN Ambassador, Mohammed al-Farra told the Security Council about the root of the Arab–Israeli tensions: 'If one looks deeper, one will find that the real causes are ideological and the acts, deeds and behaviour based on the destructive thinking of Zionism, calling for more immigration, more expansion, more expelling of Arabs – acquiring more of their lands.'[44]

Of course the Arabs played into the hands of the Israeli expansionists. The policy of the Fatah guerrilla organization and its leader Yasser Arafat was to generate an atmosphere of confrontation that would lead to an Arab–Israeli war, which Arafat was sure the Arab side would win.[45] There is plenty of evidence to suggest that President Nasser of Egypt really did not want war with Israel in 1967, but blundered into a hopeless confrontation. Indeed the Israeli Chief of Staff, Yitzak Rabin, frankly stated: 'I do not believe that Nasser wanted war. The two divisions he sent into Sinai on May 14 would not have been enough to unleash an offensive against Israel. He knew it and we knew it.'[46] But the Israelis who desired a showdown with the Arab states exploited Nasser's unnecessarily provocative military manoeuvres.

Equally foolish were the fiery speeches of Nasser's puppet, PLO leader Ahmed Shuqairi, whose extremist rhetoric heightened tensions. Arab leaders understood that Shuqairi's bluster meant nothing, but Zionist propaganda used the PLO leader's verbal excesses to convince the world that the Arabs planned to exterminate all Israelis. The Arabs, however, have produced documents indicating that Shuqairi never threatened to drive the Jews into the sea, as is frequently charged.[47]

On 5 June 1967, at 7am, the powerful Israeli Air Force launched its surprise attack against Egypt which was shortly followed by a massive ground invasion of the Sinai. The Egyptian Army's division of Palestinian volunteers put up a stubborn fight for Gaza, which is not surprising in view of the brutal Israeli occupation of the strip in 1956. But by the afternoon of 7 June Gaza town fell to a column of Israeli tanks. In his memoirs Defence Minister Moshe Dayan relates that before the invasion Yigal Allon had suggested that the Palestinians in Gaza be transferred to Egypt, but that he vetoed the scheme because it was a 'barbaric and inhumane act'.[48] More likely the Israelis realized that a mass expulsion from Gaza of the whole population would be impractical in view of the militancy and determination of the Strip's residents, but after the war a large number of refugees were deported from the troublesome region.

Before the conflict sizeable quantities of arms and ammunition had been buried in Gaza's orange groves in anticipation of another Israeli occupation. Resistance did not end with the surrender of the Egyptian Army in Gaza. Indeed it would take the Israelis years to suppress the rebellious population of Gaza, made up of hopeless refugees who felt they had nothing to lose.

From the very beginning of their occupation in June 1967, the Israelis continued where they had left off in March 1957. As a resident of the Gaza Strip, Abu Hassan, recalled:

I don't think any of us escaped the suffering. A few weeks after the Strip had been occupied, the Israelis embarked on a programme of forced deportation. On one occasion, the Israeli army rounded up all the men from my quarter and herded us into Jaffa school. The Israelis had two local *mukhtars* [village headmen] with them who told the officer in charge each man's profession – 'he's a labourer, that one's a teacher' and so on. The Israelis picked out the ones they wanted, put them on trucks and sent them to Jordan. I remember another time the army arrived in trucks early in the morning and grabbed all the young men they could find. Those of us who were around began protesting, but the Israelis told us not to worry because they were only taking the youths for a few hours to help in the disposal of those killed in the Sinai during the war. We never saw those young men again. As soon as the work had been done, their identity papers were confiscated and they were forced to cross the canal into Egypt.[49]

These deportations did not end with the summer of 1967. The Israelis had a policy of 'thinning out' the teeming population of Gaza. They were particularly interested in getting rid of those whom they considered to be 'troublemakers' or educated people who could serve as leaders of an opposition movement. During 1968 the Israelis 'encouraged' tens of thousands to leave Gaza (see Chapter 3). There would also be efforts to 'thin out' the population of the West Bank.

But first Israel had to deal with Jordan's Arab Legion. During the 1948 war the Arab Legion had provided the Israelis with their only serious opposition, but in June 1967 King Hussein had qualms about opposing the Zionist juggernaut. He realized that the Israelis were casting covetous eyes on Jerusalem and the West Bank. However Arab passions, particularly Palestinian passions, were too much aroused for Hussein to sit out the conflict. If he had not come to Egypt's aid when his ally was attacked he would have been blamed for the Arab defeat and could easily have lost his throne.

On the afternoon of 5 June fighting erupted in Jerusalem when the Arab Legion began shelling Israeli positions. But the Legion did no better than the Egyptians. With their domination of the air, the Israelis advanced with lightning speed against the Jordanians. Brigadier David Elazer, the northern front commander, swept southwards from Jenin towards Nablus while Colonel Ben-Ari descended from the Jerusalem area towards Hebron in the south. By the late morning of 7 June the Jordanian forces, who had lost their entire Air Force and most of their armour and suffered fifteen thousand casualties, were soundly defeated. The remnants of the Arab Legion scurried towards the East Bank. Elazer's and Ben-Ari's columns stopped at the River Jordan.

But for the Israelis the major prize was the Old City of Jerusalem which had been held by Jordan since 1948. At 8.30am on 7 June Defence Minister Moshe Dayan, who had advocated restraint, succumbed to cabinet pressure for the 'liberation' of the Old City. An infantry attack was launched against the final Jordanian strongpoint overlooking Jerusalem; artillery and air support were not used, in case they damaged the holy places. Within hours the city sacred to Jews, Moslems and Christians fell into Israeli hands.

The Arabs living in the Moghrabi quarter adjacent to the Temple Mount were not well treated. This area contained the Dome of the Rock and the Al-Aqsa mosque, which were sacred to Moslems. Here too was located the Wailing Wall, which religious Jews look upon as the centre of their faith; the Arabs living in the area were equally devoted to the site above the Wailing Wall where, it was said, Mohammed had ascended into Heaven.

Immediately after their conquest, the Israelis began making the entire religious complex of the Wailing Wall and the Dome of the Rock into a tourist attraction. Floodlights were set up and bulldozers were brought in to wipe out the homes of 135 Arab families. The 650 evicted Palestinians lost most of their possessions in this swift operation. Afterwards an old woman was found in the ruins of one house; she died a short time later. The haste of the operation was in order to 'create facts' before international opposition to the brutal measure could materialize. The destruction of the Moghrabi quarter in Jerusalem was one of Israel's first violations of the Fourth Geneva Convention Relating to the Protection of Civilians in Time of War, which was signed by the Jewish state in 1949. There would in fact be constant violations of this agreement by Israel in the occupied territories over the next few years.

By Thursday 8 June, the fourth day of the war, the Israelis had completed the occupation of the West Bank. Moshe Dayan notes in his memoirs that on that day he visited the newly occupied area: 'During that tour, I gave a policy directive to the GOC Central Command that he was to act in accordance with our intentions to establish permanent Jewish settlements in the Mount Hebron and Jerusalem areas.'[50] Right from the first day of the occupation, the Israelis were making plans to carry out the type of settlement that was so dear to Rabbi Kook and the other ultra-nationalists. The evidence does not support the claim that Jewish settlement of the West Bank was a reaction to Arab refusal to sign a peace treaty. Indeed on 16 June Yisrael Galili, the Information Minister, told reporters, 'Israel cannot return to the 1949 armistice and boundaries determined by those agreements.'[51]

Of particular immediate concern were reports that the Israelis were expelling Palestinian civilians from their West Bank homes. At the UN Jordan complained that refugees from the 1948 war who were living in UN West Bank camps were being 'coerced and compelled' by Israelis to flee over the River Jordan. The British made a similar charge of forced evacuation directly to Prime Minister Levi Eshkol; this accusation was denied by government radio: 'The Israeli authorities are not applying such pressure and are not encouraging the people to leave. Political circles say there is no intention of changing their policy. On the contrary every effort is being made to restore full services to the inhabitants of the territory controlled by our forces.'[52]

A United Nations report notes that with regard to the flight of the Palestinians from the West Bank in 1967, 'the truth seems to be somewhere between an Israeli statement that "no encouragement" was given to the population to flee and the allegations about the use of brutal force and intimidation made by refugees'.[53] But most of the exaggerated claims of widespread Israeli atrocities were politically motivated charges fabricated by various Arab governments and not by the refugees. The Israelis encouraged the Palestinians to flee in 1967 with threats made over loudspeakers, deliberate destruction of homes and making buses available to take the West Bank residents to border crossings.

There is no evidence of widespread Israeli atrocities in 1967 such as had taken place in 1948, when in villages such as Deir Yassin, Dawayma and Elabun much of the population was massacred and the remainder expelled from their homes. There were several reasons why the Israelis were less brutal in expelling Palestinians in 1967 than in 1948. For one thing there was the glare of publicity; in view of the expulsions in 1948, the media (now including television) was watching what happened to the civilian population in the occupied territories much more carefully. Of course the 1967 war was much briefer than that of 1948, which lasted months and allowed more fighting behind which atrocities could be covered up. Most importantly, atrocities were not 'necessary' in 1967, since almost two decades later the fear of what had happened in 1948 was enough to make many Palestinians flee of their own accord.[54]

But all over the West Bank the Israelis 'encouraged' Palestinians to cross over into the East Bank so that the 'liberated' territory could be as depopulated of Arabs as possible. Dr Almad Natsheh later told a UN panel what happened in Bethlehem, a predominantly Christian town not far from Jerusalem. He recalled that, when the army entered Bethlehem, the Israeli tanks were preceded by a civilian car with a loudspeaker which blared: 'Everyone must leave their homes and go to Jericho.' According to Dr Natsheh, 'They wanted to empty Bethlehem. They wanted to from the very first moment of occupation. They wanted to do what they did in 1948, empty the territories of their population.' But the people of Bethlehem called each other on the telephone and decided to stay in their homes despite

Israeli threats that their houses would be demolished on top of them.

Dr Natsheh spoke to the Israeli in the car with the loud-speaker. 'You have no right to do this. You are an occupier. All right, occupy. There are international laws. You have no right whatsoever to expel people from their homes.'[55] He has no doubt as to the aim of the Zionists. 'They wanted to make a vacuum in the territories and the Israelis always denied the existence of this car and yet the whole population of Bethlehem could bear witness to this.'[56]

Palestinians were not the only witnesses. A French nun, Sister Marie-Thérèse, saw Israeli soldiers driving through Bethlehem with loudspeakers warning the population: 'You have two hours to leave your homes and flee to Jericho and Amman. If you don't your house will be shelled.'[57] She added: 'The first wave of Israeli soldiers were decent humans and courageous, doing as little damage as possible, the second wave was made up of thieves and looters and sometimes killers and the third wave was more disturbing still. It seemed to act from a resolute desire for systematic destruction.'

In the strategic Latroun salient north of Jerusalem the Israelis were soon pushing out the Palestinian villagers, who numbered around ten thousand, from their homes in Beit Nuba, Inwas and Yalu. Sister Marie-Thérèse and others from the Companions of Jesus Order overcame consider-able obstacles placed in their way by the Israelis to get to the Latroun area. The nuns 'saw what the Israelis did not want us to see. Three villages were systematically destroyed by dynamite and bulldozers. Alone in a deathly silence don-keys wandered about in the ruins. Here and there a crushed piece of furniture or a torn pillow stuck out of the mass of plaster, stones and concrete. A cooking pan and its lid were abandoned in the middle of the road. They were not given time to take anything away.'[58]

Sister Marie-Thérèse's observations are verified by Amos Kenan, an Israeli journalist who served in the army during the war. Kenan, assigned to the village of Beit Nuba, notes that when they entered the Latroun area the Israeli soldiers 'were ordered to block the entrance of the village and prevent the inhabitants returning to their villages from their hideouts after they heard Israeli broadcasts urging them to go back to their homes. The order was to shoot over their heads and tell them not to enter the village.'[59]

A number of villagers attempted to return to Beit Nuba, but some Arabic-speaking soldiers in Kenan's platoon went over to the Palestinians and told them that they could not return to their homes. Kenan recalls that the Arab villagers were a pathetic sight. 'There were old people who could hardly walk, murmuring old women, mothers carrying babies, and small children. The children wept and asked for water. They all carried white flags.' The Palestinians begged to be allowed back to their homes. They had been wandering for days and were desperate. Some of the Israeli soldiers asked their officers if something could be done for the Arab civilians. They were told, 'Why do we care about the Arabs anyway?' The platoon commander went to headquarters and was told the villagers had to be driven out.[60] Kenan notes that the expulsions in Latroun area were not an isolated incident. 'We found out that not only in our section was the border straightened out for security reasons but in all other sections too. The promises on the radio were not kept. The declared policy was not carried out.'

The Israelis did broadcast statements to the Arab populations of the newly conquered territories, which were reassuring. On 16 June Israeli Radio's Arabic language service announced, 'Every military commander in the West Bank region has technical advisers to help him in dealing with civilian affairs in the area under his command such as public services, food supplies, currency, transport, economy and refugee affairs in co-operation with UNRWA.'[61] But for many weeks after the war, people continued to flee across the Jordan both as a result of Israeli intimidation and because of their fear that the atrocities of 1948 would be repeated. As in 1948, the Arab side did everything possible to halt the flow out of Israeli-controlled areas. On 15 June the Voice of Palestine radio station announced: 'The chairman of the PLO, Ahmed Shuqairi, appealed once again to Palestinians in usurped Palestine in the West Bank of the Jordan and the Gaza Strip not to leave their homes.'[62]

In only a few villages in the West Bank did the Israelis expel the population at gunpoint, since they had more subtle methods that were effective. A common ploy was to make it easy for the Palestinians to cross over into the East Bank. On 15 June Israeli radio announced:

A special transport service for Arab civilians who want to be transferred from the Old City of Jerusalem to Jordan began operating today. This was announced by the West Bank headquarters. People who want to leave are carried from the Nablus Gate to Jericho by special buses. From Jericho they cross the Jordan river to the eastern bank. Similar arrangements have also been made for Arab population centres in other areas in the West Bank.[63]

Israeli loudspeaker trucks roamed through the West Bank announcing the availability of the buses that would take the frightened civilians over the Jordan. At the Allenby Bridge large groups of Palestinians crossed each day in the last half of June; the men carried all their family's possessions, while the women tended the crying children. Israeli soldiers cursed when the hordes of new refugees became confused and blocked the crude crossings; occasionally they fired their weapons in the air to get the attention of these frightened people.

Once the homeless Palestinians crossed to the East Bank they were on their own, since the Jordanian authorities had no administrative machinery set up to process them; the small country's resources had been exhausted in the brief conflict. Members of UNRWA, which had cared for the original refugees of 1948 for the past nineteen years, worked desperately to care for the new homeless. On 3 July 1967 the UNRWA staff in Jordan reported: 'The temporary accommodation in schools where five or six families were living in one room posed a serious health hazard.'[64] Many other refugees were put up in tents. It was 1948 all over again.

There was, however, great pressure on Israel from the

United States and other countries to allow refugees to return to the newly conquered areas. In order to placate world public opinion, on 2 July the Israeli cabinet, despite the opposition of Defence Minister Moshe Dayan, decided to permit West Bank refugees to return under certain conditions. Those desiring readmission were given from 10 July to 10 August to complete Israeli application forms which would be distributed by the International Committee of the Red Cross (ICRC). But, ignoring the objections of the Red Cross, the Israelis demanded that the displaced persons must provide proof of residence, health and customs clearances and be given a security check. The Israelis made it clear that they would only accept back people who had left between 5 June and 5 July 1967.

King Hussein's government greatly favoured the return of the refugees to their West Bank homes. An official spokesman in Amman announced: 'The West Bank of the Kingdom is an integral part of its territory and the right of those who have moved from it to return to their homes and property is sacred and natural.'[65] The Jordanian government wanted the refugees to return in order to prevent the settlement of Jewish immigrants and the annexation of the newly occupied territories by Israel. King Hussein promised money and food to those who agreed to go back, and warned that those who failed to apply for readmission to the West Bank would not be helped on the East Bank, which was swamped by the new influx. King Hussein assured the refugees that they need have no fears if they returned, since somehow the West Bank would be regained.

The Jordanians made every effort possible, including many concessions, in order to facilitate the return of the refugees to their West Bank homes. On 5 August Nils-Goran Gussing, the UN Secretary-General's special envoy on refugee affairs, reported to Ralph Bunche in New York on the progress that was being made.

ICRC Jordan confirmed secret meeting with direct negotiations in presence ICRC representatives took place as scheduled 4 August afternoon at Allenby Bridge on Israeli side, between Israel and Jordan representatives, who were

Tekoa Foreign Office and Doctor Yussef Zehni, Secretary General Red Crescent. This is considered very important step towards reaching quick solution of this big humanitarian problem. Jordan negotiator had full power of decision which apparently was not the case of his counterpart, who stated that he had to refer to his government certain technical questions. This is considered to be due to differences of opinion within Israeli government, where only a very small majority is in favour of return of refugees.[66]

Gussing spoke to the Jordanian Foreign Minister, who complained, he reported, that 'only 60 per cent refugees now willing to return to West Bank, majority of whom are UNRWA refugees'. This figure is not surprising considering the intimidation which had forced the refugees to flee. But in view of the overcrowding in the East Bank refugee camps, it is easy to understand why the Amman government wanted as many as possible to return to the West Bank.

However, problems soon developed. It was originally anticipated that all administrative arrangements for the repatriation of the Arab refugees would be quickly completed. But government sympathizers with Rabbi Kook's view of the West Bank as an integral part of Eretz Yisrael were gaining in ascendancy. These ultra-nationalists included Menachem Begin, leader of the right-wing Gahal bloc, who was a member of the cabinet in the national unity government which had been formed on the eve of the Six-Day War. In the summer of 1967 Begin had not yet publicly acknowledged his adherence to Rabbi Kook, but the Gahal leader was outspoken in the Israeli cabinet for retention of the conquered territories and their settlement by Jews. Begin and those in the cabinet who thought like him were not about to allow several hundred thousand Palestinians back into the West Bank, which they believed had been promised to the Jews by God.

Under the influence of this right-wing element in the cabinet the Israelis created obstacles to the repatriation process. Differences arose between the Jordanians and Israelis over the application forms to be used by the refugees seeking repatriation. The Amman government wanted only Red Cross forms, but the Israelis insisted on application blanks that bore the insignia of their state, which antagonized the Jordanians. It took weeks to agree on the type of form to be used as well as other minor clerical details.

Matters were greatly exacerbated when the Amman government played into the hands of the Israeli hardliners. On 7 August Abdel Wahab Majali, the Jordanian Finance Minister and Chairman of the Higher Committee on Refugees, proclaimed that he favoured repatriation to the West Bank since 'Every refugee should return there to help his brothers to continue their political action and remain a thorn in the flesh of the aggressors until the crisis has been solved.'[67] King Hussein added fuel to the fire by making several statements which lacked any hint of reconciliation with Israel.

On 9 August the growing sentiment in Israel against repatriation of the refugees to the occupied territories was reflected in the nation's press. A *Maariv* editorial commented, 'The venomous incitement with which Jordan is goading Arab refugees to return to Israel [*sic*] in order to harass and harm it, compels us to classify Hussein with those Arab leaders who were defeated in the war but who refuse to learn their lesson.' *Haaretz* had a similar view: 'Because we want to achieve peace, it is advisable to adopt a firm stand towards Jordan, and there is no better means of increasing the pressure than to postpone the return of the original inhabitants.' *Shearim* claimed that Israel had been conciliatory during the repatriation negotiations, but that the Jordanian authorities were 'exploiting these concessions with evil intent'.

Nils-Goran Gussing noticed the hardening of attitudes in Israel. He reported to Ralph Bunche on 12 August, 'Israeli authorities inclined to feel that if refugees are returning only to cause trouble, it is better not to let them come.'[68] But he spoke to Jordanian officials who assured him of their 'spirit of co-operation' and willingness to implement the repatriation agreement.

At an Israeli cabinet meeting on 13 August a slim majority defeated a motion to cancel the entire readmission arrangement. Nevertheless it was decided to make tougher security checks and to slow down the approval of applicants. It was also agreed that no new crossing points would be approved and, most importantly, that the deadline for repatriation would not be extended past 31 August.

On the 18th the first group of approved refugees, totalling 350, returned to the West Bank. Amman Radio announced:

> The Secretary of the Higher Ministerial Committee for Refugee Affairs, Colonel Abdullah ar-Raf'i, told reporters that the Jordanian government had asked through the International Red Cross for an extension of the deadline, which expires at the end of August, to enable all refugees to return to their lands. It has also asked that the number of refugees returning to the West Bank be increased to about five thousand daily. He added: 'We have adequate resources to ensure the orderly return of this number . . .'[69]

King Hussein's regime was determined to do everything possible to encourage the return of the refugees. The following day Ralph Bunche indicated in a letter to Lawrence Michelmore, Commissioner-General of UNRWA, the lengths to which the Amman government would go in order to encourage the refugees to return:

> Concerning the Jordanian request that the Agency discontinue rations to UNRWA-registered refugees on the East Bank who do not return to their homes on the West Bank. We entirely agree with your view that such action would not be consistent with the humanitarian tasks of UNRWA. Should the same request concerning this group be repeated to you in the future we think you could justifiably deny it.[70]

Clearly the often-repeated Israeli claim that the Arab side wished to maintain the refugee camps in order to use them as a weapon against Israel is not supported by the evidence. In 1967, as in 1948, it was the Israelis and not the Jordanians who prevented repatriation. About forty thousand applicants involving one hundred and seventy thousand individuals requesting repatriation to the West Bank were transmitted by the Jordanians through the Red Cross to the Israelis. According to the Jordanians the Israelis approved 4673 applications involving 16,266 people. The Israelis claimed to have approved twenty-one thousand people. But not all of these returned. In some cases not all members of the family were approved, and some people refused to return without a child or elderly parent. And the Israelis gave only a few hours' notice for each day's list. Thus only fourteen thousand people out of over two hundred thousand refugees in Jordan returned by the 31 August deadline.[71]

The Israelis stubbornly refused to extend the period for repatriation. The Information Minister, Yisrael Galili, claimed that the Jordanians had decided to exploit the repatriation for 'hostile purposes'. He cited statements by Jordanian officials, who, he claimed, had attempted 'to use the West Bank inhabitants to disturb public order and carry out anti-Israeli activities which clearly indicated Jordan's negative intentions'.[72]

Publicly the Israelis tried to pretend that it was the Arabs who prevented repatriation of the West Bank refugees. On 27 August Israeli Radio accused King Hussein of 'intentional procrastination' and turning the refugee question into a 'political game'.[73] In his memoirs Moshe Dayan gave his explanation of why so few returned: 'They had to submit their applications through the Jordanian government. Jordan held them up and placed obstacles in the way of the potential returnees.'[74] But in his report of 15 September that year the UNRWA Commissioner-General, Lawrence Michelmore, stated that 'The Jordanian authorities did all that was humanly possible to ensure that those whose applications to return were approved were promptly informed and were given every assistance in re-crossing the river.'[75]

The only concession the Israelis would make to international pressure to allow the refugees back was to agree to admit the seven thousand who had not used their permits before the 31 August deadline. But because of various restrictions only 880 of these returned. In addition 8130 people who had been absent from their West Bank homes during the Six-Day War were allowed back under a family reunion scheme.[76] But this still was only a tiny fraction of the 230,000 and more who had fled or been encouraged to leave. Under Order 125, issued by the commander of the Israeli Defence Forces in the West Bank, any person who was absent from his home on 7 June 1967 and attempted to return without Israeli permission was to be considered an infiltrator and as such liable to any term up to life in prison. The official Israeli position was given by Moshe Dayan when he stated: 'The return of refugees who have fled to the East Bank during the war can only be considered within the framework of general peace negotiations with the Arab countries.'[77]

But there was no prospect for peace negotiations since the Israelis were firmly holding on to the West Bank, Gaza, the Golan Heights and Sinai. The Johnson administration had no stomach to pressure the Israelis out of the occupied territories, as had been done by Eisenhower after the Suez war. On 11 June 1967 Harry McPherson, an aide to Lyndon Johnson, warned the President, 'The Israelis don't intend to repeat 1956. We would have to push them back by military force in my opinion to accomplish a repeat of 1956; the cut-off of aid would not do it.'[78] McPherson was obviously exaggerating. Then, as now, Israel could not survive without the military, economic and diplomatic support of the world's strongest nation. The threat of a cessation of that aid or the cutting off of contributions from the American Jewish community (Eisenhower had considered ending the tax-exempt status of organizations which raised funds for Israel) would have forced the Jewish state to take a much more conciliatory attitude towards the occupied territories after the Six-Day War.

A myth has been created that Israeli intransigence over the occupied territories was the unavoidable result of the hardline attitude of the Arabs. But the evidence is otherwise. As we have seen, before the war was over Dayan planned permanent Jewish settlements on the West Bank. Soon afterwards he told an American TV audience, 'I don't think we should in any way give back the Gaza Strip to Egypt or the western part of Jordan to King Hussein.' On 12 June the Prime Minister, Levi Eshkol, stated: 'There should be no illusions that Israel is prepared to return to conditions that existed a week ago.'[79]

Information Minister Yisrael Galili made it clear that Israel could never return to the 1949 Armistice lines, which had been 'completely erased' by the Arab armies.

On 19 June President Johnson outlined his 'Statement of Principles for Peace' in the Middle East. Realizing Israeli intransigence, the plan was broad and amorphous. Its five principles gave no hint of American intentions for the Middle East.

1. The recognized right of national life.
2. Justice for the refugees.
3. Innocent maritime passage.
4. Limits on the wasteful and destructive arms race.
5. Political independence and territorial integrity for all.

Significantly Johnson added: 'We are not the ones to say where other nations should draw the line between them that will assure the greatest security. It is clear however, that a return to the situation of June 4 1967 would not bring peace. There must be secure and there must be recognized borders.'[80]

Israel and its American supporters had little need to fear that Johnson would demand an Eisenhower-style pull-back as had occurred in 1956. But Johnson's support for Israel came with a price. He wanted the help or at least the acquiescence of the powerful American Zionist lobby for his ill-fated Vietnam venture. Walt Rostow, Johnson's national security adviser, notes a discussion he had with a leader of the American Jewish community who proposed that, in exchange for Johnson's backing for Israel's hardline policy, he would be willing to drum up support for the South-east Asia war in the Jewish community. Rostow was told of the line which would be used: 'The whole fate of Israel depends on the credibility of US commitments. If the US were to fail to meet its commitment in Vietnam, what good would its commitment to Israel be?' Rostow recommended Johnson to endorse this campaign: 'I think this is a first class approach and I told him so.'[81]

By late summer 1967, Israel had taken a hard line with regard to the defeated Arab states. The Israeli cabinet repeatedly announced that the status of Jerusalem was non-negotiable after annexation was decreed in June. There was no offer to evacuate other occupied territory, nor was there any sign of flexibility by Israel with regard to the return of the 1948 or 1967 refugees.

Under the circumstances no Arab government would negotiate with Israel. To do so would have meant a further humiliation for regimes which had been so badly trounced on the battlefield. Neither President Nasser nor King Hussein nor any other Arab leader could have survived in office if they had accepted the status of Jerusalem as non-negotiable, or Israel's claim to the right to settle Jews in Hebron or other West Bank areas. It was inevitable that the Arabs would respond in kind to Israel's hard line.

Thus in late August thirteen Arab heads of state met at Khartoum in the Sudan. There was some opposition to the presence at the meeting of Ahmed Shuqairi of the PLO, who interrupted King Hussein to say that only Palestinians could decide the future of the West Bank. On 1 September Shuqairi stalked out of the conference. On the same day the delegates agreed on 'the main principles by which the Arab states abide, namely: no peace with Israel, no recognition of Israel and no negotiations with it, and insistence on the rights of the Palestinian people in their own country'.[82]

The United Nations, which was still considered the major forum in international relations, grappled with the problem of the occupied territories immediately after the Six-Day War. Israel's chief backer, the United States, made it clear that it would not accept a resolution demanding total evacuation from the occupied territories. Various proposals were advanced but failed to receive sufficient support.

In November 1967 a compromise was reached based on Resolution 242, a British draft which called for 'Withdrawal of Israeli armed forces from territories occupied in the recent conflict'. The United States and other supporters of Israel had resisted the use of the term 'all territories' or even 'the territories', thus making it arguable that Resolution 242 does not call on the Jewish state to make a total evacuation. But the Arabs and their supporters took comfort in the clause that emphasizes 'the inadmissibility of the acquisition of territory by war'; this, it is pointed out, is an implicit call for Israel to return all territory captured during the Six-Day War. Much ink has been spilt over the various interpretations of Resolution 242. Britain has refused to give an official interpretation, while Lord Cadogan, its then UN Ambassador, has stated only that the Resolution spoke for itself. But Leslie Glass, Lord Cadogan's deputy, is probably correct when he states that the British had 'almost total withdrawal in mind except the straightening out of certain minor salients'.[83] Indeed this was clearly the interpretation of most of the countries which voted for the Resolution.

The general assumption during the period was that, after negotiations, Israel would return the Golan Heights to Syria, Suez, Sinai and Gaza to Egypt and most of the West Bank to Jordan in exchange for diplomatic recognition and a guarantee of her territorial integrity. The Palestinians were not yet considered a party to the diplomatic manoeuvring and no one seriously discussed setting up a Palestinian state on the West Bank. In Resolution 242 the Palestinians are mentioned only indirectly in a pious hope for a 'just settlement of the refugee problem'.[84]

On 23 November the PLO, which was still controlled by Egypt, issued a condemnation of Resolution 242 which it rejected because it 'ignores the right of the refugees to return to their homes'.[85] The PLO also disapproved of the Resolution because of 'its treatment of the question of withdrawal of Israeli forces as superficial rather than being a decisive demand'. At the time Yasser Arafat and his Fatah guerilla organization was still outside the PLO, but they and the other guerilla groups would soon join and take over the organization. The members of Fatah feared a return of the West Bank to Jordan since that would destroy any chance for the creation of a Palestinian state. However, Arafat's fear of a return of the occupied territories to Egypt and Jordan was unwarranted. He failed to understand the growing influence of the ultra-nationalist right wing in Israel, including Rabbi Kook who saw the West Bank as the heart of Eretz Yisrael which had been promised to the Jews by God. But in the days immediately after the war the conquering hero of Israeli expansionism was Moshe Dayan; the centre of attraction, in the words of a popular tune of the day, was 'Jerusalem the Golden'.

2
JERUSALEM THE GOLDEN

As he passed the Wailing Wall, Moshe Dayan could hear the ecstatic chants of thousands of Israeli worshippers who had come to the most sacred site of their faith to commemorate, on 17 June 1967, the first Sabbath since the close of the Six-Day War. However, the Defence Minister was not in East Jerusalem primarily to visit Jewish holy places but to meet Moslem religious leaders at the nearby Aqsa mosque which was in the Haram esh-Sharif sacred compound, one of the three most revered locations of the Islamic faith. Dayan and his party felt an abrupt change of atmosphere as they passed through the Moghrabi gate from the Jewish to the Moslem area. 'It was as though we were suddenly cut off from a world filled with joy and had entered a place of sullen silence. The Arab officials who received us outside the mosque solemnly greeted us, their expressions reflected deep mourning over our victory.'[1]

The group of Moslem clerics meeting Dayan, headed by Sa'aduddin al-Alami, Mufti of Jerusalem, and Sheikh Abdel Hamid Sayih, the chief Moslem judge of the city, had good cause for their gloom. On 11 June the Israeli cabinet had agreed almost unanimously on immediate annexation of Jerusalem, which would be implemented before the end of the month.[2] Dayan had come to announce to the Moslem leaders that, with some restrictions, they would retain control of their holy compound. The Defence Minister had to act quickly before Jewish religious and nationalist extremists could put pressure on the Israeli government to seize the compound, which was also sacred to Jews.

In his conversation at the Aqsa mosque Dayan told the Moslem leaders that 'the one thing we would introduce was freedom of Jewish access to the compound of Haram esh-Sharif without limitation or payment'. Dayan added: 'This compound as my hosts well knew was our Temple Mount.'[3] Dayan noted that the Moslem leaders 'were not overjoyed' by his decision – they had no alternative, however, but to accept it. The Defence Minister did, however, reassure the Arab clerics of their control of the compound, and asked them to resume religious services the following Friday. Thus on 23 June 1967 five thousand people prayed in the Aqsa mosque, including a thousand Moslems from Israel who had not been able to worship at the Holy Places before the war since it had then been in Jordanian territory.

In view of the occupation, King Hussein's government discouraged Arabs from attending services in the Haram esh-Sharif compound since this was regarded as collaboration with the occupiers. On 30 June Amman Radio announced: 'Israel's assertions that it will ensure freedom of access to the Holy Places are false. The question is not one of accessibility to the holy places but of sovereignty over them, which is an established historical right of the Arabs who have been entrusted with the holy places for about thirteen hundred years.' The Mufti of Jordan, Sheikh Abdullah al-Qalgili, was not impressed with Israeli assurances. He declared: 'As for Friday prayer in Aqsa mosque, Moslems should not go there to perform prayers as long as the enemy of Islam calls for the holding of such prayers to deceive the world and legalize their seizure of the Holy Places and mosques in the territories of Moslems.' The Mufti defiantly added: 'Moslems throughout the world are sinning greatly by not resorting to a holy war to save Aqsa mosque from Jewish hands.'[4]

Moslem leaders in Jerusalem took a firm but less extreme position against the Israeli presence in the Holy Places. The Moslem religious and political leadership of the city held a series of meetings and on 24 July they sent a memorandum to the Military Governor of the West Bank; it was signed by twenty-two notables including the mayor of East Jerusalem, Ruhi al-Khatib, the president of the Moslem Appeals Court and Sa'aduddin al-Alami, Mufti of Jerusalem. In this memorandum the Arab leaders conceded that the Israelis had the rights of a military occupier but they refused to recognize their sovereignty, 'because the Israeli Knesset has no authority to annex the territory of another state'.[5]

The Jerusalem notables protested at Israeli interference in Moslem religious affairs including the censorship of sermons, infringements on religious courts, encroachments on holy property and the visiting of the Aqsa mosque by Israeli men and women 'dressed in an immodest manner which offends both the principles of religion and Arab and Islamic customs'. The memorandum noted that 'Islamic jurisprudence explicitly stipulated that Moslems must control all of their religious affairs and forbids non-Moslems to take charge of the religious affairs of Moslems'. The Israeli authorities were informed that 'until the termination of the occupation' a Moslem religious organizational framework would remain which would be similar to that which had operated during the last non-Moslem government of the Old City of Jerusalem – the British Mandate.

The religious situation in Jerusalem was exacerbated by Shlomo Goren, the Chief Rabbi of the Israeli Army, who announced his intention of holding Jewish religious services on the Temple Mount which was within an area sacred to Moslems. When Rabbi Goren and his followers entered the holy grounds by way of the Moghrabi Gate they pushed aside Arab guards and held a prayer service that ended with the blowing of the ram's horn. Although Rabbi Goren was forbidden by the Israeli government from holding further services in the Haram esh-Sharif compound, the controversy did not die down. Indeed Moslems were further enraged when the Israeli Minister of Religious affairs publicly stated that Jewish religious rights to the Temple Mount took precedence over Moslem claims.

On 22 August a *fatwa* (religious pronouncement) was issued in the name of the Moslem leaders in Jerusalem. It was written in sharper terms than the 24 July declaration and its contents were broadcast throughout the Arab world. The Moslems in Jerusalem recognized the right of the Jews to the Wailing Wall but reaffirmed that their own Holy Places were equally inviolable. They referred to a compromise between the two communities worked out by the British Mandate authorities in 1933, and which the Moslems urged should be respected during the Israeli occupation. The *fatwa* stated: 'This decision settled the dispute between Jews and Arabs over the Holy Places and became an international instrument, the enforcement of which is obligatory. Under no circumstances can the dispute be brought up again.'[6]

Jewish Orthodox and nationalist circles continued to agitate over the Temple Mount, despite the ruling of the Chief Rabbinate that, due to the sanctity of the grounds, Jews were forbidden entry to the entire Temple Mount area lest they inadvertently enter the place where the original Holy of Holies stood. However, the religious extremists claimed that they had pinpointed the Holy of Holies in the centre of the rock foundation on which the Dome was built; thus they made repeated attempts to hold public prayers on the Temple Mount, especially during Jewish Holy Days. However to a substantial degree Dayan's decision of 17 June remained in force since, except for one gate, the Temple Mount remained in Moslem possession. Jewish and Arab police were under orders from the Israeli government to prohibit Jews from holding prayer services in the Haram esh-Sharif compound. But the Temple Mount was to remain a bone of contention in Jerusalem.

There was in fact considerable controversy about the status of all of Jerusalem and its citizens. The Israelis annexed not only East Jerusalem but the surrounding region as well, including Kalandia Airport and several Arab villages. The hundred and twenty thousand Arabs in this area were considered resident aliens of Israel, since few took advantage of an offer to exchange their Jordanian for Israeli citizenship. As aliens they could not vote in national Israeli elections, but they could participate in Jerusalem municipal elections and carry Israeli identity cards.

Foreign governments, including that of the United States, have refused to give official recognition to the annexation of

Jerusalem and the surrounding territory. When Israel proclaimed the annexation on 28 June the State Department responded with a statement which made the US position clear: 'The hasty administrative action today cannot be regarded as determining the future of the holy places or the status of Jerusalem in relation to them.'[7] On 4 July the UN General Assembly adopted Resolution 2253 (ES-V), calling on Israel to 'rescind all measures taken and to desist forthwith from taking any action which alters the status of Jerusalem'.

But the Judaization of the eastern part of the Holy City proceeded. Arab banks were closed and their funds appropriated, while the Israeli currency and tax system were introduced. There was in fact much resentment by Arab inhabitants of Jerusalem, which had previously been part of Jordan, a country with low taxes; now they were shocked to find themselves subject to the regulations of one of the most highly taxed nations in the world. Moreover they clearly could not expect equal treatment from the social, medical and welfare system enjoyed by Israel's Jewish population. In particular Jerusalem Arabs resented the compulsory 'Defence Loan' assessments, used to support the Israeli military machine which had conquered their city. Since they considered themselves occupied but not annexed, the Jerusalem Arabs protested that the imposition of the Israeli tax system on them violated international law and numerous United Nations resolutions.[8]

Another complaint of Jerusalem Arabs was the confiscation of their property for the construction of Jewish settlements. Eventually tens of thousands of Jews were moved on to land that was Arab property. In January 1968 the Israelis confiscated a thousand acres of privately owned Palestinian land, some of which was expensive real estate. The area included the former no man's land between the Israeli and Jordanian lines, a strip of territory on both sides of the Ramallah road, large areas in Mount Scopus and the slopes of the Mount of Olives. Eventually two Jewish suburbs, French Hill and Ramat Eshkol, were built on this land. In April that year the entire Jewish quarter of the Old City, which contained 1740 rooms and 116 shops, was expropriated; most of the property was owned by Arabs who belonged to the community's leading families. Despite resistance which lasted over a decade, the area was eventually populated by Jews. In August 1970 the Israeli government seized two thousand acres of land belonging to the village of Sharafat to the south of the city; within months Jewish settlers were moving into the first of ten thousand apartments in the newly proclaimed suburb of Gilo.[9]

The aim of this building programme was to consolidate Israel's control of the whole of the Greater Jerusalem area, thus making it impossible for the Arabs ever to reacquire East Jerusalem. Right from the beginning the Israelis made it clear that the status of Jerusalem was non-negotiable. The large apartment complexes full of Jewish residents were designed to cut off East Jerusalem from the surrounding West Bank, which was administered separately.

Whereas Jerusalem was annexed to Israel and became part of the Jewish state, from the beginning the status of the West Bank and Gaza has been ambiguous. Israel considers that these areas are liberated and not occupied, since the Jews have a 'historic right' to Eretz Yisrael. It is claimed that Israel gained control through a 'defensive conquest', so that it has a better claim to the disputed territory than do Jordan and Egypt. Israel claims that Jordan illegally occupied the West Bank in 1948 and that, since its sovereignty was recognized by only Britain and Pakistan, Israel did not drive out a legitimate sovereign power in 1967. While not considered occupied, the West Bank and Gaza were referred to as 'administered territories', which makes it clear that they were not (yet) annexed to Israel.

In reality the West Bank has been ruled by a mixed assortment of Jordanian laws, ordinances going back to the British Mandate period and over a thousand orders issued by the Israeli military government. Indeed, during the early years Defence Minister Moshe Dayan governed the occupied territories as a virtual Roman pro-consul. Neither the Israeli courts nor the Knesset had the real authority to over-rule his policies on the day-to-day running of the territories. Dayan's position was greatly enhanced by the prestige, public acclaim and celebrity status he had attained since the Israeli and international press had portrayed him as the architect of victory in 1967. In the years after the war portraits of the one-eyed general could be seen not only everywhere in Israel but in numerous publications all over the world.

Unlike Ben-Gurion, Menachem Begin or Golda Meir, Dayan was a Sabra, a native-born Israeli whose world view centred on the Middle East rather than on eastern Europe. Self-confident and proud to the point of arrogance, Dayan spoke fluent Arabic which he had learnt while growing up in one of Israel's first Moshavim (co-operative settlements). He thought he understood the Arab mentality and had a paternalistic, condescending attitude toward the Palestinians, who he believed could be successfully manipulated in order to condition them to Israeli rule. He told an interviewer:

I do not have the slightest doubt that, whatever public statements are made, deep in their hearts the majority of the West Bank Arabs wish to be linked with Palestine. Although they know that this may mean, in one way or the other, that they would be within an Israeli framework. I do not want to use the word loyalty in the sense of meaning loyalty to Israel, but I must say that they would not carry out sabotage attempts or try to weaken the present rule . . .[10]

Dayan considered the Palestinians unable to rule themselves and therefore to require the blessing of Israeli overlordship. He explained: 'Co-existence for Israelis and Arabs is only possible under the protection of the Israeli government and the Israeli army. Only under their rule can the Arabs lead normal lives.' Dayan added, 'Israel should listen to the views of the Arabs and meet them as far as she can . . . but more than anything else we should persevere in the realization of our vision.'[11] It would not in his opinion be necessary or even prudent to supervise the daily lives of the Palestinians in the occupied territories. 'I believed that from the point of view of our relations with the Arabs, our international standing and even our security, the less our government interferes with the private, religious and communal lives of the Arabs, the better.'[12]

But Dayan was not very clear as to his plans for the ultimate disposition of the occupied territories. The Defence Minister objected to the annexation of the West Bank, but just as fiercely opposed the idea of a full or partial withdrawal from the occupied territories. At times he spoke of unilateral autonomy. He favoured some type of joint Israeli–Jordanian rule with the Amman government having sovereignty over the people while Israel got the land.[13]

Dayan claimed to be waiting for a telephone call from King Hussein, but he really hoped that the phone would never ring. 'It is perhaps possible to conclude peace treaties between ourselves and our Arab neighbours', he said, 'but the Arabs are asking too high a price.'[14] Of course Dayan really would have liked to annex the West Bank and expel its population; but he realized that this was impractical since there was no way, in the foreseeable future, of getting rid of the Arab inhabitants without a huge outcry from world public opinion, including Israel's chief benefactor, the United States. In September 1968 Dayan told a journalist: 'It's true that the heritage of the past remains the cornerstone of our Zionist objectives of today and that the dream of the return to the land of Israel is still the motivation behind all our political activity', but he added, 'nevertheless one has to distinguish between the past and the necessities of present reality'.[15]

Yigal Allon, the Deputy Prime Minister, agreed with Dayan that Israel should retain its interests in the occupied territories, but he saw the need for the Jewish state at least to propose an outline for a peace settlement. So on 13 July 1967 Allon set down on paper a plan which was proposed to the cabinet several weeks later. Though never officially adopted by any Israeli cabinet, Allon's plan was in various forms over the years to be a guideline for those Israelis who favoured a 'land for peace' approach during the first decade of the occupation.

Allon advocated annexation of about a third of the West Bank; the Golan Heights, which had been captured from Syria; and the Gaza Strip. The deputy Prime Minister wanted an Israeli security belt 10–15 kilometres wide running the length of the Jordan Rift, which contained a small Arab population. This would make the River Jordan Israel's military frontier with the Arab world. The Jewish state would also annex the entire Judean Desert from Mount Hebron to the Dead Sea, as well as a strip north of the Jerusalem to Jericho road, reaching and including the Latrun salient. A corridor would cut through the zone of Israeli control to connect the remainder of the West Bank with the East Bank. Allon believed that Israel should also annex most of the Gaza Strip, although he felt Gaza Port might be made available for Arab use.

It is commonly asserted that Allon advocated annexing only 'arid areas' of sparse Arab population. It should be realized, however, that the area along the River Jordan is the West Bank's potentially most lucrative and productive agricultural region. The reason why it is so thinly populated is that 88 per cent of the Arab inhabitants were forcibly evicted during the 1967 war. The Israelis did not allow any of them to return in their token repatriation programme, and they are still careful not to allow any of the Jordan Valley property owners to return across the Allenby Bridge, where Israeli customs officers keep checklists of their names.

Allon also proposed that in the portion of the Gaza Strip to be annexed by Israel the sizeable Palestinian refugee population 'should be settled in the West Bank or al-Arish district',[16] which would be returned to Egypt. Israel would keep the lush citrus-growing area of Gaza, which would be settled by Jews. Only the urban centre of Gaza City and some of the surrounding refugee camps would remain available for Arab use.

Allon insisted that his plan was consistent with UN Resolution 242, which he interpreted as calling for Israeli withdrawal from some but not all of the captured territories. His plan may never have been adopted by any Israeli cabinet, but most of the Jewish settlements during this period were built in areas designated for annexation under it.

Initially Allon appears to have envisaged a kind of Palestinian statelet in the West Bank, controlled by Israel. He described it as a 'sovereign political state with close economic and security ties to Israel'.[17] There were in fact several Israeli proposals in the early years of the occupation for a Palestinian entity linked to Israel, but this kind of scheme faded away under the influence of the PLO and Palestinian nationalism, which demanded a real Palestinian state free from Israeli control. Allon later altered his plan to include the possibility of part of the West Bank going to King Hussein if the Jordanian monarch would agree to the permanent demilitarization of his portion. The Amman government would also have to recognize Israel's right to military intervention in the area in response to any terrorism launched against the Jewish state. As if this were not enough, Allon expected Hussein to acknowledge Israeli sovereignty over Jerusalem and agree to resettle the Gaza refugees on the East Bank. Allon's only real concession was to allow a land route (but not annexation of a sovereign land corridor) between the rump of the West Bank and the port of Gaza, which would provide the Jordan–West Bank state with access to the Mediterranean.

Immediately after the war Jordan was inclined towards a negotiated settlement, but King Hussein was bound by the Arab agreement at Khartoum. Israeli UN delegate Abba Eban's impression was that right after the war Hussein reacted favourably to the 'formula' of the Allon plan, although he rejected the specific map it contained. The Jordanian monarch did not consider the annexation of Jerusalem and a third of the West Bank as 'territorial adjustment'.[18]

The Israelis continued to negotiate with King Hussein for a deal along the lines of the Allon plan. In 1970 the then Prime Minister, Golda Meir, announced that 'the Israeli government representatives have had contacts with high Arab leaders since the war'.[19] She gave, however, no details, since she indicated that the Arab side had asked for no publicity. Over the years a great deal has become known about these futile negotiations. It is said that before this meeting with Yigal Allon, Hussein asked for Nasser's support. The Egyptian President told him, 'Go and meet with them, but if you give up Jerusalem, Arab history will never forgive you.' In his meeting with Allon, Hussein told the Israeli minister, 'I can be the first Arab leader to make peace with Israel or can give up some part of Arab territory, but I cannot do both.'[20]

Many Israelis believed that Hussein could relinquish his claim to a portion of the West Bank in exchange for the return of a large share of his former domain. Indeed the 'Jordanian Option' would remain the vain hope of many in the Labour party right up to the *intifada*. Few Israelis realized that King Hussein could never retain his throne if he agreed, against the wishes of the entire Arab world, to relinquish his claim to Jerusalem and a substantial part of the West Bank. This became even more obvious with the rise of the PLO, which could portray Hussein as a traitor to the Palestinian people and the Arab world if he agreed to the Allon plan. As in most confrontations, it is those with a reputation as hardliners, such as the PLO, who are in a better position to make compromises than a moderate such as Hussein. If the Jordanian monarch had made compromises it would have been seen as weakness, but if militants such as the PLO made concessions in order to get back much of the West Bank it could be interpreted as a stroke of *realpolitik*. Thus Allon's emphasis on Jordan as Israel's negotiating partner was a fatal flaw in his initiative.

Another barrier to Allon's success was the lack of consensus in Israel on his approach. On the right hand was the Land of Israel movement, the predecessor of Gush Emunim, led by Israel Shaib-Eldad. This group included not only the activists from the far right-wing parties but also members of the Labour party. The aim of the movement was to put pressure on officials who might consider withdrawal from any 'historic territories'. There was a broad hint that a massive departure of Arabs from the occupied areas would be most desirable.[21] Since the Land of Israel movement had support from members of the ruling Labour party, no Israeli cabinet could lightly contemplate abandonment of even a small portion of the occupied territories.

At the other end of the political spectrum were Israeli moderates, who opposed annexation but would prefer the return of most of the occupied territories to Jordan and Egypt. Besides feeling that such a step would further peace, these Labour leaders felt uneasy about the annexation of territories with a large Arab population who could not easily be expelled. They foresaw that a large influx of Arab workers from the territories would become the proletariat of the Hebrew state, thus negating the tradition of *Avoda Ivrit*, the principle of Jewish labour which was at the core of Zionist ideology. The early Zionists believed that only people who actually worked the soil and factories of a country could fully possess the land. In view of the astronomically high Palestinian birth rate, twice that of the Jews, many Labour Zionists feared that Israel would become a bi-national state in which the Jews would be a minority. This would deny the entire concept of a Zionist state. Clearly sovereignty over the West Bank and Gaza was not worth such a high price. The ambivalent attitude of many in the Labour party towards the occupied territories can be summarized in Prime Minister Levi Eshkol's metaphor: 'The dowry is gorgeous but the bride is so homely.'

Moderates such as Abba Eban and the Finance Minister, Pinhas Sapir, opposed the economic integration of the occupied territories into Israel. Eban believed that all future options should be left open and that an expansionist programme would lose support abroad, most importantly in the United States. The UN envoy opposed the use of labour from the territories in Israel and the meshing of economic resources as well as the establishment of Israeli settlements. Sapir believed that by returning most of the territories Israel would be surrendering nothing. Indeed, the Jewish state would be 'freeing itself of a burden' since the retention of territories with such a large Arab population would lead to the strangulation of Israel. He told an Israeli newspaper, 'We have not come to this land, toiled and shed our blood for a state that would eventually become a bi-national state.'[22]

Sapir was willing to make any concession which did not threaten Israeli security. He objected to religious and ideological concepts being introduced into the debate on the future of the West Bank. 'Our presence in Nablus and Jericho is not that of a people liberating its homeland.'[23] He believed that security alone should determine Israel's future border, after negotiation with its neighbours. But he opposed any unilateral withdrawal from the West Bank, Gaza, Sinai or the Golan Heights before peace treaties were concluded with Jordan, Egypt and Syria.

There were, however, some Israeli leaders on the left of the political spectrum who argued that it might be necessary and desirable for the Jewish state unilaterally to evacuate the occupied territories. A spokesman of this group was Yitzak Ben-Aharon, Secretary-General of Histadrut, the Zionist Labour Federation. On 1 February 1973 he told a meeting of the Labour secretariat: 'I do not know whether the territories that we hold are bargaining cards or perhaps embers burning away at our foundations. . . . I am not at all sure that one of these days we will conclude that a certain portion of the population and certain sections of the country should not be under our control even without receiving a countersignature [on peace treaty].'[24]

On 14 February he elaborated his views in an interview with the *New York Times*. He made it clear that the crucial question for Israel was 'whether we are going to impose the present borders on ourselves. . . . Why should we wait for King Hussein's signature to give up Nablus, Jericho, maybe a portion of Hebron and with it the responsibility for 500,000 of the 650,000 Arabs who live in the West Bank?' Ben-Aharon argued that returning these areas and their residents to Jordan would restore their political rights and reduce the antagonism they harboured towards Israel. But in the early years of the occupation there was a widely felt and growing feeling that the territories could be of great economic advantage to Israel.

The 1967 West Bank harvest was particularly good, since it yielded a surplus of one hundred thousand tons for export. But the route to the usual East Bank markets was closed. If the crops were left in the fields the entire West Bank economy could collapse – which, the Israeli authorities realized, would result in increased resistance to the occupation. But they would not allow the West Bank harvest to be sold in Israel, because it would have undersold the Jewish producers by 20 per cent.

A solution to the problem was improvised. In summer the River Jordan is quite low, and in the middle there is a ford which can easily be crossed by truck. The Israelis permitted hundreds of trucks to cross the river and transfer their loads to Jordanian vehicles. On the other side West Bank trucks would simply exchange Israeli military licence plates for Jordanian ones. Tomatoes, water melons, grapes and almonds were shipped across the Jordan. When Moshe Dayan found out about the renewed trade he welcomed the development, which he saw as a sign of a return to normality which could be viewed as acquiescence to the occupation.[25]

In October the Jordanian government allowed two bridges to be built, one near Jericho and the other at Damiya, in order to maintain the trade in winter when the Jordan was too high to cross. While most of the produce consisted of exports to Jordan, some West Bank landowners with holdings in Jordan imported wheat across the river into occupied territory. Later during the year West Bank traders were allowed to use the proceeds of their sales in Jordan for the purchase of imports into the West Bank which were subject to Israeli duties. Although there was no formal agreement, both sides were well aware of the trade across the Jordan. Dayan believed not only that such trade would promote stability in the West Bank, but also that it could eventually lead to Israeli economic penetration of the Arab world via the West Bank.

But despite the well-publicized 'open bridges' between the West Bank and Jordan, Dayan's real policy was for the economic integration of the occupied territories with Israel. With regard to the population of the territories, Dayan favoured 'an economic integration and not a political integration. In other words not an annexation: we should not make them citizens of the state of Israel.'[26] He spoke of the 'autonomy of the people', but not the land and its resources. The Defence Minister saw the occupied territories as a source of cheap labour and a market for Israeli goods which could be exploited for the benefit of Israel. This kind of colonial system was preferable to allowing a huge influx of Arabs into Israel as citizens, which would change the character of the Jewish state.

On 6 November 1968 Dayan made a speech at Beersheva

in which he outlined his plans for the economic integration of the occupied territories. Several weeks later he was questioned by a Knesset member who wanted to know whether the Defence Minister had merely voiced his own views or whether they reflected official cabinet policy. Dayan realized that the questioner, Natan Peled, supported Pinhas Sapir's view that economic integration of the occupied territories was detrimental to Israel – an impediment to peace. In reply Dayan gave a fourteen-point summary of all the economic integration measures which had been officially approved by the cabinet, and denied that he had implemented economic integration of the West Bank on his own authority.[27]

He mentioned that on 7 July 1968 the committee of the Ministry of Economics, in order to relieve unemployment in the occupied territories and to supplement Israel's manpower shortage, had approved the employment of workers from the territories in Israel. This would be regulated by the Ministry of Labour and the military government in the West Bank and Gaza. Dayan also noted the establishment of enterprises in the West Bank by Israelis according to a decision of a committee of ministers on 29 September.

The Defence Minister pointed out that on 29 August the government had decided to integrate Israeli and Arab bus lines. He also mentioned the integration of electrical power grids and the cancellation of custom duties between the occupied territories and Israel. There was also a move towards allowing a limited amount of farm produce from the West Bank into Israel when it did not compete with Jewish agriculture. According to Dayan, similar measures for economic integration were being taken in Gaza, with cabinet approval.

This statement greatly disturbed Pinhas Sapir. Backed by a number of 'doves', he complained to the Prime Minister, Levi Eshkol, about the measures revealed by Dayan. But his protest achieved no result. In every area of economic life the West Bank and Gaza were being integrated into Israel. Decisions were being made which would make a negotiated settlement much more difficult. Dayan believed that, as the Palestinians became more meshed into the Israeli economy, they would become less nationalistic and give up any hope of living under their own rule. Indeed during the first decade of the occupation the people of the West Bank experienced a radical change in their way of life.

The most obvious consequence of the integration of the West Bank economy with that of Israel was the number of Palestinian workers who sought employment in Israel. Between 1968 and 1974 the number of migrant workers rose from year to year. Eventually a third of the labour force in the occupied territories was employed in Israel. Most who came were farm labourers or workers in small businesses which had been closed because they could not compete with the flood of Israeli goods into the territories. The Palestinians quickly took over the manual jobs which had previously been performed in Israel by oriental Jews; these people were now able to advance into positions as clerks, foremen and semi-professionals. Thus the influx of migrant labour transformed the Israeli social structure as much as it did that of the Palestinians.

Between 1968 and 1972 twenty-three employment agencies were set up in the West Bank. Officially these agencies were formed to regulate the job market in the interest of the workers, but in reality their main function was to satisfy the needs of Israeli business and industry by ensuring that workers were provided to fit the needs of Israeli employers. The labour agencies also helped to screen workers from the point of view of security. Palestinians received only a temporary permit, which had to be renewed every four months.

There was also a 'free market' of illegal workers who looked for employment on their own from day to day or were forced to go through Arab labour agents. These middlemen made a living procuring employment in Israel for entire crews of workers. Many of these were under seventeen and thus could not be employed legally in Israel. In the 1970s, there were about thirty-five thousand Palestinians from the territories working illegally in Israel, performing jobs which were more menial and lower-paid than those for legal workers from the occupied territories.[28]

But even legal workers were badly exploited. Despite claims of equal pay, in 1972 wages for labourers from the territories were half those received by Israeli workers. Registered legal workers were forced to pay up to 30 per cent of their salaries in taxes, national health insurance, old age pensions, unemployment insurance and sick leave, but never received benefits.[29] These unexpended taxes were held in a fund under the control of the Ministry of Finance, which used the money to benefit Israelis at the expense of the exploited Palestinians. Workers from the occupied territories tolerated these conditions because the wages offered in the depressed Palestinian economy were even lower than those offered in Israel.

Dayan's belief that the exploitation of cheap Palestinian labour would benefit the Israeli economy proved to be correct. On 18 May 1976 the Israeli newspaper *Davar* considered the question of Arab workers from the territories:

It is almost impossible to fire an Israeli worker, impossible to relocate him without his permission and without a wage increase; on the other hand an Arab worker is exceptionally mobile, can be dismissed without notice and moved from place to place, does not strike and does not present 'demands' as does his Israeli counterpart. In short, from many economic considerations, workers from the territories are a bargain for the Israeli economy. It is a labour force which economists are able to define as responding in an economically healthy manner to the demands of the economy: they exist when and where required and make a full contribution to the production cycle. As long as one does not speak in social or political terms, the workers from the territories display an excellent economic flexibility.

But some people noticed how Israel was being changed by the influx of so many Palestinian workers. In the first decade of the occupation there was a national debate on the subject. Many Israelis did not mind that most of the manual labour was being performed by workers from the West Bank and Gaza. As one farmer noted, 'If the Arabs exist, let them work. Why shouldn't Jews be the bosses? The Arab workers are naturally built for it. I have one who is fifty years old and works bent double for eight hours a day. Show me a Jew like him.' Other Israelis regretted the loss of the Jewish work ethic which had been so prevalent among the early Zionist settlers. A wife of a co-operative farmer noted: 'Today we have five Arab workers and a situation where we do nothing for ourselves on our farm. My eldest son now even refuses to cut the grass, saying, 'Let Muhamad do it'.[30]

This was truly 'apartheid Israeli-style'. The Palestinians from the territories had no rights under Israeli law. Indeed they could not even legally stay overnight. Many did so in unspeakable conditions, locked up at night like animals by their employers, so they could not be discovered by the police.

Many of the West Bank workers in Israel left farm employment at home, since it is Israeli policy to subordinate the agriculture of the occupied territories to prevent it from competing with their own. The West Bank was instead encouraged to produce low-profit crops which were neglected in Israel. These crops were processed in Israel, thus ensuring the dependence of West Bank agriculture and denying Palestinians the chance to work in factories at home.

In 1975 A. Agmon, a former Israeli agricultural specialist who was aware of all this, accused the Ministry of Agriculture of running a colonial policy in the occupied territories where he had worked. Agmon noted that the Ministry had built up legislation and procedures which prevented the free marketing of fish, grapes, dates and other produce from the occupied territories in Israel. He stated: 'It is also preventing the development of livestock in the territories for local use by limiting financing, while the left-over produce from Israel is flooding the territories without regard to the interest of local agriculture.'[31] Only agriculture 'which would not hurt a single Israeli farmer' was allowed in the territories. Agmon wrote: 'The West Bank and Gaza Strip buy tens of thousands of tons of Israeli produce. Sales in the other directions amount to only a few hundred tons, devoid of economic significance.' In view of the decimation of farming in the occupied territories, it is not surprising that between

1969 and 1977 the number of people engaged in agriculture declined by a third.

There were also few opportunities for industrial employment in the West Bank. Most production is in small workshops with modest capital. Labour for the most part is provided by the owner and his family, and so hired help is at a minimum. In 1979 there were only seven firms with more than a hundred employees, all of which were established before 1967.[32] A significant proportion of labour-intensive industry is sub-contracted from Israeli enterprises, keeping Arab workers dependent on Israeli contractors.

The absence of Arab banking facilities for credit and financial transactions is one major reason for the lag in West Bank industrial development. Another is the flood of Israeli products. In 1975, Israel sold 16 per cent of its total exports to the West Bank and Gaza. This was greater than Israeli exports to the United States or Britain. Most of the Israeli exports to the occupied territories were manufactured products – radios, TVs, gas and electric cookers and other important consumer goods – which stifled the growth of West Bank industry. This of course is a typical imperial situation, with the colony supplying cheap labour to the dominating nation which in return uses the colony as a dumping ground for its manufactured goods. And because the West Bank lacked its own government, it could not defend its means of production from outside manipulation.

With West Bank agriculture run-down and its industry stymied, and with employment in Israel limited to the most menial jobs, it is no wonder that a large part of the educated and skilled labour force in the occupied territories left to seek employment abroad. Many went to Jordan and the oil-rich Arab states of the Gulf, while others went to Europe and North America. This emigration speeded up in the 1970s, so that by 1978 over a hundred thousand people had left the occupied territories. As A. R. Husseini, an economics expert from the West Bank, has written:

We are now losing about 20,000 workers a year across the bridge, most of them skilled – teachers, doctors, engineers.

This process has accelerated particularly among educated youth. Unlike unskilled labourers, college graduates are paid relatively poorly, that is if they find jobs at all. In the last couple of years there has also been a marked increase in the outflow of skilled labourers. They can earn a lot more in Saudi Arabia and Amman. Our experience here is bitter; the ones who leave don't come back. They always rationalize in the beginning, that they are leaving for just one or two years to make enough money and come back. But somehow they settle where they are.[33]

The emigration of the educated Palestinians served the interests of the Israelis since it deprived the people of the occupied territories of their natural leaders. What was left was an uneducated proletariat that was available to serve the interests of Israeli industry without being able to offer any genuine political opposition.

Right from the beginning the Israelis exercised strict control over education in the West Bank. On 8 August 1967 a military order was issued which banned seventy-eight out of 123 textbooks then in use in West Bank schools. It was claimed that the Jordanian textbooks contained 'passages intended to inculcate hatred of Israel and the Jewish people'. But many of the forbidden materials did not involve anything anti-Semitic or even anti-Israel. The occupation authorities objected to any reference to Palestinian nationalism or to anything that linked Palestine with Arab culture. Palestinian poetry, the war of 1948 – even the crusaders – were forbidden subjects.[34]

The Israelis did not interfere in the West Bank schools operated by UNRWA. This was a reflection of a general 'hands off UNRWA' policy practised by the occupation authorities in the West Bank and Gaza. The Israelis were not anxious to antagonize the UN agency, which could create bad propaganda for them. Besides, UNRWA did invaluable work in providing services for Palestinian refugees from the 1948 war who still resided in West Bank refugee camps. On 18 March 1968 a report from the chief of UNRWA operations in the West Bank to Lawrence Michelmore, the Commissioner-General of UNRWA, notes: 'There has been

only a single military incursion into an Agency installation
and that related to a completely empty camp in Jericho. They
have even gone so far, on occasions, as to express apologies
– which, in my experience, was hardly a common occurrence
with Arab governments.'[35]

Israeli policy of not interfering with UNRWA and its
services for Palestinian refugees in the West Bank differed
markedly from the situation in Gaza, where the occupation
authorities took a decidedly negative attitude towards the
Palestinian refugees, whom they wished to expel (see Chapter 3). But even in the West Bank there was some friction,
particularly with regard to the scope of UNRWA assistance to
those whom the occupation authorities considered ineligible
for refugee status.

In his memoirs Moshe Dayan paints an idyllic picture of the
relations between the occupation authorities and the subject
Palestinians: 'In the matters which affect their daily lives, the
Arab community had no complaints.'[36] There were in fact
numerous protests by the people of the West Bank against
the Israeli intrusion into every aspect of their lives. The
Palestinians resented the curfews, administrative detentions,
demolition of homes, brutal interrogations, forced deportations and degrading roadblocks, all of which would become
standard procedure during the occupation. By 1977 approximately 60 per cent of the male population aged between
eighteen and fifty in the territories had spent at least one night
in prison. This was much higher than the number in South
Africa and would become worse in the following decade.

Demolition of homes was a favourite retaliation imposed
by the Israelis on many West Bank villages, despite Article 33
of the Fourth Geneva Convention which prohibits collective
punishments for violations of the law which have not been
personally committed. These demolitions were supposedly
aimed at punishing the population, particularly for complicity
with the guerilla organization, but in reality they constituted
a form of terrorism designed to encourage people to cross
over the Jordan. When houses were destroyed in Halhul in
the wake of a guerilla attack on Israeli soldiers, Dayan told the
inhabitants: 'Today we demolished twenty houses. If this is

not enough, we will demolish the whole town and if you don't like this policy, the bridges are open for your departure.'[37] Although destruction of homes was a widespread policy, there is considerable dispute about how many were involved. Arab sources claim that 7100 homes were destroyed in the first two years of occupation, while the Israelis admit destroying 1224 homes up to 1977.

Curfews were another commonly used form of collective punishment and inducement to leave. Often the whole male population of a village or refugee camp between fourteen and seventy years of age would be driven to a deserted spot or herded into a stockade, while the women and children were forced to remain indoors all day and night. The men were made to kneel, squat or assume other humiliating poses. This would be kept up for two or three days while the soldiers guarding them would fire into the air above their heads. The women and children, who were allowed to leave their homes for only half an hour a day, frequently lacked food, water or sanitation.

One of the largest curfews occurred in the village of Beit Sahur, which was well known for its nationalist fervour. The Israelis accused the villagers of complicity in the firing of a Katusha rocket on Jerusalem from near Beit Sahur, and as a result the population was subjected to a twenty-two-hour-a-day curfew during which they could not open doors, go out into their gardens, open windows or even stand by them. On 26 September 1969 the inhabitants protested: 'The enemy authorities detonate explosive charges near people's houses after dark to increase the pressure on the unfortunate people so as to make them leave the West Bank.'[38] The petition noted: 'The Israeli Defence Minister and the Military Governor of the district have put two alternatives before the population of the district, either go on living like this or be dispatched to the bridge.' Because of the international reaction the Israelis lifted the curfew a few days later, but there would be constant conflict between the people of Beit Sahur and the occupation authorities in the years ahead.

Another common violation of human rights in the occupied

territories was the Israeli practice of administrative detention. According to Article III of the 1945 British Emergency Defence Regulations, which the Israelis regarded as still being in force in the West Bank, any Palestinian could be imprisoned for up to six months without trial. Many people were sent to detention camps in remote locations such as Nakhl, Abu Zu'aiman and Kussimah. Most of the detainees were accused of working for the resistance, though rarely was any evidence of involvement in terrorism produced. Prisoners were denied radios, newspapers and other basic amenities. Women and children were also sometimes sent to detention camps, but they were usually accompanied by an adult male in view of Arab sensitivity about the honour of women. In 1979, under extreme international pressure, Israel issued Article 87 Security Provisions Order, which provided for judicial and administrative control over the practice of administrative detention. But abuses persisted.[39]

Most of the detained prisoners were subjected to torture, which in the first decade of the occupation was well documented by numerous international investigators. Inquiries were conducted by Amnesty International, the UN Special Committee on the occupied territories, the International Committee of the Red Cross, the London *Sunday Times* and the US National Lawyers' Guild. It was concluded that 'torture has been used in numerous instances against detained Palestinians by Israeli police, military and intelligence authorities'.[40] The methods included burning prisoners with cigarette stubs, hitting them with rods on their genitals, letting dogs bite them, administering electric shocks, suspending by the hands and blindfolding for days on end. International exposés and protests did little to end these atrocities.

Of all the human rights violations in the West Bank, seizure of land had the most serious long-range consequence. From the beginning of the occupation Palestinian land was being stolen. A particularly vicious incident occurred at Akraba, a village where the people resisted the theft of their land for use by a Nahal settlement – Fighting Pioneer Youth, an army corps made up of volunteers who combine military service with agricultural work. Previously they had set up border settlements inside Israel which were eventually turned into civilian settlements. After the Six-Day War they spread their operations to the occupied territories.

In late 1967 the Israeli army seized 100,000 dunams (1 dunam = 1,000 square metres) of land, which left the people of Akraba with very little for their own agriculture. In 1971 the Israelis confiscated the remaining land; the IDF declared the land to be a 'military training area', the fields were fenced off and the local people forbidden to enter 'for their own safety'. But the peasants rebelled: they broke through the fences and ploughed and sowed their fields as they had done for generations. It was a good year with plenty of rain, promising a good harvest. The Israelis decided to teach the people of Akraba a lesson. In the early morning of 28 April 1972 an Israeli plane flew down over the fields, spraying the area with chemical poison. Overnight the wheat turned brown and died.

When the Palestinian journalist Raymonda Tawil told the story to her Israeli colleague Victor Cygielman, the latter refused to believe it, saying, 'You exaggerate sometimes, Raymonda.'[41] But when he went to Akraba he found that the story was true. In an article published on 3 July in *Nouvel Observateur*, Cygielman described the scene of devastation as he surveyed the affected area. The villagers were shocked that the Israelis had used chemical warfare against them. 'We have cultivated the land', the mukhtar told Cygielman, 'ever since the Turkish Sultan Abdul Hamid gave it to us.'

The Israeli authorities did not deny the incident, and confirmed that they wished 'to teach the villagers a lesson'. The inhabitants of Akraba wote letters of protest to Moshe Dayan and the Ministry of Agriculture, but received no reply. Instead a government representative came and advised them not to write any more letters if they wished to get compensation for the seizure of their land. Despite international protests the people of Akraba lost their land to Gittit, a Jewish settlement – one of many that would spring up all over the West Bank.

Even though Hebron was a city sacred to Jews as well as Moslems, it seemed odd when, on 4 April 1968, a group of seventy-three Orthodox Jews led by Rabbis Moshe Levinger and Eleazer Waldman, former students of Rabbi Kook, checked into the Park Hotel, which was run by the influential Kawassma family. The rabbis had made previous requests to settle in Hebron, which had been rejected by the governor of the West Bank on the grounds that it might create political and security problems. The group now told the authorities that they would be staying at the Park Hotel for only one week during the Passover season, but this proved to be untrue: Levinger and his followers took over the hotel. They made the kitchen kosher and soon announced that they were remaining in Hebron permanently, thus renewing the bond between Israelis and the city of the Patriarchs where Jews had been killed in 1929. As Rabbi Waldman later recalled, 'We took out an option for a lifetime.'[42]

Since the Defence Minister, Moshe Dayan, was at the time in hospital and General Shlomo Gazit, co-ordinator for the West Bank, was observing the seven-day mourning period following the death of his father, it fell to Yigal Allon to deal with the incident. His sympathy with the Jews was obvious and immediate. According to Israeli Radio:

On 15th April the Labour Minister Yigal Allon visited the first Israelis who have taken up residence in Hebron. They discussed problems of employment and vocational training. The Labour Minister announced that until the newcomers found permanent posts his Ministry would employ all those seeking jobs in office work and guard duties. For the skilled workers among them the Ministry would find jobs in Jerusalem.[43]

Years later Rabbi Waldman boasted that Dayan and Allon had competed to see who would be the patron of the religious settlers. He notes that the Prime Minister, Levi Eshkol, never told them not to occupy the hotel but tried to postpone the settlement of Hebron. However, according to Waldman, Yigal Allon encouraged them to act, saying: 'If you don't create the facts nothing will come of it. Don't wait for the government's OK – just go out and do it.' Waldman recalled that Allon was entirely supportive of the religious settlers. He relates that when they complained about his famous peace plan, the Israeli Minister told them: 'Jews have to be smart. No Arab will ever accept this plan.' Waldman added, 'That was all he said. That was Yigal Allon.'[44] With Allon's help the settlement of religious Jews at Kiryat Arba near Hebron was established.

Most of the early settlements, however, were not religious. On 24 June 1967 Israeli Radio had announced: 'The United Kibbutz Council has decided that groups of Kibbutz members should establish settlement in the liberated areas.'[45] During September and October 1967, just after the Six-Day War, four settlements were established by Nahal. One was at El-Arish in the Sinai, which had been seized from Egypt, and another the Golan Heights, taken from Syria. A third Nahal settlement was established at the Kefar Etzion block, west of the Jerusalem–Hebron road.[46] This had been the site of a Jewish settlement that had been wiped out during the 1948 war. A large group of settlements in the early years of the occupation was established in the Jordan Valley along the river border with Hussein's kingdom. This area was designated for annexation under the Allon Plan. Speaking at a Kibbutz meeting on 17 April 1968 he announced: 'We must settle wherever possible in accordance with Israel's defence and security needs and the future of its borders.'[47] He added: 'The Jordan valley and the range of mountains are needed for our security. We cannot yield on this point even if there is no peace.'

The Israelis began the construction of two belts of settlements along the north–south length of the eastern border of the West Bank, one on the floor of the Jordan Valley and the other on the highlands overlooking it. A so-called Allon Plan road was constructed to connect the two belts of settlements. A total of fourteen Moshavim, six Kibbutzim, two Nahal and one Moshav settlement were built in the Jordan Valley. These settlements were initally built for security, but soon had a well-developed agriculture: tomatoes, peppers, aubergines, cucumbers, bananas, citrus fruit and flowers grew in the rich soil. A considerable profit was made selling this produce, particularly winter vegetables, to the European market.

Settlements were also established in southern Judaea, a region which Allon believed Israel should annex. However problems developed with the climate, lack of cultivable land and conflict with the indigenous Palestinian population. Only a hundred Jewish families were moved into the eleven settlements.

Difficulties also arose with the Jordan Valley settlements. The original concept was for the re-creation of the pioneering zeal which motivated the early Zionist settlers who 'cleared the land' while fighting off Arab marauders. But it soon became obvious that there were few young people in modern Israel who were motivated by the Kibbutz spirit of Labour Zionism. Thus, despite generous financial incentives to settle and enormous investment, only eighteen hundred people could be found to populate these settlements.

Towards the end of Labour party rule there was a renewed interest in West Bank settlements. On 13 November 1974 the Prime Minister, Yitzak Rabin, announced: 'The government has worked to increase the population of settlement in the Golan Heights and the Jordan Valley and, should war break out, this is the line which will determine the results.'[48] The new settlements were confined to the Allon Plan regions, including a string of satellite towns of Jerusalem proposed by the Housing Minister, Abraham Ofer. On the eve of the 1977 elections there were about 4200 Jewish settlers in the West Bank as well as forty-five to fifty thousand Jews living in the East Jerusalem area.[49] The increase in Jewish settlement in the West Bank during the second decade of the occupation would have a severe impact on the Palestinian population.

The Israelis have argued that their occupation has greatly benefited the population of the West Bank. They point to the increase in education levels, stable administration and the rising standard of living of the population to support their claim that the people of the West Bank have done well under Israeli rule. But the supposed benefits are more apparent than real.

While it is true that the percentage of the population in the

West Bank who had received no education dropped from 48 per cent in 1970 to 32 per cent in 1980, most of that education was provided by UNRWA, various religious denominations and funds from the Arab world. The Israelis were not the motivating force behind the rise in West Bank education. Their one significant contribution was in fact a negative one: to decimate West Bank industry and restrict white collar jobs for Palestinians in Israel, thus forcing educated young people to emigrate to find work.

The political stability of the West Bank during the first decade of occupation was achieved at the price of considerable repression. Dayan's claim that he left the daily life of the Palestinians alone is not true when it affected any area that was of interest to the occupiers. There was censorship, punitive repression and every other conceivable violation of human rights under laws determined by the Israelis and not the Palestinians. This was particularly true in all matters concerning the economic development of the occupied territories.

There are some statistics which suggest a rise in the Palestinian standard of living. In 1980 there were thirty-eight thousand cars in the West Bank compared to seven thousand five hundred in 1968. Only 29 per cent of the population had television in 1967, while over 60 per cent owned a set in 1980. There was a similar rise in the ownership of refrigerators, gas cookers and other durable goods. However, some observers attributed the increase in such material possessions to less positive reasons – there were few opportunities for Palestinians to invest in agriculture, financial institutions or industry, which would have created a solid boost to the long-term prosperity of their country, so all they could do with their money was spend it.

Indeed the West Bank's relative prosperity in the 1970s was not real since it was based on economic dependence on Israel rather than development of the Palestinians' own country. A major source of Palestinian income was employment in Israel, which helped develop the economy of the occupier. Indeed most of the money earned by Palestinian labour in Israel went right back to the Jewish state in the forms of the purchase of Israeli goods by the West Bank population.

Compared to the situation in Jordan and other neighbouring Arab states, which experienced real economic development in the 1970s, the rise in the availability of consumer goods in the West Bank was not particularly impressive. But there was one Arab-inhabited region which looked with envy on the West Bank. In Gaza, right from the beginning, the population experienced the full weight of Israeli repression.

3
THE GAZA EXODUS

'Bad morning to you, this is the greeting of Israel,' shouted an IDF soldier as he hustled Palestinian men over the age of fifteen from their beds at gunpoint at the Jabalia refugee camp in Gaza on the chilly morning of 29 December 1967. The refugees were gathered in groups and lined up along the walls of their huts in the A, B, C and D housing blocks of the camp. They were told to put their hands over their heads and then they were beaten with sticks and rifle butts by Israeli officers and men. The UNRWA employees who were among those rounded up showed the Israelis their identity papers, but they were 'ignored and ridiculed'.[1] The pretext for this harassment was the death of an Israeli soldier, who had been killed by a mine some kilometres from the Jabalia camp. There was no evidence that anyone from the camp had been involved.

After being lined up, the frightened refugees were then ordered to a central collection point. Soldiers standing by the side of the road beat the defenceless men as they ran by. A. L. Geaney, the director of UNRWA operations in Gaza, later noticed many 'sandals lying in the road which apparently had been left by the refugees who had been made to run'.[2]

About a thousand men were taken to a large ditch which was used to collect rainwater for the camp. There they were ordered to stand with their arms over their heads, facing the ditch, for almost two hours. Later they were forced to squat on their heels with their hands over their heads. According to the UNRWA people, 'all the time until they were ultimately released, shooting was taking place, with occasional rifle and machine gun firing and occasional bombs were thrown'.

Some of the men were brutally interrogated about the killing of the Israeli soldier. At about 10 pm it began to rain heavily, and the overnight temperature fell to 10°C (50°F). The men stood all night shivering in their pyjamas next to the flooded ditch. During this period they were starving, since it was the season of Ramadan when Moslems fast during daylight, and the camp had been under curfew for several days and nights; some of the men had not eaten anything for days. Those who asked to relieve themselves were rolled in the mud or stoned.

Next day the brutality continued. As usual, the taunts of the Israelis were designed to destroy the dignity and self-respect of the Palestinians. The refugees were forced to assume humiliating positions and to shout insults against Arab leaders, especially the Egyptian President. Those who refused to shout 'Nasser is a dog' or to make noises like a dog were beaten or thrown into the flooded ditch.

On the following afternoon, the original group of a thousand was joined by another five thousand Palestinian men from the Jabalia camp. The newcomers were harassed, but not as badly as those who had been there all night 'except that soldiers continued to shoot into the air presumably to maintain a state of anxiety among the refugees'.[3] During this period the homes of many of them were searched. The Palestinians claimed that everything of value was stolen.

In a report A. L. Geaney indicated that one of the refugees had to be taken to hospital suffering from exposure, while two others left the camp in the Agency's ambulance but refused to be admitted to hospital. He noted: 'There is no record of anyone being hospitalized as a result of being beaten but the refugees always try not to bring such matters to public notice in order to avoid further reprisals.'[4]

As a pretext to harass the refugees once again the Israelis used another attack in which an IDF soldier was wounded on 1 January 1968. In the first days of the New Year, the homes and furniture of the exiles were demolished. Even more brutal was the destruction of wells, which added to the misery in the overcrowded camps. Fishing boats, production facilities and water pumps for the orange groves were destroyed, which deprived Gazans of some of their limited opportunities for work.

In a report on 4 January Geaney observed: 'Some of the Gaza people think that the blowing up of the wells and pumps is a deliberate step to deprive labourers of work so that they will willingly leave the strip to move to Jericho.' He added, 'Perhaps it is no coincidence that we ascertained this morning that about 250 refugees from Jabalia camp were awaiting transport to go to Jericho where they are employed as labourers.' Once in Jericho, of course, the Gazan refugees could be 'encouraged' to cross over the nearby River Jordan into King Hussein's realm. The UNRWA director wrote prophetically, 'This seems to be the big push to move the refugees out of the Gaza Strip but it appears that there is a limit to what I or perhaps UNRWA can do about it.'[5]

Throughout early 1968 the Israelis increased their pressure to force the refugees out of Gaza. Passport offices were established at Jabalia and other camps to encourage them to go to the East Bank. On 17 January Israeli officials told the *New York Times* that about two hundred Gaza refugees were leaving every day for Jordan and that they wanted them to go. 'We made it easy,' they admitted 'because there are too many here.' Soon, however, voluntary emigration fell off. Firmer measures were needed.

All the mukhtars from Jabalia were called into the passport office in small groups, where they were met by an Israeli who called himself Abu Yusef. He told them that the Israeli authorities 'were planning to facilitate the movement of the refugees to the East Bank where there was more space available and that the standards at Jabalia were very low. We want to advise the mukhtars to move out.'[6] The mukhtars informed the Israeli that the refugees had no desire to leave for Jordan, but 'Abu Yusef' replied that the Jabalia area was to become a military zone and they would eventually be forced to move. He told them that they should tell their people to get to Jordan or Egypt because 'they would be sorry if they remained in Jabalia'.

On 10 July that year Israeli officials once again sent for the mukhtars of the Jabalia camp and demanded co-operation in 'causing the refugees of Jabalia camp to migrate'.[7] They specifically requested the names of those households in which the husband was abroad at the outbreak of the Six-Day War, leaving the rest of the family behind in the camp. These women, children and old people would be the first to be deported, with the transportation being paid for by the Israelis. The mukhtars resisted at first, but they were threatened with the loss of their position or even imprisonment if they refused to co-operate, so most of them reluctantly submitted lists of households from which the husbands were missing. The Israelis indicated that they were 'prepared to pay more money for the movement of complete families with the head of the family'.[8] They stressed that eventually all the refugees would have to leave Gaza; the deportation of women and children was only the beginning.

When the women were told to get ready for departure they demonstrated, tore their hair and clothes, shouted and cursed the mukhtars, whom they called traitors and accused of selling them out to the Israelis. Some of the women filed protests with UNRWA, asking them to intercede with the Israeli authorities. A few even hired a lawyer, who submitted a legal brief to the Israeli authorities stating that 'deportation from the occupied territory to territories of other states is prohibited by all international agreements and all laws and is contrary to the Security Council's resolutions and the Charter of Human Rights'.[9] The legal brief cited Article 49 of the Fourth Geneva Convention, signed by Israel, which prohibits deportation from occupied territory.

The UNRWA authorities were very concerned about the Israeli efforts to deport a large proportion of the refugees in Gaza – 330,000 out of the 434,000 Palestinians in the Strip. On 23 July the UNRWA Commissioner-General, Lawrence Michelmore, reported to the UN Secretariat that the movement of Gaza residents to the East Bank, which had dropped considerably in May and June, had risen to a hundred persons a day that month. This emigration was not voluntary. On the 27th a group of fifty-seven inhabitants of the Gaza Strip sought refuge in Jordan, after travelling via the West Bank. In their testimony they complained about 'the inhuman treatment to which they were subjected by Israeli authorities'.[10]

On the same day Michelmore gave the UN Secretariat his analysis of Israeli policy:

> . . . our general feeling is that Government is prepared to encourage this movement by money payments and indirect coercion such as threat of detention for breach of security unless persons *opt* for movement out of Strip but that simple deportation will rarely be used. We believe it likely that substantial funds are being used for this purpose.[11]

The Palestinian resistance forces in Gaza which formed the underground United National Front (UNF) opposed Israeli attempts to pressure the refugees into fleeing to Jordan. According to 'Ali', a political activist in Gaza during the late 1960s, 'The Israelis were attempting to force a mass emigration. They were inflicting all kinds of hardships on the people, ensuring that there were no employment opportunities and at the same time offering families financial incentives to leave.' Ali noted that many Gazans succumbed to Israeli pressure to leave because the Strip 'was like a big prison'.[12]

The UNF tried to persuade Gazans not to emigrate, since it would be a disaster for their cause if the Palestinians left their homeland. The movement 'distributed leaflets against emigration, visited people who were thinking of leaving, and wrote slogans on the walls'. Ali even travelled to Ramallah on the West Bank on the pretext of visiting relatives in order to speak to Gazans who had taken money from the Israelis and were on their way to Jordan. He stated, 'Usually I managed to convince them to change their minds.' It is not clear if the UNF used threats of violence to persuade Gazans not to proceed to the East Bank.

There is no doubt, however, that the Jordanians ultimately resorted to force in order to keep Gazans out of their country, which was already flooded with new refugees whom it could not absorb. On 28 July the Jordanians charged Israel with trying to force fifty thousand Gazans to emigrate to their country; they asked the UN as well as the British and Americans to help stop the flow of refugees, whom they were determined to keep out.[13] Indeed the Jordanians stopped busloads of Gazans who had been coerced by the Israelis into crossing over to the East Bank. Tensions flared, and there was an exchange of mortar and machine gun fire between the Arab Legion and the Israelis on the 29th. The Amman government complained to the UN about the Israeli effort to dump fifty thousand Gaza refugees into Jordan against their will.[14] But most Western journalists refused to accept the Arab claim that the Gazans were leaving involuntarily. However, on the 31st the *New York Times* reported: 'Although the Israelis deny the charge, they make little effort to conceal their desire to see the refugees leave the densely populated strip.'

The Israelis continued their campaign to convince all concerned that the refugees were leaving Gaza voluntarily. On 2 August Israeli Radio broadcast a statement by General Mordecai Gur, the IDF commander in Gaza, who said that 'the departure of refugees from the Gaza Strip is very natural, especially in view of the fact that during the twenty years of Egyptian rule refugees could not leave the Gaza Strip'.[15] Ignoring the complaints made by UNRWA to the Israeli government, Gur claimed that 'according to the heads of the UN Relief and Works Agency, the general situation of refugees in the Gaza Strip has in no way deteriorated'.

The same day the Israeli newspaper *Hamodia* referred to the reports spread by the Arabs about the expulsion of Palestinians from the Gaza Strip. The paper expressed 'surprise that the UN Secretary-General found it necessary to declare that he cannot investigate these allegations although the UN has eyes and ears in the region in the form of UNRWA'. *Hamodia* added: 'One can understand why the Arabs have to fabricate such rumours but it is difficult to understand why the Secretary-General does not see how ridiculous and absurd these rumours are'. In fact UNRWA had compiled a file on this subject which was examined by the Secretary-General of the UN, U Thant, who sent the file to the Israeli government along with a request that 'the Government of Israel will take urgently any action that may be necessary to suspend any measures which may have been taken with the object of inducing the deporting against their will of inhabitants of Jabalia camp'.[16]

The Israeli Ambassador to the UN, Yosef Tekoa, responded to several UN inquiries about his government's policy of forcing refugees to leave the Jabalia refugee camp, denying the allegations and claiming that the emigration out of Gaza was purely voluntary. He offered as proof a visit to Gaza on 25 July by the Defence Minister, Moshe Dayan, who had spoken with refugee leaders in Jabalia. 'In the course of a two and a half hour discussion, these Arab notables were encouraged to raise every question of concern to them and they did so with great freedom. The allegations with regard to Jabalia camp were never mentioned as they undoubtedly would have been if there had been a basis to them.'[17]

Meanwhile, according to Israeli Radio, eighteen foreign correspondents from Europe and the United States were taken on a tour of the Jabalia camp, where they spoke to several mukhtars who 'made it clear that the military administration authorities have not exerted any pressure in attempting to terrorize refugees in the camp into leaving the Gaza Strip'.[18] But of course Palestinian refugees could hardly be expected to be candid about Israeli transgressions in the presence of the occupation authorities.

Unfortunately the Israeli version of the exodus from Gaza after the Six-Day War has been generally accepted in the West. The Arab claims that the movement was not voluntary are usually dismissed as propaganda, but the newly available UN documents (recently declassified at my request) suggest that considerable pressure was used by the Israelis to persuade the refugees to leave Gaza. After July 1968 the rate of emigration decreased, although it remained substantial. In all about forty-five thousand people left the area between July 1967 and December 1968.[19] On the eve of the *intifada*, Prime Minister Shamir revealed what had happened in 1968 as a threat to the Palestinians (see pp. 227–8).

The scheme to transfer a large part of the population of Gaza to Jordan must be seen within the context of the Israeli attitude to the ultimate disposition of Gaza. The Allon Plan envisaged the annexation of most, if not all, of the Strip by Israel. As early as the summer of 1967 both Moshe

Dayan and the Prime Minister, Levi Eshkol, made it clear that Israel intended to retain Gaza, which they both hinted would eventually be annexed.[20] Various plans were proposed about what should be done with the Arab population. From the Israeli point of view mass deportation to Jordan and/or Egypt was the ideal solution, but everyone understood that this would not be acceptable to world public opinion.

In August 1968 a committee appointed by Levi Eshkol advanced 'a plan to transfer 150,000 to 250,000 refugees from Gaza to the West Bank'.[21] The plan called for 'small-scale projects for refugee settlement which should be launched while stressing the humanitarian character of the project'. The committee recommended that the refugees themselves and UNRWA should participate in drawing up the details. It also proposed that the refugees should be resettled in inhabited areas and not in new camps in Egypt or Jordan. Of course it was understood that the refugees would go to areas of the West Bank destined for return to Jordan under the Allon Plan.

In his memoirs General Ariel Sharon, who led the fight in the early 1970s against the Gaza resistance, claims that he proposed the settlement of seventy-thousand Gaza refugees in the West Bank. He also states that he recommended that 'we take twenty to thirty thousand Gaza refugees' and 'settle them in Nazareth, Acre, Ramle and other places according to local ability to absorb'. But the refugees whom Sharon wanted to settle in Israel would be collaborators who required Israeli protection.[22]

In January 1971 Dayan announced in an Israeli television interview that he wanted the 'Gaza people to be citizens of Israel' if they gave up all thought of resistance.[23] However, he added that 'the normalization between us and the Strip would not be possible before the refugee problem was settled'. Clearly the Defence Minister wanted the annexation of Gaza, with citizenship for the remaining residents after most of the refugees had been 'resettled'.

The Israeli aim of annexing Gaza after the deportation of the refugees caused a great deal of resentment among the Strip's population. On top of their overcrowded living conditions they were enduring a poor economic situation.

The immediate consequence of the 1967 war was a drastic deterioration in Gaza employment. Service jobs with the Egyptian Army and the UN Emergency Force disappeared, while trade, smuggling and tourism with Egypt came to an end. The port of Gaza was closed and the fishing and construction industry virtually collapsed. In 1966, on the eve of the war, employment in Gaza was estimated at seventy-one thousand, but in 1968 it had declined to forty-five thousand. Thus there was a 17 per cent unemployment rate, with twenty thousand more people out of work than at any time before the war.[24]

Gaza's economy, which was always far weaker than that of the West Bank, was even more completely absorbed and dominated by Israel. By 1973, 58 per cent of Gaza's exports and 91 per cent of imports involved Israel. Industry in Gaza, which under Egyptian rule amounted to only a handful of workshops, had a chance to grow after 1967. But the lack of capital investment by private and public sources contributed greatly to its strangulation. The political instability of the area made any form of investment by local Arab entrepreneurs very risky, and Israelis had no reason to invest in industry that might compete with their own. Israel's closure of all Arab banks and financial institutions in Gaza after 1967 and its refusal to allow the establishment of credit institutions in Gaza deprived the Strip's infant industry of a critical source of funding.

As a result of the stagnation of Gaza's agriculture, as well as its industry, employment in Israel was the only alternative. Between 1968 and 1972 Israeli labour bureaus were set up in Gaza despite the active opposition of the PLO, which resented the use of Gaza as a source of cheap labour to develop the Israeli economy while the Strip's own industry and agriculture were neglected.

Military resistance to the occupation was initiated by the remnants of the PLA (Palestine Liberation Army), which had served under Egyptian command during the war. Aided by substantial quantities of arms left by the fleeing Egyptians, they were soon joined by other resistance groups including Arafat's Fatah and Habash's Popular Front for the Liberation of Palestine (PFLP), both of which gained many recruits in the camps, which were crammed with unemployed refugees eager to fight to end the Israeli occupation. The Palestinian resistance forces were attracted to Vo Nguyen Giap's theories of national uprising, and so they modelled themselves on the South Vietnam insurgents; they also admired the Algerian resistance against the French. They began by establishing a network of regional command headquarters in Gaza, which in turn controlled local cells. Through this command structure money was funnelled by Fatah and the PFLP from abroad.

But the strategy of guerilla warfare was flawed from the outset. As the former resistance fighter 'Ali' notes: 'In Vietnam and Algeria the guerillas could hide themselves in the jungle and mountains; in Gaza, all we've got is a few orange groves and the nearest thing we've got to a mountain is a sixty-metre hill called Shojaiya!'[25] Another problem for the resistance was its fragmentation. Fatah and the PFLP, as well as other, smaller, groups, failed to co-ordinate their efforts, which made it much easier for the IDF to suppress their activities.

The resistance began in the first year of the occupation with strikes, demonstrations and isolated grenade attacks. The Israelis responded by restricting movement in and out of Gaza, and by imposing frequent curfews, deportation, detention without trial, ID checks and severe collective punishments. On 23 January 1968 UNRWA director Lawrence Michelmore wrote to Ralph Bunche that 'the whole policy in Gaza is tougher than in the West Bank. The reprisal actions do seem excessive.'[26] They would get worse as resistance mounted.

In spite of (or perhaps because of) Israeli repression, by the spring of 1970 the resistance movement had grown stronger. Residents of the Strip who commuted to work in Israel became the object of attack from guerilla groups. Collaborators were subject to reprisals: Palestinians killing other Palestinians would become a disturbing feature of the resistance movement for decades to come. Typical was an Israeli Radio report of 24 July 1970.

Two local residents were murdered last night in Jabalia refugee camp, in the northern Gaza Strip. At about 0300 today, unknown persons broke into the house of Muhammad Yunis Qumash, nineteen, dragged him outside, and shot him dead with automatic weapons. Members of his family were afraid to leave the house at night. They waited until morning to inform the police of the murder. The police found near the body of the youth the body of another man, about fifty years old. The identity of the latter has not yet been clarified.[27]

The same newscast noted that on that day six other Palestinian civilians had been wounded and that three had been killed in Gaza earlier in the week.

During 1970 the IDF paid more and more attention to Gaza terrorism. On 2 September the commander of Israeli forces in Gaza, General Menachem Aviram, was interviewed by *Ha'aretz* about the growing situation in the Strip. Aviram blamed the violence on the residue of the Egyptian-sponsored PLA, saying, 'There is a nucleus of persons who are far more nationalistic than in Judaea and Samaria.' He also noted an interesting difference between the West Bank and Gaza, which helps explain the greater degree of terrorism in the Strip. 'The Egyptian authorities tried to eradicate the influences of members of prominent families rather than rely on them, while the Jordanian authorities based their rule on the prominent and well-established families.' Thus in the West Bank there was a ruling elite whom the Israelis could deal with, while in Gaza 'there is no one upon whom to base contacts with the population'. When the General was asked why the Gaza Strip was not isolated from the rest of the Arab world in view of its remote location, he replied, 'A common frontier with the enemy exists over the airwaves. Every house, café and shop in the Strip can receive broadcasts twenty-four hours a day.'

A few days after the Aviram interview came news of the famous 'Black September' fighting in Jordan between forces loyal to King Hussein and the Palestinian guerilla organizations, which was followed by the ejection of the PLO from Jordan. As 'Ali' notes, 'King Hussein's expulsion of the Palestinian resistance from Jordan was a severe blow to the guerillas because it was the operational headquarters and the centre for arms supplies.'[28] But the resistance in Gaza, though weakened, continued the futile struggle.

In January 1971 the Israelis began a serious crackdown after the murder of two children of a family of new Anglo-Jewish emigrants who were visiting Gaza. For several years Dayan's policy in Gaza had been 'Let them kill each other', since almost all the casualties of terrorism had been Palestinians. This policy came under criticism from Major-General Yeshayahu Gavish, former commander of the southern front, and General Ariel Sharon, his successor, who believed that Israel had to demonstrate its mastery of Gaza by suppressing the resistance groups. Sharon states that after the Israeli children were killed he told Dayan, 'Moshe, if we don't take action now we are going to lose control.' The Defence Minister replied, 'You can start.'[29]

Sharon, who had made a reputation as leader of the infamous 101 Commando Unit which launched numerous raids on West Bank civilians in the 1950s, carried on the campaign against the Gaza resistance with his customary energy. Eighty shopkeepers were put on trial for having closed their businesses during a strike protest; this effectively broke the PLO-ordered strike. A military court tried curfew violators. Gaza residents who held Egyptian citizenship were deported to Cairo. Vigorous searches for terrorists were conducted. Most significant was the decision to move the tough border police, comprised of Druze and Bedouin Arabs, into the Gaza Strip. These Green Berets supervised the frequent curfews in the refugee camps and conducted offensive patrols. On 16 January Israeli Radio gave an honest explanation as to why the border police were so feared.

Every suspect element, even in the slightest, receives harsh treatment. The interpretation of 'suspect element' was broadened considerably and includes curfew breakers regardless of age or sex, residents who show any kind of hesitation or opposition about body searches, residents who attempt to complain in one way or another about any order given them by police and soldiers, and occasionally – as is often likely to happen – residents involved in misunderstandings with patrols. . . .[30]

Other units of the Israeli Army, though not as brutal as the infamous border police, were also far from gentle with the Gaza Palestinians. As a result there were international protests about the excessive use of violence in Gaza. An officer and ten enlisted men were put on trial on charges of 'unwarranted violence, including use of batons and truncheons against a number of residents and causing damage to buildings'. Three other officers, including two of high rank, were given administrative reprimands for authorizing violence or failing to control their men. At the same time Israeli psychologists, sociologists and education specialists were asked to work out methods to prepare young soldiers mentally for enforcement operations and searches in occupied areas. On 17 February Dayan admitted that 'during the period of intensified action in the Gaza Strip which had in general brought positive results, some mishaps had occurred'. But he stressed that this misconduct was 'attributed to the action of a few soldiers'.[31]

But far more than a few Israeli soldiers were involved in the mistreatment of Arab civilians in Gaza, and this brutality greatly increased as Sharon implemented his programme to eradicate the Gaza resistance. He ordered the demolition of the houses of suspected terrorists. Mukhtars were required to sign pledges to report to the Israeli authorities every case of assassination, beating or threats; if they did not, they would be removed from office. It was also decided to set up a security fence around the Gaza Strip's border to prevent the infiltration of supplies to the resistance forces.[32]

One of Sharon's major innovations was the division of Gaza into tiny defined sectors patrolled by small squads of Israeli soldiers who got to know every tree, irrigation ditch, orange grove or other potential hiding place in their assigned area. Sharon bypassed the chain of command and spoke directly to his troops, who were told what he expected of them. He also used collaborators cleverly and was able to exploit the organizational weakness of the resistance movement. As Gaza resident Abu Muhammad recalls:

> The organization of cells in Gaza was supposed to be on the traditional triangle system, so as to minimize what people knew and could potentially give away. It didn't work out that way because we all knew too much, too many names. Many times I saw young fighters strutting around the camp with their Kalashnikovs and their faces uncovered so that any collaborators knew who they were. It was crazy.
>
> After I was recruited I went to meet my contact in his house and there I was introduced quite openly to the whole cell. Three months later, two of them were arrested and I knew it was only a matter of time before the soldiers came for me – most of the fighters were caught because of information extracted from their comrades under torture.[33]

Sharon's innovations included the installation of electric lighting to improve security and the ploughing of wide roads through the crowded refugee camps; this made matters easier for patrols that had previously been stymied by the congested housing, which had sometimes presented an impenetrable barrier to Israeli forces. It was, of course, resisted by the refugees because of the difficulty of finding alternative housing in the tiny Gaza Strip for those whose dwellings had to be demolished, but the Israelis saw this situation as a way of reviving their scheme to resettle Gaza refugees.

On 8 July 1971 Dayan visited the director of UNRWA operations in Gaza and told him that the Israelis intended to move some of the refugees out of their homes 'so that roads could be built or widened for security reasons'. Dayan stated that the displaced refugees would be accommodated in other locations in Gaza or in El Arish, part of the Sinai territory captured from Egypt in the Six-Day War. At a meeting several weeks later the Israeli authorities assured UNRWA officials that El Arish was being used only because there was no better housing available in Gaza. But UNRWA officials were not satisfied with this explanation and tried unsuccessfully to persuade the Israelis to give up their scheme.

The Israelis showed their usual brutality towards the Gaza residents. The refugees were given between two and forty-eight hours to move, and in some cases they were notified in the middle of the night. The man of each household had his identity papers taken away to ensure compliance. The refugees were told that there was good accommodation for them in El Arish and that transport would be provided, but these promises were not kept. An UNRWA report made after the resettlement noted: 'It is evident that for many their present living conditions must be worse than before and that the health hazard must be greater.'[34]

Several months later a British parliamentary group visited Gaza and El Arish. A Conservative MP, Jock Bruce-Gardyne, observed some refugees who had been brought to Sinai. 'The families there might just as well really have been dumped down in a ghost town of the American Middle West because El Arish is to a substantial extent a ghost town.'[35] Bruce-Gardyne spoke about the relocation with some IDF officers who tried to defend the deportations, which they said were necessary because of the overcrowded conditions in Gaza. But the Palestinians saw the relocation as 'part of a concerted move to disembarrass the Israelis of the whole problem by shifting the refugees or as many as possible gradually out of the Gaza Strip into Israeli-occupied Sinai, with a view to the hope that if eventually Sinai were returned to the Egyptians the Palestinian refugees would go with it'. What he saw in Gaza and Sinai convinced Bruce-Gardyne that the Palestinians had a point, since he noted: 'It did seem to me that the scale of demolition was hardly to be reconciled exclusively with the demands of security.'

Bob Edwards, a Labour MP, also spoke to Israeli military personnel in Gaza, several of whom were very candid. One official revealed the Israeli aim: 'We are going to get fifty thousand people out of Gaza as soon as we can.' This was in addition to the tens of thousands who had already been coerced into leaving. Another Israeli told Edwards: 'We are going to develop the shores of Gaza into a great holiday establishment.' This presumably would occur after the refugees were expelled, leaving only a small Arab population in the Strip. So Israelis could enjoy Gaza's one great resource, its beautiful, unpolluted beaches.

An UNRWA report indicated that 14,704 people were displaced by Israeli authorities in the summer of 1971 for security reasons. Some went to the West Bank, some remained in Gaza, and about four hundred families were sent to a site in El Arish called Canada Camp because it had previously been occupied by a Canadian contingent of UN peace-keepers. Some of the Palestinians sent to Canada Camp came back to Gaza, but there was widespread fear in the Strip that the Israelis planned to relocate all the refugees. After a successful general strike in Gaza, the Israelis once again abandoned their relocation scheme.[36]

Sharon's proposal that Jewish settlements should be established in Gaza was more successful. The southern front commander believed that the Jewish enclaves built on state-owned land would serve as fingers dividing the Gaza Strip for security purposes. Sharon saw a political purpose in the settlements, since they would provide a rationale for the Jewish state to retain control of Gaza even if the disturbances intensified. The settlements proposed by Sharon in Gaza were eventually built; even more than in the West Bank, they proved to be a serious drain on the scarce land and water resources of the tiny territory.

After a few months the campaign against the Gaza resistance began to show results. In November 1971 Dayan announced that thirty-seven terrorists had been killed and 361 arrested. Sharon relates that between July 1971 and February 1972 his forces killed 104 terrorists and arrested 742, while only two civilians were accidentally killed during these counter-insurgencey measures. Sharon claims to be proud of the humane methods used by the forces under his command.[37]

As the resistance waned, the Israelis thought it desirable to put Palestinians in charge of municipal affairs. In September 1971 Rashad al Shawwa, a prosperous citrus merchant and a known supporter of King Hussein, was appointed mayor of Gaza. Shawwa found that he had to walk a tightrope between the Israelis, who believed he had contacts with the resistance, and nationalist elements who felt that local government officials should be elected and not appointed by the occupiers.

Mayor Shawwa focused his attention on the economic revitalization of Gaza's citrus industry, which had suffered from destruction sustained during the fighting as well as from various trade restrictions imposed by the Israelis. He was, however, able to secure export markets in Jordan. He also promoted the development of cultural organizations in Gaza, including the Red Crescent Society, a community-based health clinic, a lawyers' association and a women's guidance union. But Shawwa's efforts to improve Gazan life after the revolt proved to be of limited success because he was unable to deal with the basic problem of so many people crowded into such a small space with so few resources.

In 1972 Shawwa was asked to extend his municipal services to the Beach refugee camp on the outskirts of Gaza. He refused, on the grounds that this would compromise the refugee status of the camp residents. As a result the Israelis dismissed him from office. But the occupation authorities were not able to find a suitable local replacement. Thus they introduced direct military rule in the Gaza Strip. The Israeli military governor assumed all the powers of his Egyptian predecessor and Israelis were appointed to head all municipal social services.[38]

In 1975 Shawwa allowed himself to be reinstated as mayor, but by then there was a new tide rising in the occupied territories which made Shawwa's conservative pro-Jordanian policy seem outdated. The PLO, which after the Six-Day War had been taken over by Yasser Arafat's Fatah and the other guerilla organizations, had gained the undisputed leadership of the Palestinian people.

4
THE EMERGENCE OF THE PLO

Sharpshooters kept watch while hundreds of New York police and Federal guards manned wooden barricades to keep back crowds of demonstrators and curiosity seekers. The unprecedented security at the UN Building in New York on the morning of 13 November 1974 focused on the US Army helicopters which landed at the rear of the skyscraper. Yasser Arafat, chairman of the Palestine Liberation Organization, emerged from one of the helicopters, wearing the baggy pants, checkered Kufiyyah head-dress, open shirt and ill-fitting jacket which was rapidly becoming his trademark around the world.

But despite his scruffy appearance, Arafat came to New York with greatly enhanced prestige. In June that year the Palestine National Council (PNC) had passed a resolution which, for the first time, proposed the establishment of a Palestinian state that might be limited to the West Bank and Gaza as an intermediate step before the creation of a democratic secular state in all of Palestine. Three weeks before Arafat's UN appearance the summit of Arab heads of state, meeting in Rabat, Morocco – to the great disappointment of Jordan's King Hussein – designated the PLO as the 'sole legitimate representative of the Palestinian people'. Arafat's New York visit marked the recognition of the PLO as a major factor in any negotiation on the future of the occupied territories.

The Israelis, however, refused to accept the PLO as a negotiating partner. For days in advance of Arafat's visit, pro-Zionist crowds flocked to Hammarskjold Plaza near the UN Building to hear vote-seeking New York politicians denounce the PLO as a gang of 'terrorists and murderers'. The Israeli Prime Minister, Yitzak Rabin, thanked the Zionist supporters, 'Jews and non-Jews', who demonstrated at the UN headquarters and 'expressed sympathy and support for Israel in its present protest against the United Nations General Assembly's decision to invite the terrorist representative to take part in its discussions'.[1]

The PLO's 'terrorist representative' was creating quite a problem for the UN in other ways besides security. On his own authority the Algerian Abdul Aziz Bouteflika, President of the UN General Assembly, had decided to grant Arafat the protocol courtesies accorded to a head of state, including the use of a special chair which was placed on the podium for chief executives to sit in before and after they had given their address. UN officials, fearing the inevitable protests of the Israelis and their American supporters, worked out a compromise – Arafat would stand next to the chair but would not actually sit in it.[2]

In his speech Arafat gave an overview of the Israeli–Palestinian conflict, which was aimed at the largely Western TV audience. He referred to Israel as 'the Zionist entity', but made several conciliatory gestures towards the Jewish state. The PLO leader indicated that he wanted a solution whereby Jews would not be forced to return to their original homeland. 'When we speak of our common hope for the Palestine of tomorrow, we include in our perspective all Jews now living in Palestine who choose to live with us there in peace and without discrimination.'[3]

Arafat spoke of a single democratic non-sectarian state in Palestine, populated by Jews, Christians and Moslems, but also hinted at a two-state solution comprising a Palestinian state on the West Bank and Gaza next to Israel. The PLO chairman could not yet openly advocate a two-state solution because of internal opposition within the PLO from extremist elements, but he later recalled, 'I said enough for people of good will, even Israelis of good will, to understand that I was offering a very big compromise.' According to Arafat, he was sending a signal that the PLO was willing 'to settle for a little homeland of our own in order to have peace with Israel until the day when the Israelis decide of their own free will to join with us in the creation of the democratic state of our dreams'.[4]

Arafat's hope that the signals of moderation in his speech would be picked up by the Israelis was a vain one. Israeli UN Ambassador Tekoa was not happy with the PLO chief's visit to the world organization. 'Today these murderers have come to the General Assembly certain that it would do their bidding. Today the rostrum was defiled by their chieftain', he said.[5] The following day the Israeli Foreign Minister, Yigal Allon, announced: 'Israel will not recognize nor will it negotiate with the organization which calls itself PLO both because it has set itself as its aim the destruction of the State of Israel and because of the means it is using to achieve its objective.'[6] But if the Israeli government was not impressed by Arafat's appearance at the UN, the people of the occupied territories reacted with unbridled enthusiasm.

Palestinian journalist Raymonda Tawil recalled that on the day of Arafat's appearance at the UN 'there were strikes and demonstrations all over the occupied territories'.[7] She noted that 'after years of hostility and indifference, the world acknowledged the existence of the Palestinian people and recognized the PLO'. A wave of euphoria swept the West Bank. Palestinians gained a sense of pride, and the spirit of resistance was rekindled in the occupied territories.

In many cities young people clashed with police and security forces; in Hebron, Ramallah, East Jerusalem and elsewhere sporadic demonstrations went on over a period of many days. The *Jerusalem Post* reported that at Jenin a seventeen-year-old girl was killed in the midst of a club-swinging, rock-throwing melee between police and demonstrators. The Israelis reacted to this display of public feeling by closing schools and arresting community leaders, who were deported to Lebanon; among them were a member of the Ramallah Chamber of Commerce and the president of Beir Zeit College. At the UN the PLO claimed that ten Palestinians were killed and fifty wounded in the West Bank demonstrations.

There were also economic reprisals. Shops which had supported a strike were permanently closed by the occupation authorities. West Bank towns in which demonstrations had occurred were punished by being cut off from their markets in Jordan, and their citizens were prohibited from visiting that country. It was several weeks before the West Bank returned to normal.[8]

The demonstrations put to rest the Israeli claim that the PLO lacked support in the territories: there could no longer be any doubt that it was Yasser Arafat and not King Hussein who represented the interests of the Palestinian people. Arafat issued a statement on recent events in which he noted that 'the Israeli clique are persisting in their Nazi and barbarous operations against our people in the occupied soil'. He added: 'This is a land of peace and that peace should embrace all of it, a peace based on justice and on the national and pan-Arab rights of the Palestinian people.'[9]

Arafat's call for peace and an end to violence was not taken seriously in the West, where the media revelled in portraying the PLO as a gang of terrorists. From the very beginning, both sides in the Israeli–Palestinian conflict were guilty of gratuitous acts of violence directed against civilians. Indeed, many more Palestinian civilians were killed by deliberate Israeli bombing of refugee camps, massacres of villages and other atrocities than Israeli civilians who fell victims to PLO terrorism. But various hardline Palestinian factions purposely staged their atrocities to attract the attention of the press and television, which were only too eager to play up the incidents in all their gory detail.

After the Civil War between the PLO and the Jordanian Army, there was a wave of terrorism by various extremist Palestinian factions who were expelled from the Hashemite Kingdom. In May 1972 Japanese 'Red Army' units working for George Habash's PFLP attacked Lod Airport near Tel Aviv, killing twenty-five civilians. King Hussein called the attack 'a crime which has been concocted by sick people and carried out by sick people'.[10]

Later that year 'Black September', a terrorist faction within

Arafat's own Fatah organization, launched an attack on Israeli athletes at the Munich Olympic Games. In a statement issued on 7 September after the attack, Black September claimed that 'our fighters had strict instructions not to harm the Zionist hostages unless in self-defence'.[11] This may have been true, as there was no massacre until the German police opened fire. However, this fact was largely ignored by the Western press, which gave scant coverage to the Israeli reprisal raid three days later on refugee camps in Lebanon and Syria, in which hundreds of civilians were killed. But the desecration of the Olympic Games by Black September had shocked the world and attracted well-deserved universal condemnation.

During this period very few PLO commando operations took place in the West Bank. There were occasional grenade attacks on IDF patrols but, despite Palestinian claims, Israeli casualties were very low.[12] The massive 'Liberation Warfare' in the West Bank, which the PLO had hoped for, never materialized. The terrain was not helpful, since there were no forests or mountains from which a guerilla force could operate. Unlike Gaza, where the population consisted of desperate refugees, the majority of West Bank residents were more settled and less interested in armed conflict with the Israelis.

In the early years of the occupation, most members of the West Bank elite did not favour the PLO. While the PLO at that time emphasized a militant stance towards the Zionist state, almost all West Bank political groups – both conservative and leftist – sought a peaceful solution that would lead to Palestinian–Israeli co-operation. The dominant portion of the elite, which included West Bank conservatives who had gained prominence during Jordanian rule – such as Anwar Khatib, former governor of the Jerusalem district, and Hikmat al-Masri, former Speaker of the Amman Parliament – hoped for a return of King Hussein's rule. Many leftists supported a reunion with Jordan, but they insisted on a revision of the former power relationship so that the East Bank would not dominate as it had before 1967.

Thus in March 1972, when King Hussein proposed a

'United Arab Kingdom' that would reunite the East and West Banks, his scheme was received with interest by some West Bank leaders, although it was soundly condemned elsewhere. Hussein proposed that the new state would have two autonomous regions with considerable local authority, including separate parliaments and administrations. Defence and foreign policy would be the prerogative of a federal government headed by the King. Amman would be the federal capital as well as the East Bank capital, with Jerusalem serving as the capital of the West Bank.[13]

To give his plan credibility, Hussein created a ministry for the occupied territories and increased his financial subsidies to West Bank institutions and municipalities. He appointed a politician of Palestinian descent, Zaid al-Rifai, as prime minister and increased the number of Palestinians in his cabinet. He also authorized the formation of the National Union party in the West Bank and appointed as its chairman Mustafa Dudin, from Hebron.

There was some support for the King's plan in the West Bank. On 20 March the pro-Jordanian Jerusalem Arabic-language newspaper *Al-Quds* urged the West Bank population to study the King's plan carefully, and to consider that it offered a possible way of ending Israel's military occupation. The mayor of Nablus, Handi Ka'an, who at one time had favoured the overthrow of Hussein, wrote, 'If we find the plan acceptable, it is not out of love for the king or his regime. The unity of the two banks gives expression to a natural connection between the two populations ... let us not forget that the West Bank was conquered from Jordan and Security Council resolution 242 calls for its return to Jordan.'[14]

But despite this flicker of interest from certain West Bank elements, the plan was rejected everywhere else. The PLO vehemently denounced it, and was supported by virtually every Arab regime. On 16 March the Israeli Knesset passed a resolution denouncing Hussein's idea since 'the historic right of the Jewish people to the Land of Israel is beyond challenge'.[15]

Hussein's proposal for a United Arab Kingdom was made

in order to prevent pro-Jordanian candidates being defeated in the West Bank elections that the Israelis planned for the spring of 1972. By conducting municipal elections, the occupation authorities hoped to demonstrate their liberal rule and thus counter charges of human and civil rights violations. The elections would also demonstrate 'normality', which was always a prime consideration of the military rulers of the West Bank.

Unlike Jordan, the PLO was uncompromising in its opposition to the elections; and in February 1972 it issued a statement urging non-participation. The appeal was made by the well-respected Kamal Nasser, a former West Bank resident who had become a member of the PLO executive committee after being expelled from his homeland. The elections were called 'a Zionist–colonialist plan', and the PLO executive committee warned all who supported or participated in them that it would 'not stand idly by in the face of attempts to liquidate the Palestinian problem by Zionists and colonialists and traitors who co-operate with them'. Nasser warned his West Bank compatriots that the immediate object 'of holding these alleged elections is to turn the conflict between the people and the occupation into a struggle between different groups of the people with Palestinians fighting among themselves instead of fighting the enemy'.[16]

There was, in fact, already considerable opposition to the election from many West Bank residents. A group calling itself the Popular Resistance Front, which represented 'all nationalist forces, parties, resistance organizations, personalities and trade unions', also urged West Bank residents to boycott the election. It was claimed that the Israelis' aim was to perpetuate the occupation, to legalize all their crimes, including 'the annexation to their empire of the Arab territory they have seized', and to give the impression that 'the people of the occupied territory have accepted occupation by the Zionists'.[17]

The Popular Resistance Front statement mentioned the 'threats and intimidations' used by the Israelis to force people to vote. These included imprisonment and deportation, as well as suggestions by Israeli officials that any businessmen who did not participate would be cut off from their markets in Jordan. There were also suggestions that municipal councils which did not co-operate would be replaced by the direct rule of Israeli Army officers.

The major Israeli newspaper *Ha'aretz* reported how senior members of the al-Masri and Tugan clans of Nablus were persuaded by Israeli officials to participate in the elections. They were 'called in the evening from their homes to the offices of the military government in Nablus from whence they were helicoptered to the Judaea and Samaria Area Command Headquarters in Beit-El'. The three community leaders were 'pale and frightened' as they were browbeaten by military officials including the Defence Minister, Moshe Dayan.

It was explained to the men that if the Nablus families did not present candidates in the election, the military authorities would exercise their option as heirs of the Jordanian regime and take control of the factories owned by these families, in which the Amman government had been a partner before 1967. Furthermore, shipping goods from Nablus across the River Jordan would be forbidden if they did not co-operate.[18] Under such pressure the Nablus notables, in common with many other West Bank community leaders, caved in.

The councils elected in 1972 were largely conservative and pro-Jordanian. The survival of this traditional elite was assured by the nature of the electorate, which was restricted to male property owners over the age of twenty-one. Israeli pressure also helped prevent the election of nationalist candidates who leaned towards the PLO. But despite the victory of the pro-Jordanian element there was a perceptible move in the direction of the PLO. That year two Arabic-language newspapers, *Al-Fajr* and *Al-Shalab*, appeared in the West Bank. Unlike the pro-Hashemite *Al-Quds*, the new publications advocated a PLO-led Palestinian state.

After years of occupation and no end to Israeli rule in sight, a definite spirit of militancy could be felt in the West Bank. In April 1973 demonstrations broke out when Israeli commandos raided PLO headquarters in Beirut, killing in their homes several PLO leaders including Kamal Nasser, formerly from the West Bank. The ensuing West Bank protests marked a turning point in the Palestinian national consciousness, since they were co-ordinated with simultaneous demonstrations by two hundred thousand Palestinians in Lebanon, who marched in the funeral procession of the dead PLO leaders. During the West Bank demonstrations, the PLO flag was displayed for the first time in place of the Jordanian banner that had previously been used as a rallying point. It was clear that the West Bank was no longer docile. As the Israeli Foreign Minister, Pinhas Sapir, commented, 'All the talk of gradual rapprochement between Israel and the Arabs in the occupied territories over the last six years has begun to evaporate in the light of harsh reality.'[19]

Also significant at this time was an appeal to the United Nations signed by a hundred prominent West Bank and Gaza citizens associated with a wide variety of political factions.[20] The document made no reference to a return to Jordanian or Egyptian rule, but demanded 'the right to self-determination and to sovereignty over their territories'. Though vaguely worded, this was an indication of the rise of national consciousness.

In the summer of 1973 the Palestinian National Front (PNF) was formed by numerous West Bank groups, including the communists, Arafat's Fatah faction, the Pan-Arab Ba'ath party and Hawatmeh's DFLP, as well as representatives of trades unions, professional associations, student councils, women's organizations, merchants' associations and Islamic religious organizations. The PLO claimed that the PNF came into being in response to a call by its Palestine National Council, while the communists asserted that it was created by local West Bank initiative.

A statement accompanying the setting up of the PNF on 13 August announced that the Front was formed 'in response to a call from the Palestine National Council' and that the West Bank PNF 'was an integral part of the Palestine national movement as represented by the Palestine Liberation Organization'. This document did not openly endorse a two-state solution and denounced 'all conspiracies aimed at liquidating the cause of our Palestinian Arab people and renouncing their rights, whether they are Zionist plans such as the Palestinian entity, civil administration, autonomy and the Allon Plan or King Hussein's plan, the American solution or similar settlements involving liquidation or surrender'.[21]

But conspicuously absent is the hope for a 'democratic secular state in all of Palestine', which was official PLO policy. Many West Bank National Front leaders supported a two-state solution. Indeed, because so many PNF members, especially the communists, favoured a return to 1967 borders, George Habash's extremist PFLP did not join the PNF.

The biggest boost to the PLO and its PNF allies, and the severest blow to the pro-Jordanian forces in the West Bank, came when King Hussein failed to join the 1973 Arab–Israeli war in October. Hussein's caution, at a time when many believed that Jordan's intervention might have tipped the scales in favour of the Arabs, cost him the loyalty of his former subjects in the territories. The strong surge of national pride felt in the West Bank during the war benefited the PLO.

Many West Bank labourers showed their support for the war effort by staying away from their jobs in Israel. The PNF spread the slogan: 'An Arab working in an Israeli factory is equivalent to an extra Jewish soldier at the front.' When a journalist asked the striking workers why they stayed at home during the conflict, they replied, 'Out of solidarity with the Arab armies'.[22]

After the war the West Bank PNF supported the PLO moderates, who wanted a more realistic policy based on a two-state solution. The Palestinians in the occupied regions realized that Israel was a permanent element in the Middle East which was not about to be merged into a democratic secular state covering the whole of Palestine, since the Jews would never accept a state based on Arab majority rule. Much of the PNF's support came from the communists, who under the direction of Moscow wanted a negotiated settlement between Israel and the Arabs which would be brokered by the superpowers.[23]

While most PNF members wanted a genuine two-state solution, they rejected any 'conspirational plans' aimed at 'the liquidation of the Palestinian cause'. This scheme was the civil administration plan of the Communications Minister (and later Defence Minister) Shimon Perez, who promised the formation of a federal union 'of an Arab and Israeli state; each state having a constitution and a separate government that would take care of domestic affairs. In addition, there would be a supreme institution for the union to take care of financial, foreign and defence affairs.'[24] Although it sounded impressive, under the Perez plan the 'supreme institution' would be controlled by Israel, thus giving the Jews jurisdiction over the armed forces, taxation and emigration, leaving little more than garbage collection for the Palestinians to administer in what would supposedly be their country. This was just another variation of the Israeli autonomy proposal, which was designed to put a figleaf over Israel's imperial rule in the West Bank and Gaza.

As they made clear when Arafat appeared at the UN, the Israelis refused to consider the PLO as a negotiating partner in a diplomatic solution to the future of the occupied territories. An editorial in the liberal Israeli newspaper *Ha'aretz* declared, 'The PLO has no standing whatsoever in the peace process . . . because in principle Israel is not committed to consider any organization of Arabs of Palestinian origin who abandoned the area of mandatory Palestine at any time.'[25]

People suspected of supporting the PLO were treated with an iron hand by the occupation authorities. On 4 November 1974 Israeli Radio reported that four residents of the West Bank who were 'engaged in hostile activity against the Israeli authorities and have been among the initiators of a petition in support of the PLO were deported across the border'.[26]

One of the best-known deportations had already occurred in December 1973, when eight Palestinian leaders, including Dr Walid Qamhawi, a Nablus gynaecologist, and Abd al-Jawwad Salih, the mayor of Al-Bira, were banished to Jordan. According to Dr Qamhawi: 'Just half past midnight on the tenth day of December, the day of the anniversary of the Universal Declaration of Human Rights, the doorbell rang.' When Dr Qamhawi opened the door, 'about twenty Israeli soldiers dashed into my house, into all the rooms in the house, not caring who was sleeping, who was not, whether there were ladies in the house, whether they were clothed or not, just intruding themselves on their privacy without any warning'.[27] The soldiers ordered Qamhawi to get dressed immediately. Five minutes later, they blindfolded him and shoved him into a car. Soon afterwards, he was transferred to an armoured car; when his blindfold was removed, he saw other people in the vehicle.

All the others were also well-known champions of Arab–Jewish reconciliation and compromise. However, as they refused to become Israeli puppets but preferred a two-state solution, they were considered dangerous by the occupation authorities who did not want a genuine negotiated settlement. The soldiers were particularly brutal to the mayor of Al-Bira. According to the Israeli lawyer Felicia Langer, Salih 'had served the city's inhabitants throughout the occupation without fear, daring even to let a sculpture be erected symbolizing the injustice done to the people. He too was ready to extend us a friendly hand but not when the other hand was holding a machine gun.'[28]

Salih recalled the way he was treated at the time of his arrest: 'They crushed my legs, my feet, with their rifle butts and they wounded me and although I was bleeding they didn't even care to give me first aid.'[29] His feet and hands were closely bound as he was dragged into the armoured car. Dr Qamhawi noticed that he was in a bad condition. The other prisoners recognized the mayor, calling out, 'He is our brother, you can't do anything to him.' The Nablus doctor did the best he could for the injured man.

The eight deportees were taken to Wad Araba, a stretch of desert between the West Bank and Jordanian territory. They were read a proclamation ordering their expulsion, against which they protested, and then their captors left. The beleaguered men walked for hours in the desert until they were picked up by a Jordanian Army patrol.

The speed of the expulsions was deliberate. Felicia Langer notes that 'the banishments were carried out in such a way that there was no possibility of appealing to any court or committee'. But even so, protests were made. Six West

Bank mayors sent telegrams to the Israeli Prime Minister, the Defence chiefs and the United Nations. The deportees came to Allenby Bridge over the River Jordan, where they demanded that Israeli soldiers should allow them to return home. They stood on the bridge holding banners, which attracted worldwide publicity.

In Nablus on 15 December a number of Palestinian women organized a demonstration. They demanded an end to the expulsions, the return of the deportees, and no more detention without trial for Palestinian political prisoners. The wife of a deported Nablus teacher, Arabi Musa Awad, was among the crowd and the writer Ruth Levin spoke to the depressed woman about her husband. 'He was banished from his city and its rocky surroundings where he was born, where he lived, where he worked, he was separated from his wife, his house, his sons, his books, his hundreds of pupils.'[30] The entire West Bank supported the Nablus women in their protest.

Deportations did not end, however; indeed during 1974 they were stepped up. The military occupation government wanted to crush the influence of the PNF, particularly the communists, who formed the core of the popular front and strongly advocated a two-state solution. Such a political position was considered dangerous by the Israelis, as it made their argument that the sole aim of the Palestinians was to destroy Israel look ridiculous.

In early 1974 six leaders of the PNF were deported, including Suleyman Najjab, head of the West Bank Communist party. According to an article published on 1 September that year in the Israeli newspaper *Davar*, the deportees included all active leaders of the Communist party, and were 'chiefly representatives of the class of young educated Arab teachers, engineers, and those active in the underground professional associations'. The paper quoted a representative of the occupation authority, who said, 'They were not arrested for their ideas which after all can be heard all over the West Bank. The fact that they were organized represents a danger to Israel, since the Front also planned to realize its ideas.'[31] The occupation authorities feared that the PNF communists would attempt to implement their goals of a peaceful transition to a two-state solution, which the Israelis considered a greater threat than that of the Palestinian extremists, who loudly proclaimed their desire to destroy Israel.

Just as they feared the conciliatory attitude of the West Bank PNF, so too were the Israelis uneasy with the growing moderation of a PLO which was moving towards a two-state solution that would include the State of Israel. A moderate PLO was more dangerous because it could gain international recognition as the legitimate representative of the Palestinian people. The Israeli Labour party, which was in power until 1977, preferred to deal with King Hussein, because they believed he was more likely to acquiesce in territorial compromise and/or Israeli autonomy over the West Bank. Israeli right-wingers would rather there were no negotiations at all, as their aim was the eventual annexation of the territories.

At the outset of the occupation there was no question of negotiation with the PLO, in view of its extreme position. Since 1948 the Palestinian resistance had taken a stance of total rejection of Israel and Zionism. Their goal was simply the return of the exiles and the expulsion of the Zionists who had forced them from their homes in Jaffa, Haifa and Beersheva that year. The PLO charter of 1964 made no reference to a Palestinian state. This was a period when Pan–Arab ideology was still dominant and the charter assumed that Palestine would be liberated from the Zionists, to become a province in a giant Arab state that would stretch from North Africa to the Gulf. The 1968 charter stated that only Jews who 'were living permanently in Palestine before the beginning of the Zionist invasion (generally given as 1917) will be considered Palestinians'. It assumed that all other Jews would have to leave after Palestine was liberated from Zionism.

In the days after the Six-Day War Arafat's Fatah group developed the concept of the 'Democratic State of Palestine'. This would be a non-sectarian republic encompassing all of Palestine, to include Christians, Jews and Moslems who would live in peace and enjoy equal rights. At first Fatah was ambiguous about which Jews could stay in Palestine, but eventually all Israelis were considered potential citizens of this future state that would be formed after the defeat of Zionism. Both Hebrew and Arabic would be official languages in schools, government and commerce. Palestinians who had fled in 1948 and 1967 would be invited to return, and there was even mention of possible additional Jewish immigrants, subject to the capacity of the state to absorb them.

It was in 1968 that Fatah began floating the idea of having as its goal the formation of a democratic secular state in all of Palestine. There was considerable opposition from extremist elements and even within Fatah itself. But on 1 January 1969 Fatah's central committee passed a resolution declaring that 'the ultimate objective of its struggle is the restoration of an independent and democratic Palestinian state in which all citizens of whatever religion will enjoy equal rights'.[32]

As Arafat later explained: 'What we in Fatah were telling the world even in those days was "No" to the Jewish state, but we were saying "Yes" to the Jewish people in Palestine . . . on one condition – you must be prepared to live among us as friends and as equals, not as dominators.'[33] Israelis, of course, had a somewhat different view of Arafat's proposal, which meant that they would be a permanent minority in a 'democratic secular state' flooded with returning Palestinians – and Palestinians had one of the highest birth rates in the world.

At the 8th Palestinian National Council (PNC), held in Cairo in February–March 1971, the PLO endorsed Fatah's concept. The resolution stated: 'The armed struggle of the Palestinian people is not a racial or religious struggle directed against the Jews. That is why the future state that will be set up in Palestine liberated from Zionist imperialism will be a democratic Palestinian state.'[34]

That the proposal for a future democratic secular state in Palestine was not well received by the Israelis is not surprising. The plan was not properly thought out. If the Jews were being granted the right of self-determination in Palestine, why were they being denied the right to form their own state but instead being forced to be a minority in an Arab state? Was it democratic for the PNC or any other Arab body to set out the structure of a future state without consulting their future Jewish fellow country-men?

There was, in fact, no evidence to support the absurd claims of various PLO leaders that many Israelis wanted or would ever accept such a state in which they would soon be a minority. Many Jews had come to Israel to avoid remaining in countries where they felt discriminated against or had been persecuted because they were a minority. Besides, were all the decades of Arab–Israeli conflict to be instantly transformed into close co-operation in the new state?

It was very easy for Zionist propaganda to equate the goal of eliminating the State of Israel with the massacre of Jewish citizens. In view of the Holocaust, many Jews were all too ready to believe that the democratic secular state was a codename for genocide against the Jews. Indeed the PLO failed to alter its charter to make it clear that all Israelis would be welcome to remain in this future democratic secular state of Palestine. Clearly there was a need for an intermediate solution.

Soon after the 1973 war, the central committee of Fatah declared itself in favour of a state in any liberated part of Palestinian territory. As the Fatah intellectual, Abu Iyad, wrote, 'in order to move forward towards the inter-confessional demo-cratic society of which we used to dream, we had to establish our own state even in an inch of Palestine'.[35] While technically not abandoning the idea of a democratic secular state of Arabs and Jews in all of Palestine, Fatah proposed as an intermediate step a mini-state in part of Palestine (the West Bank and Gaza, though this was not stated).

Other Palestinian factions including Ahmed Jebril's PFLP–GC (Popular Front for the Liberation of Palestine–General Command), the Iraqi-backed ALF (Arab Liberation Front) and especially George Habash's PFLP resented the PLO's growing moderation under Fatah leadership, particularly the concept of a West Bank–Gaza state. As early as 4 August 1973 Habash declared that a mini-state in the occupied ter-ritories 'is part of the imperialist conspiracy to liquidate the Palestinian problem .... The aim behind the submission of this idea is to split the resistance movement.'[36] In November that year, after Fatah adopted the mini-state concept which it hoped would become PLO policy, the PFLP, ALF and PFLP–GC came together to form what would later be called the Rejection Front, to oppose any Palestinian–Israeli settlement.

In a long speech delivered in December Habash outlined his opposition to a West Bank–Gaza mini-state. He particularly feared that the formation of a secular state would mark the end of the struggle against Israel to gain the rest of Palestine. There were, from his point of view, many other serious problems associated with such a mini-state. Habash told his audience: 'Have we realized that such a state will be squeezed between Israel on one side and the reactionary Jordanian regime on the other?' The PFLP leader was troubled about the economic viability of a West Bank–Gaza union. But his principal concern was the size of the mini-republic. 'This state will be six thousand square kilometres, 22.5 per cent of the surface of Palestine. And the rest of our people? An essential contradiction will exist between this state and the Palestinian masses from the 1948 areas (Israel) whose vital questions will not be solved by this state.'[37]

Habash opposed any negotiations to create a mini-state. In response to a question posed after his speech, the PFLP leader raised what would become a familiar cry of the rejectionists when he characterized a Palestinian state composed of Gaza and the West Bank as a plot concocted between Arafat and the Americans – presumably led by the devil himself, Henry Kissinger! (This is ironic, however, as Arafat tends to blame almost all problems in the Middle East on the former US Secretary of State.) In view of such bizarre attitudes, it is not surprising that the rejectionists would engage in insane acts of terror.

In April 1974 Ahmed Jebril's PFLP–GC, a group which supported Habash's rejectionist position, launched an attack on Kiryat Shimonah, a town near Israel's northern border. Hostages were seized and demands made. According to the Israelis, the three terrorists murdered everyone they could find, before killing themselves. The PFLP–GC claimed that the three commandos and eighteen children were killed when the Israelis stormed the building while negotiations were taking place. Regardless of the cause, the taking of innocent children as hostages was not only inhumane but completely self-defeating from a public relations point of view. The commandos left a letter to Arafat, stating: 'We have given our lives in the confidence that our sacrifice and that of all our martyrs will not be sold for surrender solutions.'

After the attack, Jebril's PFLP–GC issued a communiqué which opposed 'any defeatist solution of the Palestinian problem, rejects the Palestinian mini-state and reaffirms that it will continue the revolutionary struggle until the total liberation of Palestine'. Jebril explained the reason for the attack: 'We have launched an operation against Kiryat Shimonah, the capital of Upper Galilee, situated within the 1948 borders, to underline that our liberation struggle is not limited to the West Bank and Gaza.'[38]

That terrorist operation, which cost so many lives, was condemned around the world. But in the occupied territories there was a different reaction. A young Palestinian in Nablus told a French journalist that the attack on Kiryat Shimonah 'was murderous and the PFLP–GC was trying to annoy Arafat. But no one can forget that a year ago Kamal Nasser and his two companions were assassinated in Beirut by Eleazar's men. Yes, I am not afraid to say so, everyone here is rejoicing over Kiryat Shimonah.'[39]

Of course, it reveals the depth of Israeli–Palestinian hatred that anyone would take pride in the attack, but it should not be surprising that Palestinians saw it as just retribution for the atrocities that they had suffered at the hands of their enemies for so many decades. The greatest tragedy is the effect of such terrorism in stifling Arafat's efforts to promote Palestinian moderation.

Even more disturbing than Kiryat Shimonah was the raid the following month on Ma'alot, another Upper Galilee town. This time the attack was launched by Nayif Hawatmeh's Popular Democratic Front for the Liberation of Palestine, later to be known as the Democratic Front for the Liberation of Palestine (DFLP). During this period, this leftist group was a strong supporter of Arafat's moderate policy; indeed it frequently led the way. In March that year Hawatmeh was interviewed by a Tel Aviv newspaper and assured the Israelis that the Democratic Front wanted 'peaceful relations between Palestinians and Israelis'.[40] He indicated that since the democratic secular state of Arabs and Jews in all of Palestine was not yet possible, a mini-state in the West Bank and Gaza and the return of the 1948 Palestinian refugees to Israel would lead to an eventual total reconciliation of the two communities.

But on the night of 13 May three of Hawatmeh's men slipped across the border from Lebanon into Israel and broke into a building at Ma'alot, shooting several of the inhabitants. Then they seized ninety teenagers in a nearby school and demanded the release of twenty-six Palestinian terrorists in Israeli prisons to commemorate the twenty-six years of Israeli independence then being celebrated.

At 7.05 am on 15 May Israeli Radio announced that the Defence Minister, Moshe Dayan, and the Northern District Commander, General Raphael Eitan, had arrived on the scene. Shortly afterwards it was reported that the terrorists belonged to the Hawatmeh faction. Later in the day Israeli Radio informed the public: 'The Cabinet has decided to release the terrorists asked for, in return for the release of the students in Ma'alot.'[41] But the Israeli cabinet did not keep its word. Despite the explanation in Dayan's memoirs, which is not particularly convincing,[42] it appears that the Israelis never intended to release the Palestinian terrorists from prison, but planned all along to storm the building.

Palestinian reports stressed that the commandos did not kill any hostages until the building was stormed. This is probably true, but their logic, which blames the Israelis for the massacre, appears flawed: 'The martyred fedayeen [commandos] are heroes of the Palestinian people. They are not terrorists. Terrorists are those who fight an unjust struggle. Those who fight in a just struggle are humane and revolutionary; hence, the Zionist stubbornness and false arrogance are responsible for forcing the fedayeen to resort to killing and throwing bombs,' said the Voice of Palestine radio station on 16 May.[43] Shortly after the atrocity, Hawatmeh's group issued a statement: 'The Palestinian people are determined to escalate their struggle and defeat the usurpers in the occupied territory in order to determine the Palestinian people's fate and build their national authority on their own soil as a step on the path of their great struggle to liberate the whole of their homeland and to build the democratic Palestinian state.'[44]

The net effect of Palestinian terrorism is a hotly debated issue. The 1974 attacks on Kiryat Shimonah and Ma'alot probably made the Israelis more intransigent and netted the Palestinians a great deal of negative publicity and a terrorist image which they have yet to shed. And the raid on Ma'alot greatly strengthened the Israel hardliners, who did not want any accommodation that would require them to relinquish control over the territories. But where would the Palestinian cause have been without terrorism? Arafat had an ambivalent attitude towards the subject, at times seeming to tolerate or even encourage terrorism and at other times claiming to discourage it or even threatening to execute the perpetrators. While realizing its dangers, Arafat believed it was a useful negotiating card. He is quoted as saying: 'As long as the world saw the Palestinians as no more than a people standing in line for UN rations, it was not likely to respect them. Now that they carry rifles, the situation has changed.' According to the leftist Israeli journalist Uri Avenery, Prime Minister Yitzak Shamir justified his own past as a terrorist by saying the PLO would not have achieved anything without employing terrorism.[45]

The Israelis have exploited the terrorism issue to gain sympathy for their cause, but the total number of casualties has been very small.[46] According to former UN Under-Secretary General Brian Urquhart,

> The Israelis are brilliant at creating myths and then getting the rest of the world to accept them as truth. There is a great myth that the Israelis are frightened of the PLO as a military force. They are not. They can handle the PLO as a military outfit with both hands strapped behind their backs. What the Israelis are really frightened of is the political PLO.[47]

Indeed during their more candid moments Israeli leaders have admitted that they welcome Arab terrorism. According to Thomas Friedman, the *New York Times* correspondent in Jerusalem in the summer of 1988, he spoke to 'one of the most senior Labour Party cabinet ministers' who bemoaned the recent conciliatory position of the PLO. The minister told Friedman, 'If you ask me, the sooner the Palestinians return to terrorism, the better it will be for us.'[48]

A giant step towards Palestinian moderation came in June 1974, when 187 delegates attended the 12th Palestine National Council, held in Cairo. As at all such meetings there were heated disputes between the numerous PLO factions. This fragmentation has characterized the PLO for decades; it can be traced to a variety of causes including the diaspora of 1948, the interference by Arab states which controlled various Palestinian factions and the individualistic nature of the Palestinian Arab character, but the most important reason is the influence of ideology. If, as Marx said, religion is the opiate of the masses, then surely ideology is the opiate of intellectuals. Since Palestinians are the best-educated people in the Arab world, they have been plagued by a wide variety of socialist, Pan-Arab, Nihilist and Marxist-Leninist ideologies.

In the months preceding the PNC meeting the various PLO factions sharpened their debate over whether the Palestinian resistance movement should accept 'a national authority' (that is, a mini-state) in the West Bank and Gaza as an intermediate step towards the eventual creation of a democratic secular state of Arabs and Jews in all of Palestine. In February that year the General Secretary of the Democratic Front, Nayif Hawatmeh, who supported Arafat and Fatah in the initiative for a mini-state, spoke out against Habash's PFLP and the other rejectionist Palestinian factions, saying that they

claim that a national authority would not have the means necessary for economic subsistence and would not be able to survive on the West Bank and in the Gaza Strip ... There is our homeland whether it has the economic means of survival or not, although we should bear in mind that the economic potentialities of Palestinian territories after 1967 are greater and more promising than those of many African and Asian countries.[49]

In a rousing conclusion to his speech Hawatmeh suggested that setting up of a West Bank–Gaza mini-state would make it possible 'to wage a long war of national liberation until the imperialist Zionist entity is finally defeated, no matter how long it takes'. This sentiment was no doubt warmly received by his audience, but many Palestinian leaders realized that the creation of a mini-state in the West Bank and Gaza would mark the end of armed struggle to liberate all of Palestine.

In May 1974 Ahmed Jebril, leader of the PFLP–General Command which supported Habash's Rejectionist Front, gave his view. He noted that 'in the history of the national revolution, a central position is occupied by ideology'. Jebril denied that he wanted the massacre of the Jews. 'The armed Palestinian revolution is not an aggressive chauvinist socialist movement directed against the Jews with the aim of annihilating them.' What he wanted was 'a national democratic struggle aimed at eliminating the Zionist imperialist entity ... and the establishment of the secular democratic state in which all citizens, regardless of their religious beliefs, will enjoy the rights of citizenship'.[50] While accepting the democratic secular state, Jebril did not go along with the mini-state concept.

The hardline Palestinian resistance groups sent token delegations to the PNC. Fatah pushed hard for agreement on a political programme that would include a clause calling for a mini-state as an intermediate step to the ultimate goal of a democratic secular state in all of Palestine. In January 1973 the PNC had passed a programme which opposed 'proposals for entities and for the establishment of a Palestinian state in part of the territory of Palestine and to resist these proposals through armed struggle and through mass political conflict linked with it'.[51]

The representatives of Habash and Jebril and their allies argued that this language should be retained by the PNC.

Eventually, agreement was reached on a ten-point pro-gramme.[52] UN Resolution 242 was rejected by the PNC because it 'deals with our people's cause as a refugee prob-lem'. Point Two of the programme was the most important: 'The PLO will struggle by every means – the foremost of which is armed struggle – to liberate Palestinian land and to establish the people's national, independent and fighting authority on every part of Palestinian land that is liberated.'

For the first time in their history, the Palestinians had set themselves a goal which was not the liberation of all of their homeland. There was no 'liberation of Palestine' but only 'liberation of Palestinian land', which was a reference, of course, to the West Bank and Gaza. Other points in the plan were hardline; these, especially Point Eight, were obviously included to placate the rejectionists: 'The Palestinian national authority after its establishment will struggle for the unity of all the confrontation states for the sake of completing the liberation of all Palestinian soil as a step on the path to comprehensive Arab unity.'

In view of Point Eight and other provisions of the pro-gramme it was easy for the Israelis to ignore the compromise being suggested, and to stress instead the negative aspect of the PNC position. According to General Yehoshafat Harkabi: 'Israel is expected to withdraw from the West Bank and expose its population centres to attacks from bases a few miles away, without any obligation on the part of the Palestinians. I consider such a position strange and extremely objectionable.'[53]

Shortly after the PNC meeting the Rejectionist Front was formed in order to prevent the implementation of the ten-point programme. According to Abu Iyad, the Fatah leader, support for the rejectionists came from a variety of sources, including 1948 refugees who saw nothing to gain by a West Bank–Gaza mini-state. Many wealthy Palestinians living in the West and in the oil-rich Arab states could support the PLO extremist factions since they were not suffering under Israeli occupation, and thus they could afford to hope for unattainable solutions. And of course intellectuals, distanced from reality, supported various extremist factions out of ideological considerations.[54]

A few weeks after the PNC Habash issued a communiqué which gave his interpretation of the programme. The PFLP rejected Resolution 242 in any form and ruled out any compromise or negotiations with Israel.[55] Habash's group claimed that their acceptance of the ten-point programme at the PNC was based on a misunderstanding, since originally Point Two had rejected not only recognition of Israel, but also negotiations with the Jewish state. Since neither Habash nor any of his top aides was at the June conference, the PFLP claimed that the rejection of negotiations was dropped without their knowledge.

The Rejectionist Front included Habash's PFLP, Jebril's PFLP–GC, the Iraqi-backed Arab Liberation Front (ALF) and the tiny Front for the Palestinian Popular Struggle (FPPS). Although the PFLP left the PLO executive committee, the Rejectionist Front did not actually leave the PLO. It formed an internal opposition which rejected all conciliatory gestures, including the Arab heads' of state meeting at Rabat in Morocco which declared the PLO the sole representative of the Palestinian people, and even Arafat's appearance at the UN in November 1974. The Rejectionist Front found little support in the occupied territories where there was great desire for a negotiated settlement based on a two-state solution.

In November 1974 a leading member of the West Bank PNF committee stated in an interview: 'Of course, a ministate does not solve our problems, because all refugees could not return to their homelands. To exist between two enemy states, Israel and Jordan, would be difficult.' He indicated that a new Palestinian state would have many economic and social problems. 'But the establishment of such a state', he said, 'would enable us to rebuild ourselves culturally and politically. Freedom and independence are very important in themselves, whatever the problems.'[56]

The communists were the most consistent force within the PNF that supported a two-state solution. In its January 1976 issue their underground newspaper, *Al-Watan*, made an appeal to the PLO 'to assume its responsibility without hesitation or delay'. The West Bank communists wanted the PLO to abandon the 'democratic secular state' slogan because it 'has not won the agreement of an important segment of residents of the state to which it is proposed'. *Al-Watan* added that it was aware 'of the reality of the strong pressures on the PLO leadership, and of extremist declarations from what is called the "rejection front", but none of this justifies conflicting declarations and contradictory stands or the occasional return to unrealistic slogans whose hardness does not serve to advance the Palestinian struggle'.[57]

There were, however, some within the PLO who were working for moderation. Chief among these was Said Hammami, who in March 1975 outlined in a speech a possible settlement based on a two-state solution. Hammami carried on extensive negotiations with the leftist Israeli, Uri Avenery, who was told by Hammami that the speech he had delivered at a London seminar and published soon afterwards had been approved in advance by Arafat.[58] Hammami envisaged close future co-operation between Arabs and Jews:

> Consideration should be given to the maintenance of open frontiers between Israel and the Palestinian state and to permitting, even encouraging, a mutual interpenetration of commerce, industry and cultural activities. Within reasonable limits and having regard for the need to provide for the ingathering of the exile Palestinians, one need not exclude the idea of allowing Israeli Jews to live in the Palestinian state . . . provided they accept Palestinian citizenship and provided a corresponding concession were made to enable Palestinians to go to Israel.

Hammami (perhaps speaking for Arafat) attempted to reconcile a two-state solution with the PLO position of ultimately forming a democratic secular state in all of Palestine. He told his audience that it might eventually be possible 'to live together within a reunited Palestine, while maintaining, through cantonal arrangements and a constitutional division of legislative and administrative powers, the distinctive character of each'. Hammami was interested in a genuine federal arrangement in which the central authority controlling defence and foreign policy would be shared by Arabs and Jews. This contrasted with Israeli federation schemes in which their own countrymen would control these functions, leaving the Palestinians as a subject people.

Sabri Jiryis, another PLO moderate, spoke out forcefully for a reconciliation with Israel. While claiming to support the idea of a single state in all of Palestine, he argued that it could not yet work because of the comparative backwardness of the Palestinians. Jiryis believed that only a two-state solution was possible in the immediate future; he did not see the Palestinian mini-state as a 'fighting authority'. He wrote, 'To think that a Palestinian state could continue to fight Israel after it has been established is a joke', adding, 'Our people know that even if they say the fighting will go on, it simply cannot.'[59]

Jiryis believed that a two-state solution had wide support. 'If you let the people inside the occupied territory choose between life under occupation and the establishment of a Palestinian state, I think 95 per cent would be for the Palestinian state. It is in their interest.' As to the economic viability of a Palestinian state, Jiryis saw no problem. 'The Arab states interested in this solution promised Arafat they would give the state something like one per cent of their national income for such and such years.' The PLO moderate was candid as to why the Arab states would be so generous to the new state: 'They would like to get rid of Palestinians who make trouble inside their countries.'

In view of the PLO's growing moderation and the continuing Israeli repression in the West Bank, Arafat was fast replacing King Hussein as the recognized leader of the West Bank Palestinians. This would be tested in the second municipal elections, which the Israelis announced for 1976. They hoped to find a West Bank leadership which would co-operate in their plan to introduce a permanent civil administration to replace military occupation. Of course, civil administration would be a thin camouflage for continuing the imperialistic rule of the Israelis, who would retain military and economic control while handing out petty administrative responsibilities to pliant Palestinian municipal leaders.

The Jordanians had an ambivalent attitude towards the 1976 elections which they feared that they might lose, in view of their declining influence. The PLO tacitly consented to candidates participating in the election. A 1973 Jordanian law making women eligible to vote had been extended to the West Bank. Even more significantly, men without property could vote for the first time, which greatly increased the chances of the PLO. The Rejectionist Front, led by the PFLP, opposed participation in elections that they saw as 'a loophole through which the enemy hopes to arrive at the creation of a subservient Palestinian entity' that will 'co-operate with the enemy to the utmost limits within the perspective and the horizons he desires, as an alternative to the armed struggle'.[60] Most West Bank Palestinians ignored the rejectionist call for a boycott of the election.

A serious problem, however, developed in February 1976, when a Jerusalem magistrate affirmed Jewish prayer rights in the Haram esh-Sharif (Temple Mount). Rioting quickly spread to Nablus and Ramallah and later to Jenin and Hebron.[61] Most of the protesters were students, who were becoming the mainstays of West Bank demonstrations. The protests lasted for months, resulting in the death of several students and many more being injured.

There was some violence connected with the election itself. At Ramallah a collaborator named Jahno killed a man called Halil Isa Liflawi and injured a woman in a dispute involving the campaign. The Liflawi family asked the Israeli lawyer Lehia Tsemel for assistance. Jahno, who was very rich, was authorized by the Israelis to carry a gun, which he used to kill his victims. Lehia Tsemel wanted Jahno to be tried in a civilian court, but the Israelis insisted on using the military court over which the occupation authorities had greater control.

Tsemel told a UN committee that Jahno came to court 'without handcuffs, without real guards . . . with the best suits'.[62] There were reports that the collaborator had a television set in his cell where he received visitors. The man whom the people of Ramallah called 'the real governor of the city' was acquitted of the murder of Halil Isa Liflawi, but found guilty of attacking the woman. He received, however, a sentence of eight months, which was the length of time he had spent in jail awaiting trial. Thus the collaborator walked out free.

In Hebron the Israelis interfered on behalf of their old friend, the pro-Jordanian Sheikh Ali al-Ja'abari. When Dr Ahmad Natsheh presented himself as a candidate against Ja'abari, the local election committee tried unsuccessfully to keep him off the election list. Intimidation was also used: Natsheh's wife received strange telephone calls, one of which threatened, 'Aren't you afraid that your husband is a candidate against Ja'abari who is the head of the Mafia? He has killed so many people. Aren't you afraid your husband will be killed like them?'[63] However, Natsheh was not scared off. He came from one of the largest clans in Hebron, so he could not easily be intimidated by Ja'abari and his Israeli protectors. Indeed, Ja'abari was reluctant to run, since he realized that the tide of public opinion in the West Bank was running against him and the other anti-nationalist candidates. The Israeli newspaper *Ha'aretz* reported that the Defence Minister, Shimon Perez, had a meeting with Ja'abari in order to persuade him to run for office.[64]

In order to help Ja'abari, on 28 March, two weeks before the election, the Israelis deported Dr Natsheh and another PNF candidate. Dr Natsheh told a UN committee, 'I was expelled for two reasons; the first was to get me off the election scene, the second was to frighten people.'[65] Fahed el Kawassma now became the leading nationalist candidate for the post of mayor of Hebron. Kawassma refused the Israeli request that he run on a joint list with Ja'abari; realizing that he was beaten, Ja'abari withdrew from the race, thus ensuring Kawassma's election.

In Nablus Bassam Shak'a was elected mayor; other nationalist candidates were elected to the city council, while the pro-Jordanians held only two seats. In Ramallah the PNF candidate for mayor, Karim Khalaf, won, while the pro-Jordanians kept only one seat on the city council. In all, the National Front candidates won a clear victory in two-thirds of the twenty-four areas where elections were held. The only major success for the anti-national forces came in Christian Bethlehem, where Elias Freij was elected mayor.

The victorious nationalist candidates were invariably described by the Western media as 'radical mayors'. But this is surely a misnomer. Most were well-educated, establishment types who were radical only in that they desired an end to the occupation and the establishment of an independent state in the West Bank and Gaza. Between 1976 and the *intifada* the Israelis did not hold any more municipal elections in the occupied territories, since they knew that these would only reaffirm the widespread support for the pro-PLO Palestinian nationalist forces.

Despite the portrayal of the newly elected West Bank municipal officials as radicals, the Israelis fully realized that they supported Arafat's approach of seeking to form a mini-state in the occupied territories. Knowing that the West Bank delegates would support Arafat's two-state policy, the military government refused permission for fifty delegates from the territories to attend the 13th PNC, scheduled to be held in Cairo in March 1977.[66] Yitzak Rabin and his Labour government feared that a moderate PLO would create expectations in the USA and elsewhere for an Israeli response.

Even without the support of West Bank delegates, the 13th PNC continued on the path towards increased moderation. In its platform it declared, 'The PNC has decided to continue the struggle to regain the national rights of our people; in particular, the right of return and self-determination and establishing an independent national state on the national soil.'[67]

The rejectionists came to accept this position. The ALF and Jebril's PFLP–GC rejoined the PLO executive committee; only the PFL remained excluded. However, eventually even Habash accepted the mini-state formula. He told a British journalist that after the establishment of the Gaza–West Bank state he was prepared to work for the creation of a democratic state for all Palestine by exclusively political means, provided the Israelis were willing to engage in a dialogue. According to Habash, 'If we can settle our complete problem with the Jews now living in Palestine by peaceful means, very good. Only a criminal would reject that. I am not a criminal. I just don't believe the Zionists want to live with us as equals.'[68] In 1977 a new Israeli government would come to power that would confirm Habash's worst fears.

5
CAMP DAVID

It had been a brilliant election campaign for the Likud party, which had transformed the image of its leader, Menachem Begin, from a wild, unpredictable warmonger to a modest grandfather whose frugal habits contrasted with the corruption-tainted Labour party. Early in the morning of 18 May 1977, with the election results in, it was clear that Begin would be Israel's next prime minister. Israelis had lived under Labour party rule for nearly three decades. Not surprisingly, there was wide interest and considerable apprehension as to how Begin, the former leader of the Irgun terrorist organization, would lead the Jewish nation.

At a 5 am press conference, Begin struck a moderate tone when he announced that he would invite President Sadat of Egypt, Assad of Syria and King Hussein to 'come and start with us together, either in our capital cities or in a neutral place like Geneva, face-to-face, direct negotiations to sign peace treaties between their states and Israel without any prior conditions'.[1] But he also made it clear that the Arab leaders would have to accept one rather significant precondition. When asked about the occupied territories, he snapped at a journalist, 'What occupied territories? If you mean Judaea, Samaria and the Gaza Strip, they are liberated territories. They are part, an integral part, of the Land of Israel'.

Before the Six-Day War, Begin had preached about the need for Israel to conquer the remainder of historic Palestine. After the 1967 victory he urged that the West Bank be absorbed into the Jewish state. In his weekly newspaper column, he wrote, 'Were Judaea and Samaria to be torn from us, the foundation

128

of our security would be destroyed and it would collapse the chance for peace'.[2] Begin argued that the conquered territory formed a necessary barrier against invading Arab armies. But he firmly believed that Israel's chief claim to what he called Judaea and Samaria was an historical one, and one, above all, based on the Bible. The Likud leader argued that if Jews had no claim to Hebron, the Temple Mount and other portions of the ancient kingdom of Israel, then they had no right to Haifa or Tel Aviv, which had never been integral to Jewish history or religion. He also made frequent references to the Holocaust and was not hesitant to use the Nazi genocide to gain the sympathy of Americans and Europeans, whom, he claimed, had done nothing to save his people. Now that they had their own state, Jews would make sure that such a tragedy did not happen again. For the Palestinians, he had no sympathy. 'The Arabs have so many countries,' he told the Knesset before he became prime minister. 'Why do those who are called Palestinians persist in taking one from us? Do they want to live here? They are welcome. Nobody is driving them out. But I can't understand why they insist that this is their land'.[3]

Begin also believed that he could use Cold War paranoia to win over the Americans to his view of the Palestinians. 'We must persuade our American friends,' he wrote while still an Opposition leader, 'that if a Palestinian state comes into being in those territories, it will not be long before it becomes a Soviet base. I am convinced the Americans understand this perfectly'. Now at his election-morning press conference, Begin declared: 'We will now carry out a campaign of elucidation in the United States ... in Moscow there is a strategic conference to take the free world from both sides, in Africa with the help of the Cubans and in the Middle East with the help of the Palestinians'.[4]

But President Jimmy Carter, who had assumed office in January 1977, was not favourably impressed by Begin. In his memoirs he notes that he found an American television interview with Begin on 22 May 1977 'frightening'.[5] Begin told the American journalist: 'Mr Arafat and his henchmen lead a group, I may say openly, with the Nazi attitude towards the Jewish people. They want to destroy our people.'[6] He also insisted that the American journalist refer to the 'so-called PLO'. When asked if he would negotiate with the PLO if it recognized Israel, Begin replied: 'Those killers who come to kill our children; we don't ask them to recognize our right to exist . . . They cannot participate in the negotiations.' He also denied plans to announce the annexation of the occupied territories. 'You annex foreign land. You don't annex your own country. It is our land.' Begin was sure the Americans would agree. 'I will try to explain to President Carter; he knows perfectly well the Bible. I understand he knows the Bible almost by heart. So he knows to whom the country belongs!'

Some of the men around Begin were even more extreme than the new prime minister. Samuel Katz, his chief publicist, had been with Begin since his days as an Irgun terrorist in the 1940s. Katz was a proponent of the geopolitical ideas of Karl Haushofer, who had greatly influenced the Nazi theory of *Lebensraum*. Katz preached that history was shaped by geography, not economics. Israel required the occupied territories as 'living space', and thus should not give up any of the occupied territories, including the Sinai desert. He wrote: 'The consequences of a withdrawal by Israel in Sinai could be foreseen as clearly as were the obvious consequences of surrender to Hitler of the Sudetenland with its formidable fortifications'.[7] Neither did Katz recognize the legitimacy of Palestinian nationalism. 'The Arabs of Palestine are not a nation. There is no Palestine Arab nation. They were and have remained a fragment of the large Arab people. They lack the inner desire, the spiritual cement and the concentrated passion of a nation'.[8] To Katz there was no alternative for Palestinians except 'cultural autonomy' under Israeli rule.

A more important figure in the new government was Ariel 'Arik' Sharon. Sharon had helped create the Likud block in 1973, but, believing it too moderate, he had left two years later. In the 1977 election he headed the Shlom Zion faction, which gained only two seats. Begin now included Sharon in his government as Minister of Agriculture, thereby preventing him from leading an opposition movement. In his new post

Sharon was responsible for the settlements in the occupied territories. His attitude towards the Palestinians offered little hope for compromise. He was quoted as saying that any Palestinian 'who [did] not want to live in Israel as it is, well, he can sell his property and receive its full price and leave the country.'9 Sharon's ambitions were, however, for a higher post, particularly Minister of Defence.

For this post, Begin had chosen Ezer Weizman, former Air Force commander and nephew of Israel's first president. Weizman had successfully managed Begin's election campaign, and in view of his military background and family name, he was the obvious choice for Defence Minister. In the years ahead he would show a remarkable capacity for growth and flexibility, which contrasted with Begin's old cronies from the Irgun days, whose rigidity Weizman would come to dislike intensely.

The inclusion of Moshe Dayan as Begin's Foreign Minister gave the new cabinet a sense of continuity. A defector from the Labour party, Dayan joined Begin's government after the new Prime Minister agreed to certain conditions.10 The most important of these was that Israeli sovereignty would not be extended to the West Bank and Gaza. Begin also agreed that the Palestinians could retain contacts with Jordan and that the religious status quo would remain at the Tomb of the Patriarch at Hebron. At Dayan's insistence the new government pledged to accept UN Resolution 242, but the Likud government would place a different interpretation from either the Americans or the Arabs on its call for evacuation from the occupied territory. As Foreign Minister, Dayan still believed that Jews and Arabs in the West Bank 'must find a way of living together' under Israeli rule; he insisted on the Jewish right to settlement in the occupied territories. Gradually, Jews would replace Arabs, but annexation would be delayed for a future generation. Like Begin, Dayan was insistent that there must be no 'foreign rule' in the West Bank.

Dayan had accepted the Foreign Ministry portfolio as a way of regaining public favour. He had lost considerable prestige when, as the Defence Minister, he had been blamed for Israel's lack of preparation for the Arab attack in October 1973.

Many in Israel could not believe that Dayan had allowed the Egyptians to cross the Suez Canal and launch an offensive that had taken the IDF by surprise on the Jewish high holy day of Yom Kippur. The assault had been launched by President Sadat in order to regain the Sinai desert, which had been lost in the 1967 conflict, and he was joined by the Syrians, who wished to regain the Golan Heights. King Hussein decided to sit out the war, but many felt that his neutrality then, when the Arabs came close to victory, was as great a mistake as his participation in the 1967 conflict, when Jordan had lost the West Bank. After an initial advance, the Egyptians were pushed back in the Sinai while an Israeli column crossed the Canal and established themselves in a salient along the road to Cairo. Despite the Israelis regaining the offensive, the Egyptian army's good showing gave back to the Arabs the self-respect lost in the humiliating defeat of 1967.

At the end of the Yom Kippur war, the opposing forces in Sinai, as well as the forces along the Golan Heights, had to be disengaged. President Assad of Syria took a hard negotiating position. His demands that the IDF evacuate the Golan Heights as a precondition to negotiations were dismissed out of hand by the Israelis. Nevertheless, despite Assad's opposition, in December 1973 a conference was arranged in Geneva which was attended by Egypt, Jordan, Israel, the United States and the Soviet Union. Disappointing the high hopes, the conference 'temporarily' adjourned after a few meetings with the understanding that Egypt and Israel would engage in negotiations for the disengagement of their forces in Sinai.

It would take considerable help over several years from Henry Kissinger and his 'step by step' diplomacy to arrange two separate disengagement agreements between Egypt and Israel and a similar arrangement involving the Syrians in the Golan Heights. No progress was made under the Nixon and Ford administrations with respect to the status of the West Bank and Gaza.

*

When Jimmy Carter was sworn in as president in January 1977, the Middle East was already on his foreign policy agenda and much on his mind. Shortly after his administration took office, Secretary of State Cyrus Vance told a congressional committee that the new president 'believes that the Middle East must be given high and early priority'.[11] To some extent, Carter's religious background led to his concern about the lands he had read so much about in the Bible. His emphasis on human rights naturally compelled him towards sympathy for the homeless Palestinians.

During the early months of his administration Carter had dealt with Israeli Prime Minister Yitzak Rabin, who presumably still favoured the Allon Plan 'land for peace' approach, but could not raise it as official policy due to his government's commitment to its religious coalition partners.[12] Rabin thought in terms of the creation of a Palestinian entity linked to Jordan, but negotiations with the PLO were out of the question since Rabin considered it a terrorist organization. In a March meeting with President Carter, Rabin would not be pinned down about the exact border to which he would agree. He was told by Carter: 'Your control over territory in the occupied regions will have to be modified substantially in my view. The amount of territory to be kept ultimately by you would only in my judgement involve minor adjustments in the 1967 borders'.[13] He told Rabin that he considered Israeli settlements in the occupied territories to be 'illegal'.

Carter favoured the reconvening of the Geneva Conference with the United States, the Soviet Union, Israel and the Arab states in attendance. The meeting would be based on UN Resolution 242, which called for withdrawal by Israel from occupied territory. In response to a question at a news conference on 9 March 1977, Carter indicated his ideas on a final settlement of the occupied territories issue when he declared: 'I would guess there would be some minor adjustments in the 1967 borders', and added, 'there may be extensions of the Israeli defence capabilities beyond the permanent and recognized borders'.[14] The following week at a town meeting in Clinton, Massachusetts, he stated: 'There has to be a homeland provided for the Palestinian refugees who have suffered for many years'.[15] Yet, under pressure from the powerful American Zionist lobby, Carter would soon be forced to declare that he had never called for an independent Palestinian state.

The American attitude towards the Israeli occupied territories cannot be understood without consideration of the influence of the powerful Zionist lobby in Washington. No president or member of Congress could defy its wishes and hope to be re-elected to office. Leaders of the Zionist lobby have instant access to top US government officials, to whom they frequently express their wishes in letters and telephone calls. As in other presidential administrations, Carter's Secretary of State Cyrus Vance and his National Security advisor Zbigniew Brzezinski had to justify every policy move in the Middle East to the president of the conference of major Jewish organizations and to the heads of the Anti-Defamation League and the American Jewish Committee. The rising force in the Zionist lobby was the American–Israeli Public Affairs Committee (AIPAC), which would eventually overshadow other pro-Israeli groups.

In a memorandum dated 11 March 1977 AIPAC informed Brzezinski that 'a hair-trigger situation would be created by a return to the pre-1967 border lines, making a new war likely and US involvement more probable'.[16] The memorandum added that in the case of war 'a military defeat of Israel would mean the physical extinction of a large part of its population and the political elimination of the Jewish state.' Although evidence has never been produced, claims that the Arabs planned a war of genocide against the Israelis played well in America, given the anti-Arab racist stereotypes and the American media's unending portrayal of Jews as Holocaust victims. The Zionist lobby also provided high-ranking American officials with a barrage of reports and memoranda which gave them the view that the Palestinians were not indigenous to Palestine, that Israel was the only proper destination for Soviet Jews, and that a PLO West Bank–Gaza state was a threat to the survival of Israel. Arab–American delegations rarely met with high-ranking Washington officials, nor did their reports or memoranda reach the top echelons of government. The efforts of the Zionist lobby had a noticeable effect on the Carter administration's Middle East policy.

* * *

On 15 June 1977, when President Carter met with Shlomo Goren, the Chief Rabbi of Israel was assured that 'the solution of the Palestinians should be in the framework of Jordan and not a separate state'. The President also added: 'The US will not interfere in fixing of borders and will not insist on Israel returning to the borders of 1967'. The Chief Rabbi was particularly pleased by the assurance that the US would not 'impose a solution' of the occupation question on Israel.[17]

A month later, on 19 and 20 July, President Carter met with the new Israeli Prime Minister, and there ensued the first of several misunderstandings, which stemmed in part from the desire of both men to avoid a confrontation. Carter believed that Begin had accepted the principle of Israeli withdrawal 'on all fronts', including the West Bank. At their private meeting Begin made no real protest at Carter's request for withdrawal and the creation of a Palestinian entity, and Begin's reply that he would have to 'agree to differ' and would refer the matter to his cabinet was taken by Carter as a hopeful sign. At a news conference after the meeting, answering a question about his often repeated opposition to the evacuation of occupied territories, Begin said: 'I am ready to the limits of my financial capabilities to pay any sum if you prove that in any of my speeches or my articles I ever used the words "not one inch".'[18] Upon his return to Israel, Begin held another press conference at which he compared Carter to Ze'ev Jabotinsky, the spiritual father of right-wing Zionism and the Prime Minister's idol.[19] But the Carter–Begin honeymoon would not last long.

The day after Begin returned home, the Israeli cabinet conferred legal status on three settlements established under the previous government. The State Department expressed its disappointment, but Carter was forced to admit that Begin was not violating any pledge made in Washington. In their meeting Begin had promised 'to try to accommodate' Carter's request that no new settlements be built, but the President had said nothing about legalizing existing settlements.[20] Not for the last time, Begin slipped through the cracks of Carter's imprecise language.

There should have been no doubt as to Begin's intentions when, on 14 August 1977, he announced that government services on the West Bank would be standardized to those available in Israel. This was immediately recognized by the Palestinians as another step towards annexation. The Mayor of Gaza, Rashad Shawwa, sent a cable to President Carter: 'The Gaza municipal council rejects the decision of the Israeli government to extend to occupied territories health insurance and social security under pretence of bringing it in line with similar services in Israel. The Council considers the decision as an infringement of the rights of Arab Palestinians'.[21]

Begin's policy of creeping annexation convinced many Palestinians that only the PLO represented sufficient force to protect their interests. But Begin was even more insistent than Rabin that he would not negotiate with the PLO at Geneva, and efforts to persuade leaders in the occupied territories to participate at Geneva without the PLO were a failure.

Nevertheless, Carter proceeded with his plans for the Geneva conference, and in late September 1977 he met with Foreign Minister Gromyko, who indicated that the Soviets wished to be brought into the Geneva negotiations. After some discussion a joint US–USSR communiqué was issued on 1 October. It summarized the points of agreement between the superpowers, which included 'the withdrawal of Israeli armed forces from territories occupied in the 1967 conflict, the resolution of the Palestinian question insuring the legitimate rights of the Palestinian people, termination of the state of war, and establishment of normal peaceful relations on the basis of mutual recognition of the principles of sovereignty'.[22]

Some Palestinians were unhappy with the superpower declaration, which they felt was not specific enough since it did not mention the PLO or a West Bank–Gaza state by name. The Israelis, however, felt that it went much too far. When asked about the communiqué a Begin spokesman replied:

'What causes concern is the fact that the statement contains real signs of an attempt to impose a settlement on us. We will not accept an imposed settlement. This is the first thing. The second thing is that the statement talks about a Palestinian state. We will not accept this under any circumstances. The third thing is the PLO. We will not be able to sit down with the PLO. What is there that does not cause concern? Everything causes concern.'[23]

As on any occasion when Israeli interests appear to be threatened, the US–USSR joint communiqué created an uproar in the American Jewish community. Typical was a resolution passed by the Hartford, Connecticut Jewish Federation which complained that the superpower statement 'tends to break down the relationship of trust and confidence between Israel and the US' because it was drawn with 'insufficient consultation with Israel'. The Hartford Jewish group also complained that the Soviet–American statement 'elevates the Palestinian problem to the central focus in the Middle East and tends to solemnize "the legitimate rights of the Palestinians" which has become a code word for the destruction of Israel'.[24]

Begin, who was a crafty negotiator, could be tactless in his public statements. On several occasions he embarrassed the American Jewish community by loudly exhorting them to use their considerable influence in Washington on behalf of his hardline policies over the occupied territories. Ezer Weizman observed that Begin 'seemed to see American Jews as an integral part of the state of Israel'.[25] This became apparent on 4 October 1977, when Foreign Minister Moshe Dayan spoke to President Carter about the Soviet–American communiqué.

In their discussion, Dayan threatened Carter with a public Israeli disavowal of the superpower communiqué that would have created a firestorm of protest in the American Jewish community. Carter was forced to issue a statement indicating that the communiqué was 'not a prerequisite for the reconvening and conduct of the Geneva Conference'. He further agreed that the Geneva Conference would be conducted on the basis of UN Resolution 242 which treated the Palestinians as the 'problem of Arab refugees'.[26] For his part, Dayan promised that Israel would negotiate with non-PLO Palestinians. This apparent concession was included not because the Israelis contemplated withdrawal but in order to establish autonomy under Israeli rule, and thereby ensure their permanent presence and hegemony. With regard to the Palestinians, Dayan noted: 'If we reject foreign rule in the West Bank and [seek] agreed means of living together we need to involve them in talks on the subject'.[27]

Among those who noted the American capitulation to Israel was President Anwar Sadat. The Egyptian leader realized that he could not count on American initiative to bring peace since there was no chance that Carter would risk the displeasure of the Zionist lobby by putting pressure on Israel to withdraw from the occupied territories. Sadat came to the conclusion that he had to make a gesture of his own that would lead to a favourable agreement with Israel.

Sadat's first step was to send an envoy to Morocco to meet Moshe Dayan. According to the Egyptian Foreign Minister, Ismail Fahmy, 'Israel's main concern was to disrupt the Geneva Conference and isolate Egypt from the rest of the Arab world'.[28] Fahmy was shocked when Sadat accepted the Israeli interpretation of UN Resolution 242, which did not require Israeli withdrawal from the West Bank and Gaza but did call for the end of belligerence between Israel and the Arab states as well as the normalization of diplomatic relations. Fahmy considered Sadat's initiative towards Israel a disaster since he believed that Egypt could have reclaimed Sinai without recognizing Israel and surrendering the Palestinians to 'autonomy'. He pleaded with Sadat not to go to Jerusalem but the Egyptian President persisted. On 9 November 1977, Sadat told the Egyptian National Assembly: 'I am ready to go to . . . the Knesset itself and talk to them'. Sadat's offer was publicly welcomed by Begin, who nevertheless made it clear that 'Israel rejects outright and entirely the conditions posed by the Egyptian President in his speech yesterday, namely the total withdrawal to the June 1967 lines and the establishment of a state called Palestine'.[29] As he departed for Jerusalem, Sadat could have had no illusions that he would get back anything other than the Sinai desert.

Arriving in the Israeli capital, Sadat kept his promise to speak to the Knesset. Although Moshe Dayan persuaded Sadat to drop all reference to the PLO from his speech, the Egyptian President felt compelled to claim, 'I have not come here for a separate peace agreement between Egypt and Israel'.[30] In order to placate Arab public opinion, Sadat added: 'These are Arab territories which Israel has occupied by armed force. We insist on complete withdrawal from these territories, including Arab Jerusalem'. He also spoke about the Palestinians' 'right to establish their own state'.

Palestinians had mixed feelings about Sadat's visit, their ambivalence contrasting sharply with the violent anti-Egyptian demonstrations which took place in Libya, Lebanon, Iraq and Syria. A PLO call for a protest strike was ignored by Palestinians and more than ten thousand people in the occupied territories signed a petition in support of the Egyptian President's initiative. Mayor Elias Freij told an American journalist: 'I don't doubt that Sadat is committed to the PLO, I have full confidence in him'.[31] Although they may not have been as certain as the Mayor of Bethlehem, many Palestinians wanted to believe that Sadat had come to help them.

At Al-Aqsa mosque, crowds greeted the Egyptian President with cheers of 'Sadat, Sadat', but they also called out 'Remember Palestine, O Sadat'. Inside the mosque, the *imam* (prayer leader) greeted the Egyptian guest but bid him not to give up Jerusalem: 'Listen to the voice of Al-Aqsa, the voice of Palestine is mourning'. Sadat's meeting on 20 November, however, with conservative pro-Jordanian Palestinian leaders, suggested that he was looking for an agreement that would include King Hussein but not the PLO.

In his private conversations with Israeli leaders in Jerusalem, Sadat found the Begin cabinet intransigent on the West Bank but willing to make concessions on the Sinai desert. This was not surprising. Begin believed that 'Judaea and Samaria' had been promised to the Jewish people by God, but as a member of the National Unity government after the Six-Day War, he had not opposed the return of Sinai to Egypt. Sinai was not part of the Zionist vision. (In February 1919, for example, the Zionist organization had drawn up plans for a Jewish state which included Gaza, the West Bank, a portion of Lebanon and a large part of Jordan, but not the Sinai desert.[32])

In December 1977, Begin made clear his intention for the

occupied territories when he outlined his plan for autonomy. In a speech before the Knesset, the Israeli Prime Minister called for the election by the Palestinian population of the territories of an eleven-member administrative council that would run departments of education, transportation, construction, health and numerous other services. A 'reasonable volume' of Palestinians would be allowed to return to the West Bank and Gaza. Residents of the territories could obtain Israeli citizenship or keep their Jordanian nationality. The IDF, however, would be responsible for 'security and public order' in the territories, and Israelis would be allowed to purchase land and settle the West Bank and Gaza. Although Begin made it clear that 'This is our land and it belongs to the Jewish nation rightfully', for the sake of peace he agreed in his speech to leave open the question of sovereignty. He told the Knesset: 'We do not even dream of turning the territories over to the PLO', which he described as 'history's meanest murder organization except for the armed Nazi organization'. Addressing Sadat in a sarcastic aside, he noted: 'Whoever desires an agreement with us should please accept our announcement that the IDF will be deployed in Judaea, Samaria and Gaza'.[33] He also outlined his autonomy proposal to President Carter in Washington. The American President saw it as a first step, but Begin made it clear that he intended no further concessions. Negotiations soon came to a halt.

By the summer of 1978 Carter was concerned that the momentum towards a peace agreement which had been launched by Sadat's visit to Jerusalem was being lost. He therefore planned a summit meeting between himself and the Israeli and Egyptian leaders to be held at the Camp David presidential retreat near Washington DC. This meeting would decide the future of the Begin–Sadat relationship. Carter himself needed an agreement to offset the criticism he had received from the American Zionist lobby, which claimed that he was putting too much pressure on Israel. In order to placate the Zionist lobby, Carter pledged not to threaten a cutoff of military and diplomatic aid to Israel as a bargaining lever, which deprived him of his only real tool to moderate Begin's plan for a *de facto* annexation of 'Judaea and Samaria'.

Sadat, too, was in a poor negotiating position. In going to Jerusalem and recognizing Israel he had played his trump card without receiving anything in return. Breaking off the dialogue would leave him without American support, which would be a disaster as he had already broken his ties with both the Soviets and the Arab world, who had opposed his initiative with Israel. The failure of his diplomatic efforts would almost certainly lead to his resignation or deposition as president. Sadat spoke about the need to pressure Israel into concessions, but as time passed it became clear that he wanted only the fig leaf of an agreement on the West Bank in order to justify a treaty with Israel that would get back Sinai without any restrictions – his real goal.

Unlike Carter and Sadat, Begin was in a strong negotiating position. While the Americans and Egyptians could talk about the occupied territories, it was the Israelis who were in control. Begin could walk out of the summit meeting and return to Israel and proclaim himself a hero who had preserved the national patrimony from Egyptian and American machinations. At Camp David, Begin took full advantage of his strong position. In particular, he refused to agree to the evacuation of Jewish settlements in Sinai unless Sadat accepted his scheme for autonomy in the West Bank and Gaza, which was aimed at preventing a West Bank–Palestinian state. There was every reason for his negotiating strategy to succeed. Sadat's devotion to the Palestinian cause was questionable.

Defence Minister Ezer Weizman was the Israeli who gained Sadat's confidence. Weizman believed that Sadat's often expressed desire for a Palestinian state was only 'lip service' since the Egyptian president 'knew that the PLO leadership is inclined to the Soviet Union. Having dismissed the Russians from Egypt, he'd hardly welcome a Soviet foothold so close to his border'.[34] Weizman indicated that the Egyptian officials called the Palestinians 'cabaret warriors'. One Egyptian told Weizman about the Palestinians: 'We're sick of them! Take them off our hands!' The Israelis found that many Egyptians wanted to disassociate themselves from the Arab world, particularly the Israeli–Palestinian conflict. If Sadat could claim back Sinai, many in his country would not be averse to leaving the Palestinians to the tender mercies of the Israelis.

On Saturday 16 September, after almost two weeks of haggling, the outline of an agreement was worked out. Israel would evacuate its Jewish settlements from the Sinai desert, which would be returned to Egypt. There would also be an accord which provided for five years' temporary autonomy for the West Bank and Gaza, during which negotiations for the final disposal of the territories would take place. Within the West Bank and Gaza the Israeli troops would only be withdrawn into designated areas. Begin claimed that this satisfied UN Resolution 242. There would be no Israeli evacuation of settlements in the West Bank and Gaza as there would in Sinai. The return of territory to Jordan or the creation of a Palestinian state were *de facto* ruled out. Under the Camp David accord, the only realistic possibility after five years was the perpetuation of autonomy or the annexation of the West Bank and Gaza by Israel.

The accords mentioned nothing about the construction of settlements in the West Bank and Gaza, but there would be a letter from Begin to Carter promising a freeze on new settlements during the negotiations. Carter later recalled that the Israeli Prime Minister had promised a halt to the formation of new settlements for the five years of the comprehensive West Bank–Gaza negotiations. Begin, however, claimed that he had only promised a freeze for the three months provided in the accords for the negotiation of the Israeli–Egyptian treaty on Sinai. William Quandt, an aide to Zbigniew Brzezinski, recorded in his notes that there was some ambiguity in Begin's oral assurances. Secretary of State Cyrus Vance wrote in his memoirs that Begin gave Carter an assurance of a five-year freeze, but changed his position because of adverse reaction in Israel.[35] The evidence suggests that there is some truth in the recollections of both Quandt and Vance. White House Press Secretary Jody Powell told journalists:

The letter on settlements on the West Bank was originally language which was agreed upon by the President, the

Secretary of State, the Prime Minister of Israel, Foreign Minister Dayan and [Attorney General] Professor Barak. There was language agreed to on Saturday night [16 September] and it was agreed to as a part of the agreement on the comprehensive agreement [West Bank–Gaza negotiations that would last five years] as opposed to the [three month] Sinai agreement.[36]

In his speech to the nation on 18 September, Carter stated that 'During the negotiations concerning the establishment of a Palestinian self-government [that would last five years] no new Israeli settlements will be established in this area. The future settlement issue will be decided among the negotiating parties'.[37] But in an earlier draft of his speech, composed after his discussion with Begin, Carter wrote: 'There will be a freeze on Israeli settlements in the West Bank and Gaza (pending)*'.[38] This suggests that Carter had received no definite commitment on the matter of the settlement freeze from Begin, and certainly not in regard to the length of the freeze.

Immediately after Carter's discussion with Begin, reports circulated in Israel that Begin had made sweeping concessions. In the early morning of 18 September† Israeli radio announced: 'There are ministers, especially those who support the settlements and the continuation of settlements in Judaea and Samaria, who prefer to wait and learn the meaning of the clauses of the agreement talking about not establishing settlements, whether this refers to the five-year period or for ever.'[39] Shortly afterwards, Commerce and Industries Minister Yigal Horowitz told Jerusalem Radio: 'If it was correctly reported that Jewish settlements in Judaea and Samaria will be forbidden, it is very hard for me to put up with this.'[40]

Clearly, reports circulating in Israel suggested that Begin had made major concessions that could lead to a permanent ban on new settlements. Where did these reports originate? In

* Original brackets.
† 11pm on 17 September, Washington time.

his notes, Brzezinski tells us that at Camp David, Press Secretary Jody Powell was 'strongly suspicious that the Israelis are beginning to manipulate the news'.[41] Perhaps someone in the Israeli delegation feared that Begin would agree to Carter's request for a five-year freeze and leaked the story so as to create pressure on Begin from his own party. Begin himself was quick to deny the news stories of a prohibition on new settlements. He told Israeli TV: 'There is nothing like what is called a total freezing of the settlements and all this is out. This is what I told the US President. However, basically I am prepared to admit that during this period of the negotiations . . . ninety days not to establish settlements. It is possible for us to wait for three months.'[42]

Most probably, Begin considered giving in to Carter's request. A five-year freeze on settlements would have been painful but there would have been no prohibition on the expansion of existing settlements, most of which were designed to be much larger. It was whilst Begin was considering Carter's proposal on 17 and 18 September that his hand was forced when the word was leaked to the Israeli news media. The resulting ground swell of opposition in Israel forced Begin to concede only a three-month freeze. The Camp David negotiations on autonomy for the West Bank and Gaza were doomed.

Relations between Carter and Begin never fully recovered from the misunderstanding. Indeed, the Israeli Prime Minister added insult to injury when on 1 November, he announced: 'We will now add population to the existing settlements. As I had informed President Carter at Camp David specifically – several hundred families.'[43] Under pressure from Agriculture Minister Ariel Sharon, Begin proceeded with the expansion of existing settlements even during the ninety-day freeze. Once the three-month period was over, there was a rapid proliferation of new settlements.

No self-respecting Palestinian, however, could accept an autonomy plan which did not place limits on the construction of new settlements. On 2 November 1978 the *Jerusalem Post* quoted the Palestinian journalist Ziyad Abu Ziyad: 'The autonomy of Camp David is not real autonomy because the international definition of autonomy includes territory as well as population. Israel claims that it applies only to the inhabitants and not to the land. They speak of constructing settlements as though the land belongs to them'. Mayor Elias Freij declared: 'In order to have peace, Israel must dismantle and give commitments to withdraw from the occupied territory'. He added, 'Mr Begin will have to negotiate ultimately with the PLO if he really wants to find a peaceful solution to the Palestinian crisis'.[44] On 29 October 1978 Arafat told the *Guardian*: 'What they are now offering the Palestinian people at Camp David is a new slavery. The difference between Begin's original plan [of December 1977] and Camp David is essentially cosmetic'.

In November 1978 a summit of the Arab heads of state was held in Baghdad. It called for the Israeli evacuation of the West Bank and Gaza, Jerusalem, the Golan Heights and Sinai. The PLO was reconfirmed as the sole representative of the Palestinian people and there was a call for a Palestinian state. There was a hint that Israel might be recognized within its 1967 borders. A delegation was sent to Cairo with a warning that if Sadat continued the Camp David process, sanctions would be imposed on Egypt for making a separate peace at the expense of the Palestinians. Sadat scorned the Baghdad summit and refused to meet with its delegation.

Any hopes of getting Jordan and the Palestinians in the territories to join the negotiations grew dim. This was especially true after an Israeli government committee drew up guidelines for Palestinian autonomy to be implemented under the Camp David accords: 'The principle proposed for the self-rule is that it will apply to the inhabitants and not the land. In accordance with this, Israel will continue to supervise water sources in the territories.' Other provisions in the report followed the same pattern:

The source of authority of the autonomy will continue to be the IDF. The military government will remain in the territories, but will concentrate in defined places. The IDF will deploy in places agreed upon in negotiations and will continue to train in the territories.

The [areas with] self-rule will have a police force, but internal security will continue to be the responsibility of the IDF and the security services.

There are 6,500,000 dunams in the territories, of which 1,002,000 dunams are State lands. These lands will continue to be held in trust by the State of Israel and a continuation of Israeli settlements will be permitted.

Free movement from Israel to the territories and vice versa will also be continued, without any supervision.

The self-rule authority will be able to levy direct taxes, but not customs duty. It will also be forbidden to issue money or passports. The inhabitants will be permitted to use Jordanian or Israeli passports. Censorship will continue over the press and censors will supervise what is printed in the press in the territories.[45]

Begin repeatedly made it clear that there would not be a Palestinian state and refused to consider a limit on Israeli settlements or the presence of the IDF in the West Bank and Gaza. Sadat made feeble protests but realized that if he attempted to confront Begin over the West Bank and Gaza negotiations, he would not achieve the peace treaty and evacuation of Sinai which he desperately needed for domestic prestige. By March 1979 the Israeli–Egyptian peace treaty was signed.

On 25 May 1979 Begin and Sadat met at Beersheva in order to initiate the negotiations for the autonomy of the West Bank and Gaza. Progress was halted by the crucial question of the powers of the Palestinian 'self-governing authority', and the issue of sovereignty. Begin had hardened his position. His earlier plan proposed that the question of sovereignty be left open for eventual negotiation. But after Camp David and the peace treaty, Begin insisted that at the end of the five-year transitional period Israel would automatically impose its sovereignty. He also made it clear that this point was not negotiable. Realizing that Begin was intent on *de facto* annexation, Moshe Dayan resigned as Foreign Minister. He was soon followed by Ezer Weizman, who resigned as Defence Minister. Weizman was replaced by Ariel Sharon.

In the occupied territories, the Palestinians formed the National Guidance Committee (NGC) in order to co-ordinate opposition to the Camp David proposals for autonomy. The Carter administration made every effort to persuade the Palestinians to participate in the negotiations, but it was hampered by Israeli intransigence, Egyptian indifference, and the overwhelming opposition of the American Zionist lobby. When, on 1 August 1979, President Carter made statements favourable to the Palestinians, he faced the outrage of the American Jewish community. The New York Board of Rabbis notified the White House that it was 'astounded by your comparison between the plight of the Palestinians and the battle for civil rights by Black Americans'. The New York Rabbis added: 'It appears you are now prepared to support the establishment of a Palestinian state which by your own observation will be a destabilizing entity in the Middle East'.[46] Not to be outdone, the Chicago Board of Rabbis also protested at Carter's remarks and complained that 'The blatant support of the State Department for a programme of autonomy for the West Bank and Gaza has even exceeded the demands made by the Egyptians in talks with Israeli officials'.[47]

Often the American Zionists' criticism was highly emotional and not well thought out. Professor Alexander Newman of Hunter College complained to Carter of the

Anti-Jewish position of your extremist criticism of Jewish settlements on the West Bank ... It is ironic that you have no criticism for Israeli Arabs to move to occupied territories as long as they are Arabs but you are revolted by the idea that a Jew should be allowed to move into a house or property which was legally purchased from bona fide residents. This double standard in discrimination in housing places America in a hypocritical position in its stand on human rights.[48]

He did not stop to consider Israel's policy of not allowing Palestinians who were born in Haifa or Jaffa to return to the homes from which they had been expelled at gunpoint in

1948. Was this not 'discrimination in housing' and a violation of human rights? Some of the Zionist letters sent to the White House were far more irrational. A common target was presidential adviser Zbigniew Brzezinski, who was suspect because of his Polish heritage. The Carter administration made little effort to publicize that his father was honoured at the Yad-Vassem memorial in Israel for saving Jews during the Holocaust.

With Carter held back by the American Zionist lobby, there was little to stop Begin from making a mockery of the autonomy negotiations. In the summer of 1981 Israel presented a detailed proposal for the powers and responsibilities of the self-governing Palestinian administrative councils. 'Absolutely free elections' for the administrative councils in the occupied territories were promised. The councils would have authority over justice, agriculture, the civil service, education, culture, health, housing, social welfare, local police, religious affairs, commerce and industry. The proposals were rejected by the Egyptians because 'the document speaks of the local administrative rule in "Judaea and Samaria" and does not speak of autonomy that prepares the way for the achievement of sovereignty over the land for the people of the occupied territories'.[49]

The PLO's reaction was more critical:

The document which the Zionist government has published means in short using the Palestinian people to serve the authorities of the continuing occupation of our territory. What it means is to give the Palestinian people powers in the administration, in controlled education and in fish and agriculture resources, while the fundamental requisites of the state or the authority are forgotten and seized. This means that the occupation authorities want to continue the occupation not only, as they say, of the territory, but of the territory and people and to utilize the Palestinian people in safeguarding that occupation and tame them into accepting that as a final thing.

Israel will then tell the world that it has produced a solution to the Palestine question while in fact that solution, as contained in the document, is a solution of the occupation problem without terminating it in the territory.[50]

After the assassination of Anwar Sadat in October 1981, the new Egyptian President Husni Mubarak made it clear that he had no desire to negotiate an agreement on autonomy for the West Bank and Gaza with Israel. Instead, in order to decide the fate of the occupied territories, he favoured bringing Jordan and the Palestinians into direct dialogue with the US, and, eventually, with Israel. King Hussein, however, would not deal with Israel if the possibility of a Palestinian state or a return of territory to Jordan was excluded.

President Ronald Reagan made an effort to revive the Camp David process. On 1 September 1982 he announced his proposals, which included a freeze on new settlements and Palestinian control of land and water rights during a short-ened period of transition. Under Reagan's plan the US would support neither a Palestinian state nor permanent Israeli con-trol of the West Bank and Gaza. The final status would be self-government in association with Jordan. The President believed that the Palestinians of East Jerusalem should be allowed to vote for the Palestinian self-governing authority, but as for the final disposition of the Holy City, Reagan stated: 'We remain convinced that Jerusalem must remain undivided but its final status should be decided through direct negotiations'.[51]

The Arab response to Reagan's plan was generally posi-tive. Despite Reagan's rejection of a Palestinian state and his refusal to accept a role for the PLO in the negotiations, Arafat responded positively to the President's initiative. King Hussein stressed that he could not speak for the Palestinians, but he joined with Arafat to form a negotiating team in the event of a dialogue with Israel based on the Reagan plan.

Begin, however, would have no part of the Reagan plan. He told US Ambassador Samuel Lewis that he considered the day he heard about it 'his saddest as Prime Minister'. On 2 September 1982 the Israeli cabinet voted unanimously to reject the proposal, particularly its call for a freeze on new settlements. Begin once again stressed his determination to see Israeli sovereignty some day over 'Judaea and Samaria and Gaza'.[52]

Nevertheless, although no international negotiations were taking place in the early 1980s over the future of the occupied territories, the Israelis were not marking time. They were rigorously attempting to impose their version of autonomy on the Palestinians.

6
THE VILLAGE LEAGUES

In August 1981, the appointment of Ariel Sharon as Israeli Defence Minister and thus *de facto* administrator of the occupied territories sent shockwaves of concern through the Palestinian population of the West Bank and Gaza. The former head of the infamous 101 commando group which had killed so many civilians in raids on Palestinian villages in the 1950s, Sharon had also been responsible for the brutal suppression of the Gaza revolt in the early 1970s. His elevation to such a high post ten years later made Palestinians understandably apprehensive.

But when he assumed office Sharon announced 'new liberal guidelines' for the territories. Under this policy there would be fewer collective punishments, school searches would cease and roadblocks would become more humane – in short, an environment free from fear would be created for the Palestinians living under Israeli occupation. Sharon promised an 'open and attentive ear' for West Bank leaders and pledged that he would work for 'the creation of a framework of co-existence with the Arabs of Eretz Yisrael in an atmosphere of mutual respect and with a desire of implementing the government policy as set down at Camp David'.[1] Sharon was obviously hoping that collaborators would emerge who would negotiate and accept limited autonomy, which would leave Israel in effective control of the disputed territories.

But Palestinians were not taken in by Sharon's new-found moderation. A PLO communiqué noted, 'General Sharon who is now trying to appear a meek lamb through his alleged new policy – is the staunchest enemy of the Palestinian people.

His terrorist record is known.'[2] Greater insight was shown in an article in the 18 August issue of *Ha'aretz* by Yehuda Litani, who did not believe that Sharon's policy would lead to the rise of a pliant Palestinian leadership that would negotiate Camp David-style autonomy with Israel. 'Whoever thinks that somewhere in the territories there hides a leadership which fears to identify itself publicly does not know what he is talking about. The ideal Palestinian leaders who would also be acceptable to the Israeli public can be found only in pipe dreams.'

Sharon's other claim was that a West Bank–Gaza mini-republic would be an unnecessary second Palestinian state. According to Sharon, Jordan was the one and only Palestinian state which would eventually be recognized as such by the whole world. In his book Sharon repeatedly mentioned this idea: 'A Palestinian state exists in Jordan with its capital in Amman' and 'the only feasible approach is for the inhabitants of the territories to exercise their political identity as citizens of Jordan'.[3] When he became Minister of Defence in 1981 his aim was to put this theory into effect.

On 21 August Moshe Dayan told an interviewer that in principle he favoured Sharon's idea of Jordan as the Palestinian state, but 'the more we push such a situation, the more resistance we will create. As formulated I accept it. But certainly no one need be surprised that Hussein is not enthusiastic about handing over his regime to Yasser Arafat.'[4]

But most of Sharon's Likud colleagues agreed with him, including the Foreign Minister, Yitzak Shamir, who explained that the autonomy proposal 'was not meant to solve the problem of a nation lacking a homeland. . . . The Palestinian nation has a homeland and a state where it can find its natural sovereign expression. And if that country is called Jordan today, it doesn't change the fact. And we will repeat it again and again until the world understands.' Shamir was also expressing views shared by Sharon when he stated that autonomy did not mean a Palestinian state. 'We came forward with this proposal not so that it [autonomy] will become a stage on a road towards the detachment of Judaea, Samaria and Gaza. On the contrary we suggested autonomy in order to remain in these areas.'[5]

Sharon came to office with a detailed programme which would exploit the autonomy concept in order to give the appearance of moderation while in fact securing greater control over the occupied territories. An important part of his scheme was his concept of ruling the West Bank through a confederation of villages whose antagonism to the PLO militants in the larger towns could be profitably utilized by the Israelis.

But before these so-called Village Leagues could be spread all over the West Bank, Sharon moved to replace temporary military rule with a permanent civilian administration in the occupied territories. He chose as civil administrator of the West Bank Menachem Milson, who defined civilian administration as the separation 'of military and security issues on the one hand' from 'the handling of the population's problems' on the other. According to Milson the civilian administration would leave to the Army military matters such as 'chasing terrorists, dispersing demonstrations and imposing curfews. That is to say, there is a distinction between the various duties.'[6]

But two West Bank lawyers, Raja Shadeh and Jonathan Kattab, had a different view of civilian administration. To them it was:

designed to alter the status of the West Bank, unilaterally implement the Israeli interpretation of the autonomy contemplated in the Camp David Accords, give permanence to the changes Israel has introduced in the West Bank during the past fourteen years and create a semblance of terminating the occupation and withdrawing the military government. All of this is to be accomplished without granting the local inhabitants any degree or prospect of self-determination or seriously impeding Jewish settlement in the West Bank.[7]

The choice of Menachem Milson, a professor of Arabic literature at the Hebrew University in Jerusalem, as the

first civilian administrator of the West Bank was no more
welcome to the Palestinians than Sharon's own appointment
had been a few months earlier. On 1 October an Israeli Radio
report noted:

> On the eve of Professor Milson assuming the post of head
> of the civilian administration in the military government,
> some twenty public institutions in Judaea and Samaria have
> denounced what they termed attempts by the Conqueror to
> molest the rights of the Palestinians to self-determination
> and attempts to find a replacement for the PLO.[8]

It is not difficult to understand why Milson's appointment
was not well received. The professor had made it clear how he
believed the occupied territories should be ruled. In May 1981
he had written an article in the American Jewish magazine
Commentary which criticized the methods used by Moshe
Dayan when he had served as Defence Minister in the early
years of the occupation. Milson started from the assumption
that Palestinian nationalism was an artificial creation which
could not and should not be satisfied on the sacred soil of
Eretz Yisrael. Besides, there was already a Palestinian state
'whose centre is Amman'. A second Palestinian state composed of the West Bank and Gaza was impossible and, under
the right circumstances, Milson believed that Palestinians
who would realize this could be found.

Milson wrote that in the territories 'one can reach an
agreement with those who are willing to work within the
necessities and constraints of reality and accept the political
consequences'. He believed that such 'moderate Palestinians
refused moral and political support against the extremists'.
Milson faulted Dayan because, according to the professor,
the first Israeli pro-consul of the occupied territories did not
understand the Arab political mentality.

'To assure its political control over the West Bank between
1948 and 1967, the Jordanian government applied a system
of patronage (which in fact is standard in Arab politics). Economic benefits, prestigious appointments and access to the
King and his lieutenants were granted in return for loyalty.'

But Milson claimed that Dayan proceeded in a way contrary to Arab practice. 'Benefits and services were given by the Israeli authorities on the basis of non-political, objective administrative rules. Whether a person was a declared supporter of the PLO or a moderate seeking to live in peace with Israel did not matter when it came to the services offered him by the Israeli government.'[9]

He attributed this error to the *zeitgeist* of the 1960s, which held that radicals of necessity were 'genuine and honest' and the 'wave of the future', while moderates were seen as 'insincere and unrepresentative'. Milson did not share this view, since he believed that a class of collaborators in the territories could be developed who would participate in the autonomy talks planned at Camp David.

Like Sharon, Milson counted on a silent majority in the West Bank composed of the 70 per cent of the population which did not live in the main towns but in the small villages where the people were more parochial, conservative, less politicized and easier to manipulate. These simple people were thought to resent domination by the PLO militants in the towns; their loyalty, it was supposed, could be won by small concessions and gifts. So Village Leagues under Mustafa Dudin of Hebron were now being formed to organize the rural population – who would, it was hoped, accept *de facto* annexation of the West Bank under the cover of civil administration and autonomy. Milson wanted to extend the Village Leagues to every section of the West Bank and gradually to allow them to replace the Palestinian local officials who had been in office since the 1976 election. He considered the election to have been the greatest mistake of the occupation. Milson also advocated using inducements such as travel permits to Arab countries and the transfer of funds from Jordan to finance West Bank projects to persuade the Palestinians to abandon their hope for an independent state and accept autonomy.

Even pro-Jordanian moderates viewed Milson's appointment with alarm. The editor of *Al-Quds* and a strong supporter of King Hussein, Mahmud Abu Zuluf, told Israeli Radio: 'Professor Milson is the father of the theory of "divide and rule" in territories currently under Israeli control. He is bound to fail. . . . There is no division, nor should there be one, between the rural and urban population.'[10]

When Milson assumed office on 1 November there were noisy protests throughout the West Bank. Many Palestinian mayors refused to recognize the authority of the new civilian administrator, and widespread student demonstrations involved stone throwing and tyre burning, which was becoming almost traditional in the occupied territories. A general strike by East Jerusalem merchants was broken up and shopkeepers threatened with arrest. As the violence escalated, the IDF forces became bolder: in Jenin they entered schools to pursue protesting teenagers. These disturbances were the most widespread since 1976 and in some areas surpassed them.

'We are saying no to autonomy. We are saying no to civilian administration. We are opposed to the Camp David accords. We are opposed to the Village Leagues,' chanted the demonstrators in many towns. Indeed a particular target was Mustafa Dudin, the head of the Village Leagues, who was regarded as a traitor and collaborator. On 3 November Israeli Television reported: 'In Hebron students threw stones at the building of the Village League which is headed by Mustafa Dudin, the leader of the moderate camp in the area. The soldiers dispersed the students. Dudin is now protected by a special force following reports of threats to his life.'[11]

Gradually the demonstrations subsided. Defence Minister Ariel Sharon, who had appointed Milson, told an interviewer, 'We must understand the causes of tension in recent weeks . . . we have taken a new step and set up a civil administration. In the view of the radicals this is a step towards a political settlement. The radical opposition means that this is a correct step.' Sharon added: 'The perpetrator of all these activities in the territories is the terrorist organization which works through its supporters in Judaea and Samaria and Gaza.'[12]

By mid-November Sharon and Milson believed that the territories were calming down. But the PLO was determined to send a warning to the quislings in the Village Leagues. In the Ramallah area the Israelis had been particularly brutal in coercing mukhtars into joining the Village Leagues. Yusef al Khatib, the head of the Ramallah League, was in any case much hated for his shady role in transferring Palestinian land to Jewish settlers, which even an Israeli court found to be illegal.

The Palestinian newspaper *Al Fajh* labelled Khatib 'a tool of the enemy against whom the people have begun to organize'. Israeli guards were not able to protect him. On 17 November Khatib and his son Kazim were driving to the Village League Office in Ramallah when gunmen stopped the car and shot at close range. Kazim died instantly; wounded in the head, Yusef died in hospital five days later. The PLO claimed responsibility and issued a communiqué which pledged 'to strike with an iron fist the heads of all enemy agents who are involved in the agent autonomy plan throughout our Palestine territory'.[13]

Mustafa Dudin attended Khatib's funeral along with Menachem Milson and other Israeli officials. Milson eulogized Khatib, while Dudin denounced the PLO. In November 1981 the West Bank was headed for a confrontation over the policy of Sharon and Milson to rule the territories through the Village League collaborators.

Palestinians have been employed by the Zionists as collaborators from the days before the establishment of the Jewish state right up to the *intifada*. As early as 1924 the Jewish Agency founded the Arab Farmers' party for peasants in the Nazareth, Nablus and Hebron regions. The Zionists hoped to use the party to oppose the anti-Zionist Arab Executive headed by Haj Amin al-Husseini. The Farmers' party failed since the Zionists did not control the patronage in British-ruled Palestine, but the idea of organizing pliable Palestinians against the nationalist movement re-emerged after the Israelis occupied the West Bank in 1967.

Abd al-Jawwad Salih, who served as mayor of El Bireh until his deportation, described how in the 1970s Israeli officials tried 'to convince us to create committees in order to establish a representative body to implement their policies. I faced a lot of trouble because of my refusal to be involved in any political questions.'[14] Salih informed the Israelis that if they were interested in solving the Palestinian question, they must go to the PLO. But of course they refused to deal with Arafat. The occupation authorities were very insistent that Salih should set up a committee of quislings. The mayor recalled: 'Many times I have been detained and harshly interrogated in order to pressure me to accept the idea of establishing such committees.' But he and his fellow mayors refused to collaborate with their occupiers.

Several years later, the Israelis tried a new tactic in order to create a class of collaborators on the West Bank. On 1 August 1978, a small item in a Jerusalem newspaper announced the creation of a Village League in Hebron; its main objectives were stated to be 'the resolution of local disputes among villages in the most efficient and least costly method' and the encouragement 'of rural co-operatives and social and charitable societies which will work for the benefit of all villages'.[15] The leader of this first Village League was Mustafa Dudin, whom Menachem Milson would later describe as 'a man of courage and initiative and one who has a wide political experience'.[16] Most Palestinians and not a few Israelis, however, had a markedly different view of Dudin and his fellow Village League collaborators.

Mustafa Dudin was a native of Dura, a village in the Hebron district, and a member of a large clan in the region. In 1944 he had served the British rulers of his country as an officer in the Palestine Police. The following year he switched allegiance when he entered the employ of the Egyptian government, which he served for twenty years. In 1965 he went over to King Farouk's rival King Hussein, whom he served in various capacities including head of the National Arab Union party and Ambassador to Kuwait. It is not clear why Dudin left King Hussein's service, but it might be related to the sentencing *in absentia* of his brother to a five-year term for theft. After leaving Jordan Dudin came back to his village, where he was recruited by the Israelis as head of the Hebron district Village League.[17]

Dudin relied heavily on his clan as a base of support. In his home village he had the anti-League school principal replaced by Turki Abu Arkoub, one of his many relations. Abu Arkoub opened security files on nationalist-minded students, banned Palestinian newspapers on school premises and prohibited all student meetings. When someone broke into his office and burned his security files, he called in Israeli troops to discipline the students. In the village of Yatta there also were clashes between students and soldiers over Dudin's replacement of a nationalist principal with a Village League supporter.[18]

The position of supervisor of agricultural co-operatives in the Hebron area, one of the most senior local civil service posts, was awarded by Dudin to his brother Muhammad despite his earlier conviction by a Jordanian court. Under his direction the department of agricultural co-operatives was purged of its anti-League employees. But despite all the pressure put on him by the occupation authorities, Mustafa Dudin could not recruit more than five hundred Village League collaborators out of a Hebron district population of two hundred thousand. None the less the Israelis decided to start Village Leagues in other areas of the West Bank.

Dudin soon became an outspoken opponent of the nationalist forces in the occupied territories. He maintained: 'The solution to the problem is not in our hands. An independent Palestinian state is not possible, it can't live.'[19] He spoke of an eventual settlement that would put the West Bank back under the rule of King Hussein. It is clear, however, that, unlike the genuine traditionalists such as Anwar Nusseibeh or Hikmat Al Masri, Dudin's real loyalty was to the Israelis rather than to King Hussein.

The Israelis saw Dudin and his Village League as useful tools, since they needed Palestinians who would serve as pliable negotiating partners for the autonomy talks envisaged under the Camp David accords. The Village Leagues did not replace the elected municipal government officials, most of whom were loyal to the PLO, but sought to undermine their authority by dispensing favours and privileges to the peasants. Before 1978 the Israelis spent less than $3000 on the seventy-five villages in the Hebron area; but after 1978 $2 million was allotted for use by Dudin and his Village League collaborators.

The Israeli Arabic-language TV programme showed pictures of Dudin giving out funds for much-needed development projects in the Hebron area. People were told that it was not the elected mayors but the Hebron Village League who could obtain telephones, ID cards, permission to visit relatives in Jordan, agreements to sell produce in Israel, employment with the occupation authorities or a meeting with high Israeli officials.

In the Bethlehem area the Israeli military authorities appointed Bishara Qumsieh from Beit Sahur (a nationalist and pro-PLO stronghold) to head a Village League. The Palestinian metal factory owner justified his role, claiming that a Village League leader was needed to represent the interests of Christian Arabs who made up a large part of the local population. The plan to base the Bethlehem League on an alliance between Christians and the Bedouin Ta'amra tribe proved to be a dismal failure.

Only sixteen people were willing to join the League, and they included members of Qumsieh's own family. The Israeli Army now put pressure on the village mukhtars. They were reminded that under Jordanian law they were considered state officials, and should follow orders if they wished to keep their positions. Rumours began to spread that those officials opposed to the League would be replaced, but out of 120 mukhtars only one joined the League. Even halting the transfer of funds from Jordan for development projects proved to have no effect.

Bullying tactics were also used. The cars of League opponents were bombed. The Army raided and in several cases demolished the homes of nationalists in the area. Members of the Ta'amra tribe were also intimidated, but without effect. As the Ta'amra leader, Sheikh Muhammad Abu Amara, stated, 'Deportation and even death are better than the League of the military authorities. We shall die in the place we now live in but we will not agree to the League. We need no favours. God will protect us.'[20]

Elsewhere in the West Bank, the story was much the same. In the Nablus area the League was no great success. The civil authority tried to recruit Takseen al-Faris, one of the leading pro-Jordanian figures in the region, but he refused. The cause of the League was not helped when Israeli settlers planted a bomb in the old market of Nablus town; an eight-year-old Palestinian child was killed and fourteen other people were wounded. Eventually a Village League was established here under Jawdat Sawalha, a reported defector from Fatah, but he never got very far in an area known as a nationalist stronghold.

In the Tulkarem area, with the exception of the village of Hilba the League was a non-starter. An Israeli newspaper reported that in Jaba' a collaborator tried to establish a Village League but 'the inhabitants sent him away'.[21] Immediately afterwards a military force arrived on the scene and surrounded the village. The men of Jaba' were gathered in the town square and forced to lie on the ground from midnight until morning. Several youths were beaten and humiliated and told 'for their own good' to join the League, but they resisted the intimidation. Similar incidents occurred elsewhere, with the same result. In Balha, when the villagers learned that the mukhtar had arranged a meeting with the governor to discuss setting up a League they stoned his house until he agreed to cancel the meeting.

Realizing that the Tulkarem area was not ripe for the establishment of a League, the occupation authorities tried a different approach. Equally important to their plan was the acceptance of the West Bank officials of Israel's urban administration and local autonomy. This the Palestinians resisted since it implied the replacement of temporary military occupation with a permanent Israeli presence in the area. Village mukhtars were assembled and ordered to assume duties, such as registering travellers to Jordan, which had previously been conducted by the military authorities. The mukhtars refused to co-operate; some of them preferred to resign rather than facilitate the crude Israeli attempt unilaterally to implement autonomy.

The most ruthless Israeli campaign to establish a Village League occurred in the Ramallah area. Since much of the region lay on the 'Green Line' between the West Bank and Israel, it was targeted for heavy Jewish settlement so as to

IMPERIAL ISRAEL

obscure the border. Here the Israeli military played an overtly coercive role in trying to recruit for the League. The local mukhtars were threatened with loss of their notary stamps, the symbol of their office, and authority. In Kufr Naameh the local mukhtar was a staunch League opponent. One day an Israeli Army unit appeared with a bulldozer and completely destroyed his store room, which contained all his valuables. He was told: 'You know why we did it.'[22]

In general the Israelis had their greatest success in recruiting in the villages of western Ramallah, the poorest part of the district. In this area most of the labour force worked in Israel and was therefore more subject to intimidation than the eastern part, where most of the people had their own farms and received remittances from educated relatives working in the Gulf states.

Yusef Khatib, the League co-ordinator for the area, was able to play on the rivalry of his clan with the Samara clan in order to gain the support of his relatives. But despite the social, economic and political conditions in eastern Ramallah fewer than a dozen villages had active League members. The cause of the League was not helped when Khatib was assassinated in November 1981.

After Khatib's murder Mustafa Dudin and Bishara Qumsieh called on the government to arm the Village Leagues.[23] To most Palestinians this was not a desirable prospect, especially since some of the Village League members had exceedingly shady criminal backgrounds. The traditional village notables and the rural intelligentsia such as schoolteachers shied away from joining an organization which had the declared aim of combating Palestinian nationalism. The Israelis were forced to rely on socially marginal and politically ostracized elements as the backbone of the Village League: itinerant labourers, drifters, former members of the British Police Force and Arab employees of the Jewish Agency constituted the main source of Village League recruits. Mayor Salih called the Village League members 'low status, low calibre personalities who had little claim to distinction'. According to him the head of the Bethlehem League, Bishara Qumsieh, 'is a taxi driver who is illiterate, he does not know how to read or write and at one time was a smuggler of hashish'.[24] Israeli Major General Binaymin Ben-El Iezer called them 'puppets shielded by the border police'.[25]

But on 30 November 1981 the Defence Minister, Ariel Sharon, 'acceded to the requests of the leaders of the Village Leagues in the Hebron and Bethlehem districts to allow them to use weapons for their defence'.[26] Indeed in addition to arms the Arab collaborators were given communications equipment and patrol jeeps. With their Israeli Uzi submachine guns, the Village League members could be seen manning flying roadblocks alongside the Gush Emunim settlers, who believed that Palestinians had no right to any part of Eretz Yisrael. Many of these armed Palestinian collaborators would fight a quasi-civil war with Palestinian nationalists several years later during the *intifada*.

During the early 1980s the Village League leadership had other preoccupations. Despite an extremely narrow powerbase, and the active opposition of pro-PLO elements, Mustafa Dudin had grandiose plans for the Village League. Sharon received a proposal from Dudin that he be permitted to 'convene a conference of the Arabs of the territories with the intention of authorizing him to participate in autonomy talks'. Israeli Radio also reported that 'a new positive youth movement called the Democratic Youth movement has been established in Judaea and Samaria. It was founded by the area Village Leagues which maintain a political dialogue between the Palestinians in the territories and the Israeli government.'[27] On 11 March 1982 Mustafa Dudin claimed that 'the absolute majority of the inhabitants will continue to support these leagues and to rally around them, because they are the beacon which lights their way to wellbeing, peace and security'.[28] But the Village Leagues had almost no support among the population of the West Bank. Sharon decided to use other measures to counter the influence of the PLO and force the Palestinians to accept autonomy.

He now ordered that the National Guidance Council Committee, which had been established in 1978, would be outlawed in the occupied territories. The NGC had been set up to oppose the Camp David agreements, and had led the campaign against the establishment of civilian administration and the Village Leagues. Soon afterwards Sharon dismissed the mayors of Al-Birah, Nablus, Hebron, Jenin and Ramallah because they declined to have a meeting with Menachem Milson, head of the civilian administration which they refused to recognize. The mayors justified their refusal on the grounds that their towns were under military occupation and thus they would only meet with military representatives.[29]

The mayors who were dismissed had gained their positions in the Israeli-run elections of 1976. At the time the Israelis claimed correctly that these would be largely democratic and free elections, but they were disappointed to find that they yielded Palestinian officials who were pro-PLO rather than the pro-Jordanians they had expected. Now Sharon and Milson were compelled to denounce the process in order to justify the removal of the democratically elected Palestinian officials. On 26 March Milson claimed:

> These were not democratic elections, these were elections held under terrorism, intimidation, bribery. They were held when the smoke of the burning fires and the stones and the burning cars of those who were not in line with the PLO were still in the air. . . . Now three of these mayors were removed from office. That is a step towards allowing people who are not bent on the destruction of Israel, but who are willing to negotiate with Israel, to come to the fore.[30]

But no matter what actions were taken by Sharon and Milson, none of these initiatives helped to weaken support for the PLO in the territories or to increase support for the Village League puppets. Sharon had been dealt another blow on 9 March when the Jordanian government announced that all those who were members of the League were traitors. Since West Bank residents were citizens of Jordan, they were warned that they could be subject to the death sentence if they were members of the organization of collaborators.

On 11 March Amman Radio commented on King Hussein's condemnation of the Village Leagues:

The Jordanian statement has drawn the attention of our struggling steadfast people in the West Bank against getting involved in this cunning game. It is also a warning to those who have been deceived by the false allegations that these Leagues are aimed at rendering services and helping villages unaware of the grave role they are playing in servicing Israeli policy and losing Palestinian land forever.

The broadcast added: 'Jordan wants an independent Palestinian state on its western borders and not an agent enclave under Zionist domination or an extension of Israel.'[31]

Sharon's Village League policy had the opposite effect from what was intended. Instead of creating a class of collaborators and dividing the Palestinians, his initiative united the population of the West Bank. As the Israeli journalist Yehuda Litani commented, 'There is no longer a Jordanian camp confronting a PLO camp but a camp of Jordan and PLO sympathizers that is nearly united against Israel and its few supporters in the Village Leagues who are in Israel's pocket.'[32] Sharon realized that the only way to destroy the will of the Palestinians on the West Bank was to strike at the heart of the PLO.

On 3 June Shlomo Argov, the Israeli Ambassador to Britain, was shot down in front of the Grosvenor Hotel in London. The assailants were members of the extremist anti-PLO Abu Nidal faction, which was under the control of Iraqi intelligence. Abu Nidal's group were among the bitterest opponents of Arafat and were responsible for the murder of many PLO moderates. But the attempted assassination served as a convenient excuse for the Israelis to launch their long-planned assault on Lebanon. On 4 June 1982 they launched a raid on Beirut in which five hundred people died. Soon afterwards the IDF began a full-scale invasion of Lebanon.

Defence Minister Sharon and the super-hawk Chief of Staff, Raphael Eitan, believed that the destruction of the PLO infrastructure in Lebanon would break the resistance of the West Bank Palestinians to the Village Leagues and Israeli-style autonomy. Better still, Sharon hoped that if the PLO was ousted from Lebanon it could be induced to take over Jordan, which would become the Palestinian state. Sharon believed, of course, that the West Bank Palestinians would eventually emigrate to their new home on the East Bank, thus allowing Israel to colonize and annex 'Judaea and Samaria'. Eitan, whose thinking was similar to Sharon's, proclaimed after the invasion began that the Lebanese campaign 'is part of the struggle over the Land of Israel, a war against the main enemy that has been fighting us over the Land of Israel for a hundred years'.[33]

The Palestinians in the West Bank watched events in Lebanon with great concern. On 8 June students in Bethlehem and Nablus staged small demonstrations, but there were no widespread outbreaks. On the 10th the *Jerusalem Post* reported that 'frustration and an uneasy silence' had enveloped the occupied territories. Everyone knew that a few PLO guerillas could never hold out against the overwhelming onslaught launched by the Israelis against the Palestinian refugee camps in Lebanon, which would be at the mercy of Sharon and Eitan. Many people in the occupied territories realized that the extinction of the PLO would mean their own inevitable demise as well. There was a need to show at least some support for Arafat, so on 20 June the mayors of the West Bank and Gaza declared that 'despite the blow the PLO had taken in Lebanon, it continues to be the sole representative of the Palestinian people'.[34]

Sharon and the civilian administrator, Milson, saw the weakness of the PLO in Lebanon as the ideal moment to increase repression in the West Bank. On the 16th Milson dismissed the Palestinian Municipal Councils in Dura and Nablus because they refused to recognize his authority. Aba al-Fath Dudin, another brother of Mustafa Dudin, was appointed as head of the administration in Dura while Nablus was placed under the rule of an Israeli Army officer. Milson commented that 'after the PLO's defeat in Lebanon, the civilian administration will attempt to appoint moderates to public posts in Judaea and Samaria, on the assumption that they will be less prone to PLO threats'.[35]

Sharon was no less convinced that the campaign to eliminate the PLO had left the Palestinians in the West Bank subject to intimidation. He told an Israeli newspaper:

In my opinion a much more propitious framework has now been created for implementing the autonomy programme for Eretz Yisrael Arabs. Now that the terrorist organizations have been backed up and their infrastructure and capability to threaten the world neutralized, there is a better chance for talks with those Arabs who believe that the only way to a solution is their peaceful coexistence with Israel. Personally I intend to make every possible effort along this line and in the coming days I will renew contacts in an attempt to expand the range of talks. I believe the time is more favourable now and we must not miss our chance.[36]

On 24 October 1982 Sharon and Colonel Yigal Karmon, the new head of the West Bank civilian administration, met to discuss their strategy, particularly in view of signs of a growing alliance between King Hussein and the PLO, which had survived the siege of Beirut and the evacuation of Lebanon. It was agreed that the Village Leagues would receive 'massive support'. In mid-November there were Village League rallies in Ramallah and Hebron. Karmon, Milson (now a private citizen, having resigned due to ineffectiveness), Dudin and Muhammad Nasr, head of the Hebron League, were the main speakers. Nasr stressed the leading role of the Leagues as an indigenous bridge between the Jordanian regime and the Likud government. Milson called on the Palestinians to 'resist the communists, the imperialists and others who have sown strife and divisiveness in the area'. Dudin attacked 'Palestinian terrorism' and called on the Arab regions to recognize Israel.[37]

But Sharon's efforts to invigorate the Village League proved to be moribund. On 30 November the PLO, like the Jordanian government, ordered the death sentence for League supporters. The Voice of Palestine Radio proclaimed: 'People in the occupied homeland, let us pursue the agents of the suspect Leagues, let people carry out the sentence passed by the people and the Revolution against these agents. There is no place for the Village Leagues in the homeland and the agents will have no respite or safety.'[38]

The PLO consolidated its position in the occupied territories by entering into an alliance with King Hussein. He and Arafat agreed to a joint delegation to negotiate at an international conference for a Palestinian state that would be associated with Jordan. In the West Bank, the forces of Arafat and King Hussein were able to present a united front after the PLO's evacuation of Beirut.

In 1983 the Village Leagues began to disintegrate. Various leaders began to squabble among themselves. The head of the Hebron League, Muhammad Nasr, was arrested when a youth was killed by one of his men. The League's militia was ordered to return many of its firearms. There were reports of financial irregularities. Worst of all from an Israeli point of view, some of the Village League leaders announced their opposition to the Jewish settlements in the West Bank and their support for a Palestinian state. Clearly the Israeli policy of attempting to create a constituency of collaborators had proved to be a failure. The Hebron League lingered on until it was disbanded by its head, Jamil al-Amlah, in February 1988 after the outbreak of the *intifada*.[39]

Sharon's inability to crush the PLO influence in the West Bank was certainly a key factor which led to the demise of the Village Leagues. But the scheme was flawed from the beginning. It was based on the false assumption that the Palestinians living in small villages were more conservative and less politicized than those residing in the larger towns. Milson's original analysis was not correct. A high percentage of the villagers worked in Israel, where they became conscious of their status as a suppressed proletariat in contrast to the more affluent Israelis. Indeed a higher percentage of Palestinian villagers were arrested for 'subversive activity' than their town-dwelling cousins. While in prison, they were often recruited into one of the various Palestinian political factions. Thus Sharon and Milson's plan failed to take into account the changes which made their strategy impractical.

But the two men made an even more basic miscalculation. They failed to realize that, if the Village League members were given any power, they would use it to build an independent force that would eventually turn against the occupation. No Palestinian could acquiesce to Israeli policies, especially the accelerated pace of Jewish settlement of the occupied territories which occurred under the Likud government.

7
THE SETTLEMENTS

'Samaria and Judaea belonged to the Jewish people even before 1967. We've known that they belonged to us all throughout history.' So spoke a leader of the Gush Emunim settler movement, Rabbi Moshe Levinger, who added: 'We know that some day we will receive the East Bank of the Jordan as well. It's God's will.'[1] In numerous interviews over the past few years Rabbi Levinger has articulated the views of the Jewish extremists who have dominated Israeli policy towards the West Bank, creating perhaps the greatest obstacle to the conclusion of a peaceful solution of the Israeli–Palestinian conflict. Indeed Levinger has said: 'Peace in itself is not a goal. Right now the advancement of the Jewish people and the redemption process are more important than hypothetical peace.'[2]

According to Rabbi Levinger and other Jewish fundamentalists the redemption process will culminate with the coming of the Messiah as foretold by the Hebrew prophets. But certain conditions must be met before the Messiah can arrive. Chief among these is the settlement of the Jewish people in its ancient homeland. Levinger claims that the Jewish people 'can perform its mission as the link between the material and transmaterial only by living a life rooted in the soil of the promised land'.[3]

Levinger has repeatedly stated that the Jews cannot fulfil their spiritual mission within the borders of pre-1967 Israel. 'No Jew prayed three times a day that he'd come back to Tel Aviv or Haifa but for centuries we did pray to come back to Jerusalem, Hebron and Nablus. The tombs of Abraham, Isaac and Jacob are here. Hebron was David's capital.' According to the Rabbi a Jewish state encompassing all of Eretz Yisrael must be formed to await the coming of the Messiah.

The state envisaged by Levinger would be authoritarian. 'The very notion of democracy is a deceptive one. Modern notions of democracy, individual rights and self-fulfilment are the root of social and moral breakdown.' He adds: 'If in Europe and the United States a moral and democratic mission requires equality of rights for all, it is clear and obvious that in Israel what must determine rights to vote and be elected to public office must be identification with and participation in the struggle of the people of Israel to accomplish its mission.'[4] In another interview Levinger left no doubt about his attitude to Arab participation in the Israeli political process: 'I believe that they shouldn't be able to vote in national elections for the Knesset because if they could they would vote to change the purpose, the Jewish nature of the state.'[5]

Rabbi Levinger believes that the moral imperative of Jews moving into the occupied territories cannot be outlawed by the Knesset or any authority in the Zionist state. 'Certain things are above democracy. Certain principles cannot be subject to democracy. Among us *Hitnahalut* [settlement] is one of those basic moral principles. Just as we could not accept a people among us as first-class citizens if they will not accept laws against murder or theft, so too they must accept settlement in Judaea and Samaria as a basic principle of Jewish existence and a moral foundation of this state.'[6]

Like most Jewish fundamentalists, the Rabbi has no high opinion of non-Jews. 'For us, Gentiles can be divided into two groups. Those who hate us and those who would be indifferent to our destruction.'[7] His views are shared by his wife, who has also played a key role in the West Bank settler movement. Miriam Levinger believes: 'All Jews whether they are Orthodox, Reform or secular must recognize that there is only one place in the world in which they truly belong and that is Israel.'[8]

Mrs Levinger, who lives with her husband at the Kiryat Arba settlement near Hebron, boasts that she does not mingle with her West Bank Arab neighbours nor would she accept an invitation to visit an Arab home. She told an interviewer: 'I'll be very frank with you. The reason I don't encourage too close a relationship is because I saw in America that too close a relationship leads to assimilation.'[9] Her goal is the settlement of a large Jewish community on the West Bank that would be separate from the surrounding Arabs. Miriam Levinger believes that Jewish control of the West Bank is inevitable. 'If the Jews are secure in themselves and secure in their sovereignty over Eretz Yisrael then the Arabs themselves will receive the idea of Jewish sovereignty, and those who don't – well, they have somewhere else to go.'

The Gush Emunim (Block of the Faithful) movement in which the Levingers have been prominent has played a key role in the formulation of Israeli policy in the occupied territories since its founding in 1974. The Gush platform states that 'the whole land of Israel is the exclusive property of the Jewish people'; the movement demands that 'full Jewish sovereignty should begin immediately over all areas of the land of Israel which are presently in our hands'. As for the 'Arabs of the land of Israel', they are promised 'private and legal rights', but no Palestinians in any part of Eretz Yisrael should ever be allowed any national rights. There would be no wholesale expulsions, but the Israeli government 'should, by means of information and economic assistance, encourage those who are not prepared to accept Israeli citizenship for nationalist reasons to emigrate'. The Gush programme was summarized by a former leader of the movement, Eliezer Levne, who wrote: 'This country is the land of Israel and no one is a partner to sovereignty over it – except our brothers in the Diaspora who need its expanses to save themselves and to save us.'[10]

Gush Emunim has never had a formal membership list or elected leadership. But it has been very effective none the less, especially Amana (Covenant), the branch which actually supervises settlement in the occupied territories. Gush marches and demonstrations have attracted up to 150,000 people, most of whom are Orthodox Jews.

Gush Emunim must be seen as a Jewish version of the religious fundamentalism that has swept like a tidal wave in recent years through the Moslem world and among American Protestants. It shares certain similarities with Shia Moslem fundamentalists as well as American TV evangelists who were prominent in the 1980s. All these movements are characterized by their tendency to link religious beliefs with political action designed to make radical changes. Fundamentalists are unwilling to compromise with reality in their efforts to transform the world in the image of their religious convictions.

Jewish fundamentalists believe that they are living in the redemptive age – from ancient times Jews have awaited the coming of the Messiah who would deliver God's chosen people. This redemption would include the return of the Jews from exile to the land of Israel, the establishment of Jewish sovereignty over the land, territorial expansion, reconstruction of the Temple and economic prosperity. Some fundamentalist ideologues have suggested that the redemption process will be over very quickly. But Rabbi Tzvi Yehuda Kook, who died in 1982, wrote, 'Israel's redemption will proceed by gradual stages which is in harmony with what is clearly stated in the Torah.'[11]

Members of Gush Emunim believe that Jewish settlement of Judaea and Samaria, which they consider the heartland of Israel, is a prerequisite for the fulfilment of the redemptive process. One settler commented, 'My husband and I are convinced that we are living in a most faithful period. If we prove to be the exclusive proprietors of Eretz Yisrael, of the parts we have managed to liberate, it will hasten redemption.'[12] Since 1974 Gush Emunim has pressured every Israeli Prime Minister to finance many new West Bank settlements so as to secure Jewish control of the disputed territories.

Withdrawal from Judaea and Samaria is considered the ultimate catastrophe by Gush supporters. According to Rabbi O. Hadya, 'If God forbid we should return only a tiny strip of land we would thereby give control to the evil forces of *sitra achra* [Satan's camp].'[13] Shlomo Avener, one of the best-known Gush ideologues, has stated: 'There is an absolute Torah prohibition against the transfer of any portion of our holy land to foreign rule', and those who even discuss territorial concessions to the Arabs are guilty of 'profanation of the name of God'.[14] Avener has written that the principle of *Pikuach Nefesh* (preserving life rather than following religious law) does not apply to conquest, possession and settlement of the land of Israel.

Indeed Elijahim Haetzni, a lawyer who has proved to be the most articulate spokesman for Gush Emunim, has warned that the settlers would resist the return of the West Bank to Arab control. 'If amidst the shedding of blood the government tries to evacuate a hundred thousand Jews from their homes by force, a civil war will break out.'[15] There is some debate, however, within Gush Emunim as to exactly how an evacuation order might be resisted. Some argue that a civil war might be avoided if the settlers sabotaged the evacuation process, while others believe that they would prefer to remain behind to be slaughtered by the Arabs in a dramatic fashion that would force the Israeli government to reoccupy the West Bank.

Gush settlers have a totally negative attitude towards the Arabs, whom they consider potentially violent and treacherous, supporters of terrorism and ultimately inferior to God's chosen people. One woman told the Israeli writer Amos Oz that the proper role for West Bank Palestinians was to live under Jewish sovereignty and do the dirty work for the settlers. 'Isn't that the way it is in the Bible? Weren't there hewers of wood and carriers of water? For murderers that's very little punishment! It's mercy.'[16]

Many of the Gush Emunim see Palestinians and Arabs in general as the descendants of the Amalekites of the Bible, who harassed the Israelis during their wandering in the desert, preying on the weak and helpless stragglers. As a consequence God commanded the Jewish people not only to kill all Amalekites – men, women, and children – but to blot out their memory from the face of the earth. Rabbi Yisrael Hess of Bar Ilan University published an article in the student newspaper *Bat Koll* on 26 February 1988 entitled 'The Commandment of Genocide in the Torah'. The piece ended with the words: 'The day will yet come when we will be called to fulfil the commandment for the divinely ordained war to destroy Amalek.'[17]

Many other Gush fundamentalists, while not advocating genocide, believe that it is permissible for the Jews to inflict numerous other injustices on the Palestinians. Shlomo Avener, the Gush ideologue, believes that divine commandments to the Jewish people to settle Eretz Yisrael 'transcend human notions of natural rights', and that while God requires other nations to abide by abstract codes of 'justice and righteousness' such rules do not apply to the chosen people.[18] He is supported by Mordechai Nissan of the Hebrew University, who has written:

While it is true that the Jews are a particular people, they none the less are designated as a 'light unto the nations'. This function is imposed on the Jews who strive to be a living aristocracy among the nations, a nation that has deeper historical roots, greater spiritual obligations, higher moral standards, and more powerful intellectual capacities than others. This vision, which diverges from the widely accepted egalitarian approach, is not at all based on an arbitrary hostility towards non-Jews, but rather on a fundamental existential understanding of the quality of Jewish peoplehood.[19]

There is some disagreement among the Gush Emunim as to just what is to be done with the Palestinians in the territories. The super-hawk former Israeli Army Chief General Raphael Eitan has stated that, if the government implements the Gush programme, the local Arabs would be no problem. 'When we have settled the land, all the Arabs will be able to do about it will be to scurry around like drugged roaches in a bottle.'[20]

Many of the Gush Emunim favour Rabbi Meir Kahane's Kach party, which has as its principal proposal the expulsion of all Palestinians from the State of Israel and the occupied territories. Some estimates indicate that about 20 per cent of the settlers in the territories have voted for Kach in local elections. A large number, however, are members of the Tehiya party, a radical group of both secular and religious Jews who in 1981 broke away from Likud, the major right-wing party. Professor Yuval Ne'eman, the scientist-politician who heads Tehiya, has openly advocated the transfer to the Arab countries of the half million refugees from the 1948 war who are still living in camps in Gaza and the West Bank. He is supported by Moshe Ben-Yosef, who correctly points out: 'The idea of transfer has deep roots in the Zionist movement.'[21]

However, most Gush supporters believe that a dramatic expulsion of all Palestinians from Eretz Yisrael is not necessary, or even entirely desirable, since at least some Arabs will be needed to do the menial labour. It is generally believed that with strict enforcement of security laws, effective laws on Arab political and cultural activity, limited educational opportunities and deportation of Palestinian leadership elements – along with large-scale Jewish colonization – an environment can be created in which gradually the thinning out of the Arab population of the West Bank will take place.

Even before the *intifada* there was widespread support among settlers for an iron-fisted policy towards the Palestinians in the occupied territories. A 1987 poll of rabbis living on the West Bank showed that 86 per cent of those responding judged that it was permissible to use collective punishments including deportations against refugee camps, villages or extended families suspected of rock throwing or other resistance activities.[22]

Most Gush settlers believe that Palestinian resistance is to be expected, since there can never be any real peace with the Arabs until the redemption process is fulfilled. To Jewish fundamentalists (as with their Moslem and Christian counterparts) war is not a great horror to be avoided at all costs. Rabbi Tzvi Yehuda Kook has written: 'Torah, war and settlement – they are three things in one and we rejoice in the authority we have been given for each of them.'[23] Rabbi Kook decried the Camp David peace agreement and taught that war was an integral part of the redemptive process.

In view of their paranoid world view, for most Jewish fundamentalists war is unavoidable. As one settler told the Israeli writer Amos Oz, 'In general I don't believe there will be peace. The Gentile hatred of Israel is an eternal thing. There's never been peace between us and them except when they beat us completely or when we beat them completely.'[24] Jewish fundamentalists believe that Arab hostility towards them is the latest and most crucial episode in Israel's constant battle to overcome the forces of evil. According to Gush philosophy, Arab hostility springs not from any justified grievances but, like all anti-Semitism, is simply a manifestation of the world's recalcitrance in the face of Israel's mission to save it.

According to the fundamentalist philosopher Harold Fisch, the Palestinians in particular struggle against Zionism for totally malicious reasons. He sees them as the epitome of evil, as men who must surely oppose God's chosen people who have sole claim to the holy land. He writes, 'The Palestinian national identity was invented as a kind of antithesis or parody of Jewish nationhood. . . . Its aim is not to build but to destroy. It is not love of land which inspires it but hatred of the Jewish inhabitants.'[25] Fisch denies that the Palestinians have known any real suffering like the Jews, who have earned a right to their homeland. The Palestinian resistance is a 'suicidal' struggle for the elimination of the state and people of Israel. Israel must therefore recognize the Palestinians as their worst enemies and stand ready to destroy them as they seek to fulfil their collective death wish.

But the lands of the Palestinians are not the only territory desired by many Gush activists. Most see the West Bank and Gaza as only the minimal requirement for Zionist expansion. The Gush scholar Yehuda Elitzur considers that the proper boundaries of the Jewish state extend to the River Euphrates, southern Turkey and the Nile delta. Rabbi Yisrael Ariel sees the boundaries of the Zionist state as including Lebanon up to Tripoli, Syria as well as parts of Iraq, the Sinai and the oil-producing regions of Kuwait.[26] The ultimate territorial demands of Gush Emunim are unclear, but their desire to annex is unmistakable.

Their moment came in May 1977 when Menachem Begin and his Likud party came to power. Begin had long been known as an outspoken advocate of Eretz Yisrael, having written in his memoirs: 'Whoever fails to recognize our right to the entire homeland does not recognize our right to any of its territories.'[27] One of Begin's first acts after his election as Prime Minister was to visit Tzvi Yehuda Kook in order to receive the Rabbi's blessing. Begin bowed and knelt before him in what one former student called a 'surrealist scene'.[28] It was after this encounter that Tzvi Yehuda gained the fame and prestige that would last until his death in 1982. 'You could see for yourself that instead of treating him as if he were crazy, people looked upon him as upon something holy. And everything he said or did became something holy as well.' Rabbi Kook's ethos pervaded the Likud government, which placed top priority on plans to settle in the West Bank.

In September 1977 the new Agriculture Minister, Ariel Sharon, outlined his proposal to settle the occupied territories, which he called 'A Vision of Israel at Century's End'.[29] Sharon foresaw the settlement of a million Jews in the West Bank within twenty years. The previous Labour government had pursued a settlement programme that largely consisted of an effort to create Jewish suburbs surrounding Arab East Jerusalem, which would be cut off from the West Bank and thus prevented from becoming the capital of a Palestinian state. In ten years the Labour government had settled only seven thousand people in the West Bank outside the Jerusalem area. Most of them were in 'Allon Plan' Kibbutzim in the sparsely inhabited area near the River Jordan which the Labour government hoped to control permanently after negotiation at some future date with King Hussein's government.

But all of this changed after the Likud victory. Menachem Begin made it clear that 'we have an absolute right to settle in all parts of Eretz Yisrael since this is our land'.[30] Sharon was particularly concerned about settling Jews in the densely populated West Bank highlands, which were close to the Green Line border with Israel. He feared that the contiguous area of Arab inhabitants in the highlands could serve as the centre of a Palestinian state; this 'solid Arab block', he believed, threatened the coastal plain, which contained most of Israel's population but lacked 'strategic depth' in the event of a new Arab-Israeli war.[31] According to the Agriculture Minister's announcement in September 1977 two highways would be built in order to connect Israel's coastal plain to the Samarian settlements and to the Jordan Valley in order to disrupt the continuity between Arab population centres.

Sharon's conception of a vast Jewish colonization of the West Bank was embodied in the 1978 'Master Plan for the Development of Settlement in Judaea and Samaria' prepared by Mattityahu Drobles, co-Chairman of the Settlement Department of the World Zionist Organization (WZO).[32] The Drobles Plan, which was revised several times in the early 1980s, reflected Gush Emunim's intention that the occupied territories should eventually be annexed by Israel.

Like Sharon, Drobles believed that Jewish colonization could be used as an instrument of 'demographic transformation' that would change the ethnic character of the occupied territories. The new emigrants would be attracted not by political, religious or ideological considerations but by the availability of land and housing that would be irresistible to middle-class Israelis who could not afford spacious, pollution-free suburban dwellings in Israel. Most advocates of colonization believe that if a hundred thousand Jews are settled in the West Bank it would be impossible for any Israeli government to relinquish control of the territories in any future negotiations. Drobles made it clear what action had to be taken in the West Bank:

> State land and uncultivated land must be seized immediately in order to settle the areas between the concentration of minority population and around them with the object of reducing to the minimum the possibility of the development of another Arab state in these regions. It would be difficult for the minority population to form territorial continuity and political unity when it is fragmented by Jewish settlement.[33]

Drobles placed a high priority on obtaining control of West Bank land. Under the 'Fourth Geneva Convention Relative to the Protection of Civilian Persons in Time of War', which was signed by Jordan and Israel, it is forbidden for an army of occupation to seize the land of any territory it has invaded. Israel has claimed that the Fourth Geneva

Convention does not apply to the West Bank since the area was never really part of Jordan and therefore Israel is not an occupying power. This interpretation is contradicted by every competent international authority, including the United Nations and the International Red Cross.[34] While denying the applicability of the Convention, Israel asserts that it is observing its provisions in the occupied territories. Since the Convention prohibits an occupying power from seizing land and settling its citizens in an occupied territory, the Likud government of Menachem Begin had to find a way of avoiding this restriction.

The Labour governments before 1977 had seized West Bank land by claiming that it was being 'temporarily requisitioned for military purposes', which is allowed by the Fourth Geneva Convention. This subterfuge was challenged in the Israeli courts in several cases which proved to be inconclusive. The most serious legal challenge to land seizure for military purposes came in 1979, in a dispute involving the requisition of land near Nablus needed for the Elon Moreh settlement.

A group of seventeen Arabs from the village of Rujeib fought the requisition of their land since they questioned the army's right to seize land that was intended for a permanent civilian settlement. Many Israeli doves, including the 'Peace Now' movement, came to the aid of the Palestinian farmers because they saw Likud's policy of West Bank settlement as the biggest obstacle to the resolution of the Arab–Israeli dispute. In the Knesset there was bitter controversy, with many left-wing members calling Sharon a 'fascist' and a 'racist' who was an expert at 'driving Arabs from their land'.[35]

The court case was even more bitter. General Raphael Eitan, arguing that the settlement was necessary for national security, was opposed by Matti Peled, a reserve general and a member of the dovish Sheli party, and General Haim Bar Lev, a former Chief of Staff and General Secretary of the Labour party. Peled and Bar Lev disputed the claim that national security was involved in the seizure of the Rujeib farmers' land. Ironically, the government's case could survive the testimony of its opponents but not that of some of its supporters. Representatives of Gush Emunim argued that military considerations were immaterial since the real issue was the 'return of Israel to its land' as part of the redemption process.

The Likud cabinet was placed in a difficult position by the Elon Moreh case. In order to win the suit and proceed with the settlement it had to prove that the requisition of land was temporary. But Likud's ideology made it impossible for the cabinet to declare Elon Moreh or any other settlement to be temporary, since Begin's policy was openly to declare the West Bank as an eternal part of Eretz Yisrael.[36] In view of the attitude of Gush Emunim and the Begin cabinet, the Israeli Supreme Court had no choice but to rule the seizure of Palestinian land for Elon Moreh to be illegal. The court stated that the security argument

> would in itself not have led to the taking of the decision on the establishment of the Elon Moreh settlement, had there not been another reason, which was the driving force for the taking of such decision . . . namely the powerful desire of the members of Gush Emunim to settle in the heart of Eretz Yisrael as close as possible to the town of Nablus . . . the decision to establish a permanent settlement intended from the outset to remain in its place forever . . . to exist even after the end of the military rule in that area when the fate of the area after the termination of military rule is still not known.[37]

After the Elon Moreh decision the Likud government had to find a new rationale for land seizure. Besides, the Drobles Plan required very large amounts of land which individual holdings could not provide. During the 1980s the West Bank Data Base Project (WBDP), under the former Labour deputy mayor of Jerusalem, Meron Benvenisti, monitored conditions on the West Bank, including the seizure of Palestinian lands for Jewish settlements. A WBDP report noted: 'Israeli authorities in their quest to take possession of land in the territories have been using every legal and quasi-legal means in the book and are inventing new ones to attain their objectives.'[38]

The person responsible for the seizure of West Bank land

since 1967 has been Plia Albeck of the Israeli Justice Ministry. In scores of cases she had defended the government against the claims of Palestinians suing for illegal seizure of their land. She makes no pretence of objectivity: 'I believe in the Bible. I believe in the return of the Jewish people to the land.'[39] She and her staff have diligently applied a wide variety of techniques to acquire Palestinian land, especially since 1979.

Some land was gained by seizing the property of Palestinians who were expelled or fled when the Israelis invaded the West Bank in 1967. A small amount of property was seized by claiming that it belonged to Jews who had lived in the West Bank before 1948. Other land was expropiated under Jordanian law (still theoretically in force) which allowed the government to take land if it would be used for the benefit of the public. Under this pretext property has been seized for use as roads leading to Jewish settlements as well as the installation of settlement cesspools and reservoirs.

The most common method used to seize Arab property in the West Bank has been the concept of state land, which originated under Ottoman rule and carried over into British and Jordanian law. Under their interpretation of Ottoman law 750,000 dunams which comprised state land during Jordanian rule have been seized by the Israelis for use by Jewish settlers. But even this vast tract has not satisfied the Israeli appetite for West Bank land.

Plia Albeck and her department were directed by Sharon and Begin to consider all communal land which was not registered and whose Arab farmers could not document their ownership to be declared state land and thus liable for seizure by the occupation authorities. In this way 2.15 million dunams have been newly classified as state land. In May 1980 a special committee of the Israeli cabinet was set up to supervise the expropriation of property declared state land.

Much of this consisted of grazing fields on the outskirts of villages, which Palestinians had never registered since they wanted to avoid paying taxes. After the property was seized Jewish settlers arrested Palestinians who dared to enter the fields, which in many cases had been used by their families for generations. The Israeli decision to reclassify a large part of the West Bank as state land to be used for Jewish colonization is a major step towards *de facto* annexation of the occupied territories.[40]

The seizure of West Bank acreage that resulted from the state land reclassifications netted the Israeli government a considerable amount of real estate in the occupied territories. But much prime farmland was still in the hands of the Palestinians. Dispossessing these farmers, who held legal titles to their land, would have caused a worldwide outcry and generated bad publicity which the Israeli government was not willing to face; this land could best be obtained through private purchase. In 1979, Begin lifted the ban on private purchase by Jews of West Bank land which had been imposed by the previous Labour government.[41] Despite the imposition of the death penalty by the Jordanians and the PLO on Palestinians who sold West Bank land to Jews, thousands of Arabs succumbed to financial temptation. By 1983, 100,000 dunams in the occupied territories had been purchased by Jews.

Many of these sales were made through shady Arab middlemen who used strong-arm tactics and various forms of fraud to transfer West Bank land to Jewish clients. These transactions led to widespread scandal, exposed in a report published in 1985 by the left-wing Israeli Citizens' Rights Movement. Hundreds of Arabs were cheated out of their land but were afraid to appeal to the authorities. The occupation regime refused to make a serious investigation since they feared that any prosecutions would hinder the effort to colonize Eretz Yisrael. Yitzak Shamir, who had replaced Menachem Begin as leader of the Likud party, shouted at a public meeting: 'Sometimes tricks and schemes and unconventional means were used to purchase land. It is intolerable that a witch hunt should try to block this patriotic mission.'[42]

By 1987 through various means the Israeli settlers had acquired 563,000 out of 1,672,000 dunams of cultivated land as well as most of the pasture and grazing areas on the West Bank. It is no wonder that Ariel Sharon told a British journalist, 'We have won the only battle that is important in the Middle East, the battle of the land, and it's all been legal.'[43]

In the Middle East, however, the battle for land is surpassed in importance by the battle for water. This fight too has been won by the Israelis. Since 1967 Israelis have limited Palestinian use of water by placing meters on West Bank wells and prohibiting Arabs from drilling new wells. The Jewish settlers, however, have had almost unlimited access to the area's most precious commodity. By 1988 settlers were using 36 million cubic metres of water per year, while the much larger Arab population used about 110 cubic metres. On a per capita basis this meant that each settler was getting 90 cubic metres while the average Arab town dweller got 50 cubic metres, and people living in West Bank villages were getting only 25 cubic metres.[44]

Among the largest users of West Bank water were the Jewish agricultural colonists who were moved into the Jordan Valley in the first years of the occupation (see Chapter 2). These settlers saw themselves as the descendants of the early Zionists who came to Palestine filled with socialist ideals. In the 1970s the Nahal semi-military colonies of the Jordan Valley were followed into the West Bank by Gush Emunim settlers who were motivated by their religious fanaticism, for which they were willing to make any sacrifice demanded of them.

Unlike the Allon Plan Jordan Valley communities, who laid emphasis on manual labour and an agrarian lifestyle, Gush settlers were semi-urban with no real attachment to the land. They were decidedly not socialist, since each resident owned his own home and managed his own finances. But like the Jordan Valley Kibbutzim they had their own brand of ideological zeal. By the 1980s both types of ideological settlements suffered the same fate since there were simply not enough zealots willing to come to the West Bank out of socialist, nationalist or religious motivation, thus there was a need for 'yuppie' communities which attracted people for sheer materialistic reasons.

Swimming pools and shopping malls sprang up all over the

West Bank as Sharon and Drobles' scheme was implemented in the 1980s. Although most of the people in the West Bank suburban communities were drawn by economics rather than ideology, polls indicate that they often changed from doves into hawks after living there for only a short time. Thus the original goal of those who favoured large-scale West Bank settlements – that it would create a sizeable group of people with a vested interest in annexation – began to be achieved in the 1980s. Almost the entire increase in West Bank settlement was in the suburban communities, which by 1987 accounted for 85 per cent of all West Bank settlers.[45] But the Jewish population of the West Bank has not grown as rapidly as Sharon and Drobles hoped, since there were seventy thousand settlers on the eve of the *intifada*, somewhat short of the hundred thousand goal. Many of the settlements have had to rely on foreigners, especially English-speaking immigrants, to survive, since few Israelis have the religious or ideological commitment.

Located south of Bethlehem about twelve miles from Jerusalem, Efrat is one of the West Bank settlements which is home to yuppies who commute to their white collar jobs on the other side of the Green Line. In Efrat they can choose from eight types of homes, some with Italian tile roofs, Finnish wood decoration, Jerusalem stone facing and solar heating. Residents do not appear to be disturbed by the fact that Efrat's architect also designed Yamit, the Sinai settlement evacuated after the Israeli–Egyptian peace treaty.

Efrat was founded by Rabbi Shlomo Raskin, formerly of the Lincoln Square Synagogue in a fashionable part of Manhattan. Some of the Rabbi's congregation came with him to Efrat where they were joined by Jews from several other English-speaking countries including a group from South Africa. Many have returned to New York, London or Johannesburg in view of the isolation of the community from the surrounding Arab population, which was evident even before the *intifada*. By 1982, 330 units had been built but only 110 families were living in Efrat.[46]

Rabbi Raskin has enjoyed a good press in America, where he has been called 'The Rabbi of Dialogue' because of his alleged excellent relations with Efrat's Palestinian neighbours which supposedly could serve as a model for the entire West Bank. He is quoted as saying: 'I don't think I have the right to displace anyone who is living anywhere. But if no one is living there and if I have my roots there then of course I have a right to be there.'[47] However, although no Palestinians were driven from their homes when Efrat was built, many Arabs lost valuable farmland.

Ariel Sharon visited the site where Efrat was being planned and proclaimed that the new settlement would be part of a 'chain securing forever Jerusalem's unity and Jewish identity'.[48] But work did not proceed smoothly since Palestinians waged a legal battle to halt the confiscation of their land. When the inevitable decision against them was passed down by the Israeli court they resorted to civil disobedience; some threw themselves in front of the bulldozers that were mowing down their vineyards and olive trees. But as in most such cases all efforts and appeals by the Arab farmers failed, since the Israeli court held that their Jordanian land registration forms had not been completed properly. Felicia Langer, an Israeli lawyer who handled the case for the Arab farmers, commented, 'It was a typical example of Israelis finding a way around the law. But it wasn't justice. It was robbery. Theft is legal here, you know.'[49]

Some of the residents of Efrat may have less hostile attitudes than other West Bank settlers towards Arabs. Rabbi Raskin claims that there are even supporters of the dovish 'Peace Now' movement in his community. But there is reason to believe that less humane views predominate, particularly among the Jews from South Africa, one of whom told a British journalist: 'I didn't believe in one man one vote in South Africa and I don't believe in it here.'[50] Merel Cohen from South Africa confided: 'Here I find myself becoming more and more extreme. Partly it is because so many of the settlers are that way.' She added, 'What we are doing here is comparable to what whites did in South Africa. We too have imposed the rule of conquest.'

Ariel, a suburban settlement near Nablus, is also sometimes portrayed as a 'model for living together with the Arabs'. But like Efrat there is reason to doubt this public relations image. From the beginning the settlement was designed as an obstacle to a resolution of the Arab–Israeli conflict. Indeed Ariel was built immediately after the signing of the agreement between President Sadat of Egypt and Menachem Begin to show that there would be an increase in West Bank settlements despite the expectations of the Americans and Egyptians. Over 3500 dunams of land near the village of Sulfet were confiscated so that Ariel could be built, which was bitterly protested by the local population.[51]

The guiding spirit behind Ariel has been Ron Nachman, a fourth-generation Israeli who sees the community as a way of creating a permanent link between Israel and the territories. Nachman, who before 1977 had been a middle manager in an aircraft industries plant, is a staunch member of the right-wing Likud party.

In order to attract the eight thousand residents who he hopes will ultimately increase to a hundred thousand, Nachman ran a TV advertising campaign. His message was that an average Israeli could have a comfortable villa or apartment for a quarter of the price of similar accommodation in Israel. He claimed: 'Here in the heart of Samaria, here is the future.' A very attractive picture of the settlement was painted: 'We are a non-fanatical pluralistic community – 90 per cent secular, 10 per cent religious, 60 per cent Sephardic [Middle Eastern Jews], 40 per cent Ashkenazim [European Jews]. We are a cross-section of average Israel. A real melting pot.'[52]

Naomi Loney, a black American Jewish resident of Ariel, agrees: 'This place is spiritually divorced from most other settlements on the West Bank. Its attitude toward the Arabs is an enlightened one.'[53] But in an interview after the outbreak of the *intifada*, Ron Nachman, now Ariel's mayor, did not sound too conciliatory. 'We're all secular but everyone who moves here becomes right-wing. We're defending our homes.' He added, 'If the Arabs don't keep themselves under control, they will find themselves in Jordan.'[54]

Ariel is built on a huge piece of land twelve kilometres wide. Part of this area is being turned into an industrial park that it is hoped will employ thousands of people. Already some of the land has been getting tax concessions from the Israeli government, which is standard practice for all industry established in the West Bank.

Other industrial parks are located throughout the West Bank. It is estimated that about 70 per cent of their workforce is Jewish.[55] Plans call for the creation of new high-tech industrial parks all over the West Bank, which by the year 2010 will employ 83,500 people, of whom only 25,000 will be Arabs. These industrial complexes will be integrated with existing industry in Israel, thus further obscuring any distinction between the Jewish state and the occupied territories.

But despite attempts to build up the West Bank's industry, the settlement effort has been a severe drain on the fragile Israeli economy. By 1987 in constant dollar prices the Israelis had invested $3 billion in West Bank settlements. Each family which moved to the West Bank highlands cost the Israeli taxpayer (in reality the American taxpayer) $80,000, while a family settled in the Jordan Valley cost $160,000. Expenditure for West Bank settlements, depending on their size, is between 63 per cent and 143 per cent higher per capita than similar communities in Israel. Several studies indicate that economic assistance for West Bank settlements has been given while many Jewish communities in Israel, especially in Galilee, lack both economic assistance and Jewish settlers. The West Bank financial drain is unlikely to end soon. One researcher notes: 'Preferential treatment of West Bank settlements will have to be maintained for a long time, and if generous public funding is suddenly withheld, the whole structure will collapse.'[56]

Many right-wing Israelis have claimed that the settlements must be retained for military reasons. General Aryeh Shalev argues that 'in wartime these settlements are likely to provide strong bases for IDF forces passing through them'.[57] He believes that 'their very presence is likely to deter the Jordanians from sending forces into Judaea and Samaria'. Some have suggested that the settlements could serve as early warning outposts or 'trip wires' in the event of an

Arab attack. It has also been claimed that the settlements might play a useful role in 'anti-insurgency' operations.[58]

However, there is no evidence to support the argument that the settlements could play a military role of any kind. There are now sophisticated electronic devices which could easily detect any potential Arab attack long before West Bank settlers could raise the alarm. During the 1973 war the Golan Heights settlers on the border with Syria were no help to the IDF – indeed they had to be evacuated on the first day of the war. During the *intifada*, Defence Minister Yitzak Rabin called the Jewish settlers a 'burden' to his anti-insurgency operations. Israeli General Harkabi has pointed out that in time of war 'settlements are more of a liability than an asset because they require forces to protect them and are a provocation to the Arab population'.[59]

Despite the settlements' lack of value, the Israeli government, particularly the right-wing Likud party, has made it plain that no matter what it takes the settlements will never be abandoned. At the opening of a new settlement on 10 October 1982 the Minister of Energy, Mordechai Sippori, indicated why the Israeli government supported colonization of the occupied territories: 'The continuation of settlement is the backbone of the Zionist movement in the West Bank and it is the only means to defeat any peace initiative which is intended to bring foreign rule to Judaea and Samaria.' On another occasion Haim Korfu, Minister of Transportation, told a gathering: 'The settlements are a guarantee against the Palestinian state of those who hate us.'[60] From time to time the Israeli government has responded to initiatives made by Gush Emunim which push the cabinet towards West Bank colonization. But as one settler told an American researcher, 'If the government didn't want something, then it wouldn't happen no matter how hard we fought. It just serves their purpose to have it look like we pressured them into things that they would probably do anyway.'[61]

One of the things the settlers have pressed for is the extension of Israeli law to the territories. In recent years a legal device unique in modern jurisprudence has been used – to 'annex' the Jewish settlers without extending

Israeli sovereignty to the West Bank land, while allowing the Arab population to remain under Jordanian law. This is reminiscent of the old system of European colonialism, in which Europeans living in China or Turkish-ruled lands, say, were exempted from native laws but were subject to the legal system of the British, French, Russian or other colonial powers.

When Jewish housewives in the West Bank suburbs complained that Israeli home appliance companies refused to repair their washing machines because the owners resided 'outside Israel', the Ministry of Trade and Industries issued an emergency regulation that extended the insurance obligation for appliances to Jewish settlements in the territories. By scores of such small steps the legal distinction between Israel and the occupied areas has been eroded.

One of the biggest steps in this direction has been the creation of the system of West Bank regional and local councils which administer services in the settlements. These authorities run parallel to the Palestinian municipal authorities, which deal with Arabs. The budgets of the West Bank Jewish councils are incorporated into the general budgets of Israeli civilian ministries with standards equal to that of Israel proper.

The Israeli practice of creating a legal system to accommodate the settlers without extending Israeli sovereignty to the West Bank is motivated by a desire to give a veneer of legality to the settlements without provoking worldwide condemnation and possible retaliation by officially annexing the territories. As Meron Benvenisti has noted, 'It is precisely the way the Boers of South Africa have worked and are still working. Everything in South Africa is legal. But it is not the rule of law which presupposes immutable values like justice. It is rule by law. In other words, it is legal but not just.'[62]

While the system developed for the West Bank settlements may conform to Israeli national law, it is not consistent with international law. As seen earlier, the Israelis have defied the provisions of the Fourth Geneva Convention which prohibit the seizure of land. They are also in violation of the clause in Article 49 of the Convention which states: 'The Occupying

Power shall not deport or transfer part of its civilian population into the territory it occupies.'[63] The Israelis deny that the Fourth Geneva Convention with its prohibition against settlements in occupied territory applies in the West Bank. On 26 October 1977 the representative of the Jewish state declared to the General Assembly:

> Since Jordan never was a legitimate sovereign in Judaea and Samaria, the provisions of the Fourth Geneva Convention – including those of its Article 49, which were intended to protect the rights of 'the legitimate sovereign' – do not apply in respect of Jordan. Therefore, Israel is not affected by these provisions, and need not consider itself restricted by them. In other words, Israel cannot be considered an 'occupying Power', within the meaning of the Convention in any part of the former Palestine Mandate, including Judaea and Samaria.[64]

This interpretation has been denied by every competent international legal authority including the International Committee of the Red Cross, which has been given a special status in occupied territories by Articles 30 and 173 of the Convention. Although it is generally reluctant to comment on controversial questions, which might impair its impartial image, in 1975 the ICRC declared that it was of the opinion that the Fourth Geneva Convention 'is applicable *in toto*' in the occupied territories and 'cannot accept that a duly ratified international treaty may be suspended at the wish of one of the parties'.[65] The US government shared this view until the Reagan administration. At a press conference on 21 January 1981 President Reagan announced: 'As to the West Bank, I believe the settlements there – I disagree when the previous administration refers to them as illegal, they're not illegal.'[66] However, Reagan did call the settlements 'ill advised' and 'unnecessarily provocative'.

Under its leader Rabbi Moshe Levinger, the Gush Emunim colony at Kiryat Arba near Hebron was the most obvious 'unnecessary provocation' in the West Bank. Established in 1970 (see Chapter 2), from the beginning Kiryat Arba was the centre of an intense conflict between the Jewish settlement which has been called 'Miami Beach meets the Casbah'[67] and the neighbouring Arab town of Hebron. Despite its worldwide publicity the Kiryat Arba community is not large, numbering in 1983 only 2900 individuals and fewer than seven hundred families. Not all the community is ultra-Orthodox; indeed only half the residents can be classified as religious as defined in Israel.[68] About 70 per cent are Israeli-born, most of them of non-Western origin. The largest group are of North African background. The educational levels in Kiryat Arba are above average for Israeli Jews, with the Americans and Soviets having the highest education and thus playing a leading role in settlement affairs.

Opposite Kiryat Arba is Arab Hebron, which, although it is one of the largest towns in the West Bank, has many of the characteristics of an overgrown village. Ownership of land confers status in the community, where attachment to the family patrimony and rural activity play a prominent role. The Moslem character of the town is very prominent, much more so than in more cosmopolitan communities like Nablus or Ramallah. There are no cinemas or other entertainment facilities in Hebron. The selling of liquor is forbidden, and during the holy month of Ramadan no eating places are open during the day. In Hebron loyalty to Islam rivals loyalty to the PLO.

In 1976, Gush Emunim escalated its provocative activities. Rabbi Levinger and his followers made a habit of entering Hebron while flaunting their guns which, as in the Wild West, the settlers but not the indigenous population were allowed to carry. In defiance of a standing military order the Rabbi held a public prayer session in the ruins of Abraham Avinu Synagogue in the heart of the Arab town next to the vegetable market. The military governor summoned Levinger to his office and produced an order prohibiting the Kiryat Arba settlers from entering the ruins of the Hebron synagogue. Levinger tore up the order in the governor's face, saying, 'I will not accept that order because it is not legal.'[69]

Rabbi Levinger 'went into hiding' in Kiryat Arba, while

challenging the army to move against him for his open defiance of a military order. Finally the army removed Levinger, but he was not taken into custody. A compromise was arranged whereby he would report to military government headquarters for questioning and be released the same day. The army's lenient attitude to Levinger enraged the population of Arab Hebron; it also emboldened the Jewish settlers.

The man responsible for halting the encroachment by Levinger and the Kiryat Arba settlers in 1976 was Fahed Kawassma, the newly elected mayor of Hebron. Kawassma tried to walk a delicate line between the PLO nationalists, the pro-Jordanian faction and the occupation authorities, while attempting to placate Rabbi Levinger and the Gush extremists. But in the end he asserted his Palestinian nationalism. He told a UN committee investigating the West Bank: 'We would welcome the coming back to Hebron of any Jewish person who wishes to come back to Hebron but such a person has at the same time to allow us similarly to go back to our land and our homes in Lydda, Ramle, Jaffa, Haifa and Jerusalem.'[70]

According to Kawassma, on 2 October 1976 'settlers from Kiryat Arba insulted the Koran inside the Ibrahini Mosque and tore it up and stamped on it'. The Moslems of Hebron retaliated by destroying Jewish holy books in the Cave of the Patriarchs. The situation in the area became tense. On the 7th the Israeli cabinet met to discuss the crisis. After the meeting Prime Minister Rabin condemned the actions of the Arabs in Hebron, but added, 'Rabbi Levinger was trying wittingly or unwittingly to bring about a Jewish–Arab confrontation in Hebron. It must be made clear to Gush Emunim people that there is law and order in the State of Israel.'[71] Rabin's words proved to be hollow. Indeed after the Likud government under Menachem Begin came to power in 1977 the settlers of Kiryat Arba became even bolder.

In 1979 there was a further confrontation between Jews and Arabs in Hebron over a building which is known as Hadassah House. The building was erected in 1863 and was later used by a Jewish doctor, Ben-Zion Gershon, for a clinic which served both Arabs and Jews. During the 1929 riots a mob ransacked the building and killed Dr Gershon, his wife and one of his daughters. In the 1970s a surviving daughter who lived in Israel expressed an interest in reopening the non-sectarian clinic, but she was prevented from doing so by the local military governor.

In April 1979 Miriam Levinger broke into the building along with a group of women from Kiryat Arba and occupied the premises. Dr Gershon's daughter bristled with indignation over the 'illegal squatters who are allowed to remain there undisturbed – even their expenses are covered, while I would like to carry on my father's mission of serving the population of Hebron and helping to create as normal a life as possible for Arabs and Jews – I am not allowed into the building'.[72]

But Miriam Levinger was adamant in her refusal to leave. She told the Israeli journalist Rafik Halabi that her presence was 'the bone stuck in the government's throat. Here we must proclaim, "Hebron will never again be *Juden rein*".' One of her followers added, 'There may be bloodshed but we will not leave Hadassah House.' That was no idle boast. In early 1980 the Israeli government formally called for the re-establishment of a Jewish quarter in Hebron, and within a few years several more locations in the heart of Arab Hebron were occupied by Jewish settlers with active official backing.[73]

The people of Hebron bitterly resented the Gush pressure on their town. But unlike the Palestinians of Nablus and Ramallah, they are not prone to street demonstrations. Hebronites tend to keep their feelings bottled up until it erupts in a burst of violence. Thus in the early 1980s Hebron suffered terrible incidents of terrorism and counter-terrorism as the townspeople fought it out with the Kiryat Arba settlers.

On 3 January 1980 a Yeshiva student, Yoshua Saloma, was shot and killed in central Hebron. There were charges that the mayor, Fahed Kawassma, had condoned the murder of the Israeli youth in retaliation for the murder of two Palestinian teenagers in March 1979. The Kiryat Arba settler accused of the crime had been acquitted by an Israeli court, which enraged West Bank Palestinians. But in an interview with an Israeli journalist, Rafik Halabi, Kawassma denied ever linking the murder of the student with the killing of the two Palestinian youths. He commented prophetically, 'I think I should buy an apartment in Amman. They're surely going to deport me there.' He added, 'I'm tired. Things are getting serious. The Jews will extract their revenge and the Arabs will respond in kind.'[74]

As expected, Saloma's death became a rallying cry for the settlers. At the funeral Kach party leader Meir Kahane addressed the dead youth: 'Your death will be a service to our cause'; while Rabbi Moshe Levinger told the crowd, 'This young man's blood has given us life.' The Rabbi added, 'Can Israel turn its back on those who are persecuted for being Jews?'[75]

After much debate in the Knesset the Israeli government decided to make Jewish settlement in the centre of Arab Hebron permanent. Several buildings, including an old synagogue, were turned over to Levinger and the Gush Emunim settlers from Kiryat Arba. Palestinian violence was being used as a rationale to extend Jewish settlement.

In Hebron there was an immediate reaction to the plan for a Jewish colony within city limits. The mayor told Halabi, 'They're trying to undermine the peace. I will not stand by silently while they go about over-running my city. I prefer to be deported, arrested, tried — anything but the judaization of Arab Hebron.' Kawassma, who was clearly angry, went over the line when he told a meeting of supporters, 'It is not with words that we shall stand up to their measures. We shall resist the decision with deeds and by every means available.' He added, 'Just as the British Empire collapsed and the Nazis collapsed, so will these arrogant presumptuous men disappear.'[76] Clearly Kawassma's days as mayor were numbered.

On 2 May four Arab gunmen took up position on the roofs of houses across from Hadassah House and opened fire on a group of Yeshiva students, killing six and wounding sixteen. According to the Voice of Palestine clandestine radio broadcast, the terrorist attack was launched by the General Command of the Palestine Revolution Forces 'as an expression of our Palestinian peoples and our Arab nation's will to challenge and stand fast in the face of the Camp David conspiracy'. Hebron had been chosen for the massacre because it was where 'the Zionists have defied the town's inhabitants in an attempt to strengthen their aggressive presence on our land by carrying out military operations through which they have been provoking our kin in the valiant town'.[77]

The Israelis used the incident to increase still further the presence of the Gush Emunim settlers within Arab Hebron, and several more buildings were taken over. They also expelled Kawassma, along with his fellow mayor Milhem of Halhoul. The Defence Minister, Ezer Weizman, claimed that Kawassma was responsible for the murders, but neither he nor anyone else presented any evidence. Weizman pointed out that 'a radicalization can be felt in either direction' in the Hebron area.[78] Unfortunately this prediction proved to be disturbingly accurate.

The settlers formed a Jewish underground terrorist group. According to the confessions of the leaders, they obtained the blessings of Rabbi Levinger and Rabbi Waldman, a Gush Emunim leader; indeed Waldman was said to have taken part himself.[79] Among the victims of settler terrorism were Bassam Shak'a, the mayor of Nablus, whose legs were blown off in a car bomb, and Karim Khalaf, mayor of Ramallah, who was also maimed in a car bomb. A third intended victim, Ibrahim Tawil of al-Bireh, escaped unharmed but an Israeli soldier was blinded as he tried to defuse a bomb intended for Tawil.

In 1981 there were twenty-two reported incidents of settler violence in the Hebron area, most of them committed by Gush members in the heart of the city. Following the destruction in March of a shop belonging to one of the Palestinians remaining on the ground floor of Hadassah House, the Israeli journalist Yehuda Litani noted: 'The fight led as usual by Rabbi Moshe Levinger is over every house in the Jewish Quarter, over every shop. It is a constant battle house to house.'[80] In November a Kiryat Arba resident responded to the stabbing to death of a Jew by shooting indiscriminately into a crowd, injuring three children. Central Commander Moshe Levy sent him a letter praising him for his courageous action. As further retaliation for this incident the homes of

Arab suspects were destroyed and seven hundred children were expelled from an elementary school, which was turned over to the settlers and renamed Romano House.

Despite the tensions and conflicts there has been some contact between the people of Kiryat Arba and those of Hebron. Arabs come to Kiryat Arba to purchase alcohol, since this is not available in their Moslem town. Some Hebronites retain Kiryat Arba lawyers, especially for cases involving intervention with the Israeli government. But more often Jews come to Arabs, especially at the main Arab market in Hebron. Clothing, household goods, appliances and especially fruit and vegetables are purchased by Kiryat Arba residents from their Hebron neighbours. Settlers even use local barber's shops and dentists, or take lessons at Arab driving schools, while many settlers travel to Jerusalem in Arab long-distance taxis. On occasions settlers travel on Arab buses.

The residents of Kiryat Arba are forced to use Arab establishments because of the lack of services of their own. By 1985 seven hundred settler households had no more than half a dozen Jewish stores at their disposal, and shopping in Arab Hebron is preferable to making the long trip to Jerusalem for needed goods and services. Another factor is price, since everyone knows that goods and services in the Arab economy are always noticeably cheaper than similar items purchased from Jewish shops. Arab establishments may be shabby-looking, but they have lower overheads and pay lower wages to their employees and rarely deal in credit cards or similar methods of payment which raise prices. Indeed, Hebron prices are 30 per cent lower than those in the Jewish economy.[81]

Most Jews shopping in Hebron go armed. Some of them say they are overcharged by the Palestinian merchants, while others, like Gush spokesman Elijakim Haetzni, claim to enjoy haggling in Arab shops. Some settlers quote Arab merchants who say that they would not overcharge Jewish neighbours 'as if they were simply Israeli tourists'.[82] Except during periods of tension, Kiryat Arba residents are welcomed by Hebron businessmen.

A particularly serious period of tension occurred when, on

7 July 1982, a Yeshiva student, Aahron Gross, was stabbed to death in the centre of Hebron. The response was swift. A curfew was imposed and acting mayor Mustafa Natashe and the city council were removed, despite their condemnation of the murder. Soon afterwards armed settlers went on a Wild West-type rampage in Hebron, where they wrecked the Arab market. Worse was to follow. On 26 July settlers assaulted the Islamic College in Hebron with machine guns and grenades, killing three and injuring scores of others. The leniency of the government towards the Jewish terrorists outraged the people of Hebron.

In 1984 the Jewish settlers in Hebron called a debate in collaboration with their Arab neighbours. More than a hundred attended the session, which was held in the main hall of the municipality in Hebron. The large Arab turnout surprised Rabbi Levinger, who was left speechless when one of the Palestinians told him:

> Rabbi Levinger, I don't know you and you don't know me. But often I see you in Hebron, at the fruit market in the Casbah, and I feel I want to say hello to you, to stop and talk. I always stop myself because I do not want people to misinterpret me. They will think I want something from you or that I am trying to flatter you.

After pausing, the Arab added, 'Rabbi Levinger, why don't you greet me first? It is easier for you than for me to break the ice. A simple greeting would mean so much to all of us. But it has to come from you first.'[83]

Perhaps the episode is best characterized by the settler Yitzak Shimon, who noted: 'There is a fundamental flaw in the Jew. It's the mentality of the ghetto. It is a state that has passed from generation to generation. The people of Kiryat Arba behave the way that they do because they have built the perfect ghetto.'[84]

The Defence Minister, Moshe Ahrens, told a British journalist, 'We are not living in the West whatever our common heritage. We are living in the Middle East. We are living with an Arab mentality that doesn't place the same value on life as we do. What is a Jew supposed to do? Lie down and die?'[85] Ahrens denied that he approved of Jewish terrorists, but added, 'What it means is that the only language is force, the only currency is strength. I don't expect the Arabs to like us. . . . The only thing I expect from the Arabs is respect.'

In their effort to gain the 'respect' of the Palestinians the Jewish settlers inflicted numerous casualties throughout the West Bank. Between 1980 and 1984 twenty-three Palestinians were killed and 191 injured in settler violence, most of which went unpunished by the occupying army – which, however, vigorously pursued any acts of violence by the Palestinian population.

The settlers formed two terrorist groups which were responsible for many attacks on churches, mosques and schools. The 'Lifta' or Brai Yehuda Messiani group attempted to blow up the al-Aqsa mosque. Indeed there have been numerous attempts by various groups of extreme settler factions to destroy sacred Moslem sites in Jerusalem.[86]

On 19 April 1981 Israel's Attorney General appointed a special inquiry into the major Jewish terrorist actions in the occupied territories. This became known as the Karp Commission after its chairman, Deputy Attorney General Yehudit Karp. In May 1982 the Commission completed its report, but Yehudit Karp resigned from his post because the report was not made public. A censored version was finally made available on 7 February 1984, but all attempts to have the complete document released have been unsuccessful.

The bulk of the report focused on a random sample of fifteen cases in which investigation was deemed faulty or inadequate. These included cases of alleged crimes committed by Kiryat Arba residents and other Jewish settlers in the West Bank. The Karp Report noted:

The handling of many files went on for an unreasonable length of time, regardless of the sensitivity of the issue under investigation. The inquiry team takes a very grave view of the slow pace of investigation (and the pace of reporting) in cases of death from shooting. It should also be pointed out that even in those cases where the state attorney's office had given its commitment to the Supreme Court to conduct an effective investigation, the inquiry team's efforts to expedite handling were to no avail.[87]

In order to support its charge that the actions of the settlers constituted 'civil rebellion', the Karp Report cited the harrowing cases of the villages of Sinjil and Na'im, where Arab civilians were murdered by settlers:

> In both cases when the murder suspects were summoned to appear before the police they announced that they would not come, and that they dealt only with the military government. The police did nothing to bring the suspects to the police station, despite the grave suspicion, and the arrest warrant issued against the suspect in the Beni Na'im murder was not implemented, under circumstances that demand clarification. In the case of Beni Na'im, a delegation including the head of the Kiryat Arba Council and a representative of the Gush Etzion Council turned up three days later and, according to Superintendent Kalij, told the police, citing military government authorities, that there would be no co-operation, and that the police and the Jerusalem District Attorney were hostile. They said they would not convey their version of the incident unless they received instructions from the political echelon. It should be noted that one of the suspects was a member of the delegation, and that he was not questioned on that occasion. As a result, the suspects were not located, and not until six days after the incident were the police able to gather evidence (and this on a case of manslaughter, or suspicion of murder, when the suspects were well-known). This, of course, had direct implications for the investigation itself. It is hard to believe that this is how a case involving a death would be investigated in Israel.[88]

The Karp Commission concluded that the 'procedures for the bearing of IDF arms by civilians must be re-evaluated, along with the instructions they receive about opening fire'.[89] This and other recommendations of the Karp Commission were ignored by the Israeli government.

But there was no end to settler terrorism. In April 1985 twenty-five members of a suspected Jewish terrorist organization were arrested on the eve of an attempt to place bombs under six East Jerusalem buses. This Jewish plot to commit mass murder sent shockwaves through Israeli society. All the suspects were Orthodox Jews with ties to Gush Emunim. Many had studied at Merkaz HaRav Yeshiva under the spiritual father of Gush Emunim, Rabbi Tzvi Yehuda Kook.

The twenty-five were charged in connection with the assassination attempts on the West Bank mayors on 2 June 1980; the attacks on the Islamic College in Hebron in which three people were killed; a plot to blow up the Dome of the Rock in Jerusalem; and other crimes. The defendants were allowed to plea bargain, so that none of them received anything like the sentences which their crimes required.

During the investigation it was learnt that the settler underground organization had been formed in 1978 for the sole purpose of carrying out terrorist attacks which would sabotage the peace process between Israel and Egypt. In his testimony one of the defendants, Yehuda Etzion, revealed that while the underground settler terrorist organization had clear political goals, its underlying ideological motive had a fundamentalist religio-nationalist messianic character. He told a British journalist:

> For Gentiles life is mainly a life of existence while ours is a life of destiny, the life of a kingdom of priests and holy people, the Kingdom of David. We Jews exist in the world in order to make our messianic destiny a reality.[90]

Etzion made it clear that the aim of his organization was to fulfil the Gush Emunim goal of using terror to frighten the Palestinians in the West Bank so that they would flee to Jordan, which was regarded as their real home.

During the 1980s there was considerable Israeli opposition to the Gush Emunim settlements. Initially the 'Peace

Now' movement concerned itself with the peace agreement with Egypt, but its members gradually came to see the central importance of resolving the conflict with the Palestinians. The first major demonstration by 'Peace Now' against settlements in the West Bank was a rally of forty thousand on 16 June 1979. In December 1980 'Peace Now' described the West Bank settlements as a 'deliberate policy of the Likud government intended to hurt peace prospects through establishing *fait accompli* on the ground and leaving scorched earth for the coming government'.[91]

'Peace Now' advocated a moratorium on all West Bank settlements and expropriations of Arab land, the right of the Palestinians to manage their own affairs and the removal of all restrictions on the inhabitants of the occupied territories. The movement also favoured the reallocation of resources so that the money being spent on West Bank settlers could be used to help the poor in Israel. The ultimate ambition was the negotiation of a permanent agreement that would 'recognize the rights of the Palestinians to a natural existence'. But the borders of such a Palestinian state were not specified by 'Peace Now'.

Many 'Peace Now' activists were supporters of the liberal wing of the Israeli Labour party. In 1983, a number of Labour party Knesset members as well as members of several left-wing parties signed a statement calling for a freeze on West Bank settlements, and endorsed many of the aims of the 'Peace Now' movement. In the 1984 Knesset elections the Labour party supported 'territorial compromise', which provided for the retention by Israel of the Jordan Valley, the Etzion Block area, the environs of Jerusalem, the southern Gaza Strip and part of the Golan Heights; while 'well-defined, densely populated areas of Judaea, Samaria and Gaza' would be turned over to a 'Jordanian–Palestinian framework'. Since that election provided no clear-cut winner, a coalition government was formed between the Labour and Likud parties, thus rendering any implementation of the Labour platform impossible.

In the absence of any government policy to resolve the impasse over the West Bank, many Israeli intellectuals in the

1980s spoke out against West Bank colonization. Perhaps the most articulate was Amos Oz, the journalist and author who recalls a talk he gave to a group of residents at the settlement of Ofra. Oz admonished the Gush supporters for threatening 'to push Judaism back through history . . . to the extreme of fanatical tribalism, brutal and closed', and criticized them for demanding that the Palestinians 'agree to live with a status we would never accept for ourselves'.[92] He described the dilemma posed by Gush Emunim for liberals in Europe and America who accepted the outdated image of the persecuted Jew: 'We demand to be judged by a special standard in that our enormous contribution to culture be remembered as well as our terrible suffering . . . we played on the heartstrings of decent people, even making ingenious use of the guilt feelings that were caused in the Christian West.'

Oz pointed out to his Gush listeners that, because of their activities in the occupied territories, the West was wondering what the Israelis had as their ultimate goal. 'Is it really only a strip of land for refugees, a homeland, independence and peace and security as they claimed originally, or are they really cheating and is the real goal to reconstruct some nationalistic and religious fantasy?'

But in spite of the opposition of many liberal Israelis the trend towards colonization of the West Bank continued. A 1984 report of the West Bank Data Project noted:

> The political, military, socio-economic and psychological processes now working towards total annexation of the West Bank and the Gaza Strip outweigh those that work against it . . . Those processes do not yet appear to have reached a point of no return . . . however, we can say the critical point has passed.[93]

Many have tried to refute this conclusion, but without any noticeable success.

8
THE STEADFAST

In July 1985 delegates from sixty Palestinian trade unions converged on a meeting hall in Jerusalem. The conference had been organized to improve conditions for workers from the occupied territories who were employed in Israel. They had many grievances, including lack of equality in insurance, job security and other privileges enjoyed by Israeli workers. The delegates were also asking for measures to alleviate the impact of Israel's economic crisis on Arab workers, who were the first to be fired during these troubled times. The principal demand was for the government to allow workers from the territories who were employed in Israel to join Arab trade unions. Since 1979, the Israeli government had refused to recognize new Arab trade unions, preferring workers from the territories to join the Jewish-dominated Histadrut, which Palestinians believed did not serve their interests. Many of the delegates at the Jerusalem conference were members of new illegal Arab trade unions.

Israeli troops surrounded the meeting hall. Some of the delegates were told not to enter, while others, including Ismail Tabanja, a well-known Arab labour leader, were taken to prison. But these repressive actions drew worldwide condemnation from trade unionists and other groups, such as the American Peace Council. Reluctantly, the Israelis released the Palestinian labour leaders and allowed the trade union conference to meet a few days later.

The aim of the conference was not political. But one of the delegates, Ali Abu Hilal, notes that its goal of unionizing Palestinian workers from the territories was 'considered by the Israelis as a threat to the security of Israel, although it is the legitimate right of all workers to belong to a union and to try to improve their condition'.[1] Hilal recalled that Israeli delegates too attended the conference, and were able to see that there was nothing discussed or proposed that endangered the Jewish state. He also indicated that the conference was covered by the Israeli news media, who interviewed Hilal and other Palestinian union organizers, none of whom made radical demands.

But the following month the Israeli cabinet instituted practices which became known as the 'iron fist policy' in order to 'clamp down on terrorism and incidents in the territories'.[2] Many Palestinians were imprisoned, including thirty trade unionists, and some of the latter were deported. On 27 October an order was issued for the arrest and deportation of Ali Abu Hilal, who had a long record of encounters with the Israeli West Bank security authorities. When Hilal was arrested, he relates that his house was carefully searched. They found International Labour Office (ILO) reports, because Hilal was preparing for that organization a study on the conditions of Arab workers in the occupied territories. Hilal told a UN panel that the Israelis confiscated these documents in spite of the fact that he 'pointed out to the authorities concerned that they were international reports and in no way constituted a danger to Israel'.[3]

Three other Palestinians were arrested with him, including Dr Azmi Shweibi, a dentist from El Bireh, who later identified his crime: 'I considered it essential to express my point of view in public to the authorities that the Palestinians have the right to self-determination.'[4] For this he was harassed for many years. At times, Dr Shweibi was locked in a tiny cell in isolation for long periods. Over the years, his health had deteriorated; by 1985 he had advanced lung cancer but this did not spare him from the deportation order.

Michael Smith, a lawyer from New York and a member of the National Lawyers' Guild, was with a delegation of American attorneys who went to Israel in November that year to investigate the deportation order against the four Palestinians. Smith had the opportunity of meeting Dr

Shweibi's wife and children, family and neighbours, who described what happened on the night of the arrest. 'They heard a knock on the door, they opened the door, they found the house surrounded, including soldiers on the roof, by some twenty uniformed men with submachine guns.' When the Israelis broke into the house they placed Dr Shweibi under arrest, although they had no warrant; nor did they tell him the charge against him. The security people put a hood over his head and tied his arms behind his back as they led him off to the police station. Smith was outraged at the treatment of Dr Shweibi. He told a UN panel:

> It was particularly disturbing to me having come from a family of Jews who emigrated to the United States from Europe. My grandparents came from four separate anti-Semitic countries in Europe and I grew up hearing often about the famous knock on the door, and it was something that concerned my family in the United States, even though the possibility there was remote. Nonetheless, we always heard stories about the knock on the door. That is precisely what happened to Dr Shweibi and his wife and three young children when they lay in bed at two o'clock in the morning.[5]

With Michael Smith in the American delegation was Mark van der Hout, another Jewish American, who was an internationally recognized legal expert on deportation. Mary Rita Luecke, vice president of the National Lawyers' Guild, and Wilhelm Joseph, co-chairman of the National Council of Black Lawyers, were also in the group. At a press conference in Israel, van der Hout denounced the deportation of the Palestinians as a violation of 'one of the most basic rights of any person to remain in the country where she or he is born'. Ms Luecke charged that 'the use of deportation procedures appears to be a ploy by the Israeli government to avoid having to prove its case in court. The basic element of due process is the right of the accused to know the charge against him or to have the opportunity to confront witnesses against him'.[6] She was reacting to the Israeli authorities' claim that they could not reveal the evidence against the four men facing deportation because such a disclosure would compromise state security.

Renato Janack, the prosecutor in charge of the case against the four Palestinians, told the American lawyers that the men had to be deported since they were guilty of 'advocating pre-state formations'. Smith realized that in the occupied territories it was a crime to be prominent in any way. He noted, 'We met with the woman who heads the Society for the Preservation of the Family, in Ramallah. She is under town arrest. We met with the head of the Red Crescent Society in the Gaza Strip. He is under town arrest.' Smith saw the method in the Israeli madness. 'All these people are popular political and cultural leaders, and I suppose that if and when a Palestinian state were organized they would be figures in the government, and seeing that they are popular leaders now, the change in a very perverse way does make sense, that they are part of pre-state formations.'[7]

The Israelis tried to pretend that Ali Abu Hilal, Dr Shweibi and the other two Palestinians scheduled for deportation had been involved in a recent series of random killings of civilians. But when asked for evidence, an Israeli official told the American delegates, 'Well, we can't exactly prove that they did this; we can only say that these acts of violence occurred and they profited by it.' This was hardly evidence. The Americans noted, 'Due process was lacking here.'

Were it not for the seriousness of the matter, the Israeli effort to justify the deportations seems like something out of a comic opera. Smith and Joseph asked the Israeli prosecutor about the case. Under cross-examination he admitted, 'Yes, these men have not been directly charged with the acts of violence or indirectly charged', but he added, 'We feel that if they are out of the country there will be peace and quiet for at least two or three years.' When Joseph pressed the Israeli about the lack of due process, he replied, 'Yes, you are right, but nothing is perfect here.' Joseph found this explanation 'very incredible'.

Despite the American intervention, the Israelis refused to relent. For a while the four Palestinians tried to delay their deportation with appeals to Israeli courts, but in the end they gave up. Dr Shweibi explained, 'We withdrew our appeals from the Israeli court on the basis that there would be no just sentence passed against us. We considered that the deportation law was a racist law, practised purely against the Arab population.'[8] He noted that no Jew had ever been deported under this regulation.

Right to the end the Israelis were brutal. As Dr Shweibi recalled: 'A few days before we were deported, my colleagues and I were separated and put in single cells in the prison. We were handcuffed and leg-shackled, as well as having bands covering our eyes so that we couldn't see anything.' Despite his serious illness, Dr Shweibi was shown no courtesy. He laments: 'The thing which touched me most, from the human point of view, was that I was not allowed to say goodbye to my wife and children.' Neither were Abu Hilal or the other men allowed to bid farewell to their families before they were deported on 31 January 1986. Jerusalem Radio announced that the Palestinians were being deported because they were 'involved in subversive activity in the service of the Popular Front'.[9] But of course no proof was presented.

Smith asked Hilal's wife if she would join her husband in exile. Since she had spent two years in prison for violating a curfew, she had a police record which made her ineligible for readmission if she left the country. She told the American lawyer that she would not leave even if it meant that she could never see her husband. When asked why, she answered, 'Because I have to stay here. You see, if I go with him, that's what they want. They will have won if we all leave, so my duty is to stay here.' Smith realized that Hilal's wife was *sumud* – steadfast – which was the Palestinian response to the Israeli effort to seize the last remnants of their homeland.

The term *sumud* – the state of perseverance or hanging on – was coined at the Baghdad conference of Arab heads of state in 1978. The Arab politicians called on Palestinians in the occupied territories to stay put, to cling to their homes and land by any means possible in the face of Israeli efforts to push them out of the West Bank and Gaza. There was concern in the Arab world over the flight of so many people, particularly the young and educated, out of the occupied territories. A special Pan-Arab fund, Amwal-es-Sumud, was set up to help combat the collapse of the Palestinian social and economic fabric caused by Israeli colonization. Raja Shedeh, a West Bank lawyer, described the dilemma of his people: '*Sumud* is watching your home turned into a prison. You *samid* choose to stay in that prison because you fear that if you leave, your jailer will not allow you to return.'[10]

The fate planned by the Israelis for those who remained is revealed in the candid comments by an American supporter of the Jewish state: 'Every nation needs an underclass. Most Israelis aspire to professional/managerial positions. Being a member of the proletariat just doesn't carry the status it did in simpler times. Israeli Arabs in Haifa or Hebron must inevitably fill the vacuum. Those who can't tolerate it will probably leave.'[11] The Israeli journalist Yoram Binur notes, 'According to official policy, Israeli Arabs are supposed to work, eat and sleep and collaborate with the authorities. At the very most, they are allowed to express support for Jordan's King Hussein.'[12]

But some Israelis who practised *sumud* made it clear in every possible way that they supported the PLO and an independent state. Palestinians in the territories placed their red, white, black and green flag on telegraph poles, or painted it on walls and anywhere else they could display their national colours. These were activities outlawed by the occupation authorities. Michael Smith investigated the case of a man who built a house with the help of some friends. In order to celebrate the event, he baked a cake and decorated it in the Palestinian colours; the Israeli authorities heard about the subversive cake. Smith told a UN panel: 'They arrested the man and they confiscated the cake and the man. I have documentation of this . . . the man did six months in prison for baking that cake.'[13]

The status of Palestinians in the occupied territories reminded the black attorney Wilhelm Joseph of conditions in South Africa. He noted that 'all the people of the West Bank and Gaza must carry pass books, which I find particularly objectionable and very much in line with what South Africa does to its black citizens. A Palestinian must have a pass book on him at all times. That pass book restricts their freedom of movement.'[14]

There were other violations of human rights in the West Bank and Gaza. Numerous witnesses have testified about the torture routinely inflicted on Palestinians who are interrogated by the Army and border police; but this has frequently been denied by the Israelis. On 16 September 1987 Israeli Radio's English-language service announced that, with regard to the claim of a Palestinian youth that he had been tortured while in prison, 'Most of the complaints submitted in the past were found to have no basis in fact.'[15] But there is a great deal of evidence from a variety of sources which clearly indicate that, in the years before the *intifada*, torture was very commonly used by the authorities in the occupied territories.

Yoram Binur served as a lieutenant in the occupying forces in the West Bank. He recalls that suspects who were brought to a police station for interrogation were made to stand waiting in a narrow corridor. 'Two heavy-set policemen walked along the narrow passageway and hit them with bare fists and with wire cables.'[16] He notes that on one occasion in Ramallah, the tough border police 'clubbed a demonstrator to death'. Binur summarized the feeling of being a member of an occupying army: 'Whether committing brutal violence or performing acts of kindness, the sensation is the same – it is the feeling of the power one has over others.'

During his military service, Binur served as a judge in a military court in Ramallah. Such courts consisted of three judges, one of whom was a lawyer and the other two regular army officers. He recalls a case in which in his first statement a man denied the charges against him; but after spending a little time with security forces he returned to the court to confess. According to Binur, 'We all knew – judges, military prosecutor and defence attorney – by what means the confession had been procured, but the issue was never raised for discussion.'

Such situations were very common in the occupied territories.

Typical is the case of a twenty-three-year-old Palestinian carpenter who later spoke about his ordeal while he was in custody in March 1984.

I was taken to an interrogation room where there was an interrogator called Abu Dani. He proceeded to make various charges against me – closing stores in Ramallah, incitement, preparing Molotov cocktails and internal recruitment. I had done none of these things and told him so. I told him I owned a shop and looked after my family – my wife, two daughters and a son.

After this I was moved to a cell for seven successive days, with interrogation continuing day and night. There were handcuffs on my hands and a bag over my head, and there was always water on the floor of the cell. They also restricted my food. I underwent a long period of interrogation and extremely ugly techniques were used. More than once they used cold showers on me during the bitterly cold nights when there was heavy rain. Another method was for the interrogator to rub and pull at my genitals. Then I was taken to the cell for two hours and then back to the rooms.

After this, I went on trial and my detention was extended for seven days. During the seven days I was taken once at random to the court, and after the session the judge ordered me released.

After I left prison I had pains in my throat, stomach, right knee and genitals. During interrogation, I was told that I wouldn't be able to father children because of the treatment they'd dealt to my genitals.[17]

The young carpenter had been held in the notorious Al Fara prison, where thousands of suspects, many of them teenagers, were held in terrible conditions. Under military order 378, prisoners in the occupied territories could be held for up to eighteen days without access to a lawyer. The charges included throwing rocks, flying Palestinian flags and possessing forbidden literature. According to a 1984 Amnesty International report, Palestinians held in detention 'have been hooded, handcuffed and forced to stand without moving for many hours at a time for several days and have been exposed while naked to cold showers or cold air ventilation for long periods'.[18] The human rights organization notes that detainees had also been deprived of food and sleep, toilet and medical facilities, and had been subjected to threats not only to themselves but also to female members of their families.

A commission of the Israeli Supreme Court under Moshe Landau investigated the charges that torture had been used on Palestinian prisoners. In a report dated October 1987, the Landau Commission found that Israeli security agents had lied to cover up the torture and murder of detained Palestinians. But the Israeli panel noted that, since Palestinians were guilty of terrorism, they had forfeited 'the moral right to demand that the state safeguarded normal accepted' civil rights. The Landau Commission ruled that the use of 'clearly defined psychological and physical pressure' was 'legitimate' if such methods were kept under 'supervision and control'.[19] This report on the eve of the *intifada* dispelled any claim that the Palestinians in the West Bank and Gaza were living under a humane occupation. The Israelis conceded – and indeed, attempted to justify – their repression of those detained and imprisoned.

Even those who completed a prison term in Israeli jails found that their ordeal was not over. Former political prisoners in the occupied territories have their identity cards stamped on each corner with a triangle enclosed in a circle. When a former convict applies for a job, admission to a university, a driving licence or a travel permit, or makes any other request requiring official approval, he will almost certainly be turned down because of the markings on his ID card. The Israelis, of course, want such people to cross over the Allenby Bridge into Jordan, thus removing one more possible opposition leader.

It is clear that, in the mid-1980s, Palestinians in the territories were denied even the most basic human rights. The evidence suggests that they were also exploited from an economic point of view. The standard of living in the occupied territories did not compare well with that of Jordan, which in previous decades had been much more depressed economically. Real GNP (Gross National Product), the major indicator of economic activity, in the West Bank and Gaza in 1985 was less than in 1979. In many categories, such as health care and levels of employment, the standard of living of the population was lower than it had been in the late 1970s.[20] The economic growth rate was lower in the occupied territories than in Jordan and in many other Arab countries. The economic recession which started in 1982–3 lasted through the *intifada*. The emigration of the young and educated out of the territories continued. By the eve of the uprising, one out of four Palestinians had left his or her home in the West Bank or Gaza since the beginning of the occupation, due to lack of employment opportunity and a decline in basic services.

Not surprisingly, many Israeli sources claim an improvement in the health situation. According to the Bank of Israel Research Department, nutritional standards in the occupied territories were constantly rising. According to this source, calorie intake for adults in the West Bank rose from 2300 in 1968 to 2800 in 1984, while in Gaza the rise was from 2100 to 2500 during the same period. But other studies showed that during the mid-1980s many children suffered malnutrition – as many as 50 per cent in some communities.[21]

As part of their steadfastness response to military occupation, beginning in the 1970s, Palestinians attempted to build up in the occupied territories a medical infrastructure which was independent of the Israelis. There was a drive to establish autonomous health institutions and projects wherever possible, particularly in the larger towns. As in many developing countries, however, too much emphasis was placed on sophisticated medical facilities that helped only a few people, while disease prevention, particularly in rural areas, was neglected. But, for the Palestinians, the construction of hospitals under their control had a definite political purpose.

To the occupier, these hospitals and health centres were seen as 'pre-state formations' which could make the Palestinians independent of Israeli rule. In testimony before a UN panel, Dr Aziz Alabadi, a surgeon working for the Palestinian Red

Crescent, noted that 'the Israelis have prevented the construction of new hospitals, secondly, the number of beds in hospitals has fallen by 50 per cent approximately, third, several laws have been adopted to prevent doctors from practising their profession unless they obtain permission from the military commander'.[22] The physician-to-population ratio in the West Bank and Gaza was dangerously low. There were 28 doctors per 10,000 in Israel, 22 per 10,000 in Jordan, but only 8 practising physicians per 10,000 in the occupied territories. Dr Alabadi noted that there were 600 Palestinian doctors in the West Bank and Gaza who were denied a licence to practise medicine. All were medical school graduates from various countries around the world. Dr Alabadi saw this as part of a design. 'The goal of the Israeli authorities in implementing this policy is first of all to impede the improvement of health services in the occupied territories so that these health services are dependent on Israeli medical services.'

This inhuman policy had a devastating impact on West Bank health care. This was noticeable with regard to infant mortality. In Israel, this was 14 per 1000 births; in the occupied territories it was 70 per 1000 births, compared to 55 in Jordan and 60 in Syria.[23] Dr Alabadi believes that 'health services as a whole have deteriorated as a result of Israeli practices'. He was not pleased that the Israeli authorities had prevented the World Health Organization (WHO) from setting up offices and services in the occupied territories and that they would not even allow a team of WHO experts to visit the West Bank and Gaza.

In the years before the *intifada*, an alternative health movement grew up in the occupied territories. Its basic philosophy was 'reaching people with services, instead of people having to reach the services in urban areas'.[24] The alternative movement emphasized basic health services, especially preventive medicine and health education activities, as well as people's participation in the solution of health problems. It operated in open defiance of the Israeli authorities, since its clinics did not wait for government approval. This approach gained wide acceptance, since it operated along the lines suggested by the UN and other international agencies.

The Palestinian health system would be severely tested in the *intifada*.

Higher education was another area of life where Palestinians developed their own institutions on the eve of the *intifada*. The number of university students in the occupied territories became very high. Beir Zeit, founded in 1962, expanded during the occupation. Bethlehem University was founded in 1975, followed by Najal University in 1976. Other institutions of higher education were founded and expanded in Jerusalem and Hebron. These institutions have been funded by religious and charitable organizations and contributions from the Arab world. The Israelis have not financed them, and frequently harass them.

In 1978, an Islamic university was founded in Gaza with six faculties, including education, science, economics and administration, the arts and two different curricula in religious studies. Professor Mohammed Saker, who served as president of the university, testified to a UN panel on the problems he faced in trying to operate a free university under an alien occupation.[25] He indicated that his main goal was to institute a full-time programme instead of the half-day schedule. In order to do this he needed the authorities' permission to build new classroom space. After lengthy discussions with Israeli officials, he believed he had their approval for the expansion of the university and started to make preparations. Then the Israelis told him they would not allow a full-time programme at the university. Saker knew what that meant. 'Well, I realized at that time that the Israelis are not interested in real education. They would like us to have only mediocre universities without real education.'

Despite the numerous problems, Professor Saker was dedicated to keeping the Gaza Islamic University open. He realized that political agitation on campus was counterproductive. 'They want the students to come there and make demonstrations, raise the Palestinian flag, so that the Israelis can come and close the university for one month or two. We know their tricks.' Saker told the Israelis, 'You made the agitation, you sent your stooges to make that demonstration in order to close the university.' But he refused to allow the agitation that could be used to justify a shutdown.

Another problem which Saker faced was faculty. With regard to staff, he noted, 'I ask for forty, perhaps they will give permission for four.' Even these were given permission to enter Gaza only at the last minute, so that many of the invited staff had already taken positions elsewhere. Saker makes it clear that he never asked the Israelis for financial assistance to run the university. 'The funds are Islamic funds, this is WAQF [religious financial trust] money, we are not getting a single penny from the Israelis.' Indeed, the Israelis attempted to control and tax the money coming from Jordan and Saudi Arabia. The university paid $30,000 a month in taxes to the Israelis on the money coming from the Arab world.

Saker admitted that he allowed 'touchy' subjects to be taught at the university, such as courses on the Zionist movement, the history of Palestine and the Islamic world. Despite their efforts to interfere, Saker stood firm against the occupation authorities. 'I did not allow the Israelis any knowledge whatsoever of what was going on in the university from this point of view, and I did not submit to them any details of the subjects we were teaching.' The university faculty found no difficulty in obtaining copies of censored books. 'It is enough to have a single copy, we go to an Israeli dealer in Tel Aviv – of course secretly – and we ask him to publish ten thousand copies.'

But it is the Israelis who have the ultimate means of reprisal. According to Saker, 'Our university is not accredited by the Israeli authorities, the reason being that they do not want a university in Gaza and they do not allow its graduates to work in various departments in administrative health and in the municipalities in Gaza.' Thus, like other Palestinian university graduates, those in Gaza are forced to emigrate.

Professor Saker was ousted by the Israelis as head of Gaza University when he was not allowed to return after a trip to Jordan. His attitude towards the Israelis is intractable. 'Israel is an alien foreign body in this region. All the American aid, all the weapons, will still not permit an alien body to live in this region, which has a special touch, a special history, a special outlook.' Such a rejectionist attitude was much more common in Gaza than in the West Bank; it reflected the greater repression suffered by residents of the Strip.

The rise of Islamic influence in Gaza was both a cause and an effect of radical political attitudes. Islam was particularly strong at Gaza University among the numerous students of refugee or rural origin. Islam preached a puritanical lifestyle, which stood in contrast to the secularism of the leftist Palestinian political groups and the Israeli influence. There were two main Palestinian Islamic groups, the Moslem Brotherhood and its political arm, the Islamic Resistance Movement, better known by its Arabic acronym, HAMAS, and its rival, the Islamic Jihad. Contrary to many Islamic groups the world over, which seek state power as a prelude to a re-Islamization of society, the Palestinian Islamic groups, especially HAMAS, have emphasized the reintroduction of Islam in their society before the seizure of state power.

HAMAS dates back to the 1930s, when the Society of the Moslem Brethren began to spread its influence from its birthplace in Egypt to surrounding areas of the Middle East. The charter of the Islamic Resistance Movement calls HAMAS a wing of the Moslem Brotherhood in Palestine, and considers itself a descendant of the forces which revolted against the British mandate in the 1930s.

In the 1980s there were frequent clashes between HAMAS and various PLO groups. Not only did HAMAS reject the PLO as the sole legitimate representative of the Palestinian people, but it proposed a completely alternative lifestyle for young people who joined their movement. They eschewed 'frivolous' student activities such as folk dancing, theatre and excursions, which the PLO encouraged in order to stimulate Palestinian culture. HAMAS members concentrated instead on organizing study circles, communal prayers and commemorating religious occasions in public events and rallies.[26]

The central tenet of HAMAS, as spelt out in its charter, is that the land of Palestine is an Islamic trust (Waqf) to be held as such for generations of Moslems until the day of judgment.

According to HAMAS, no one has the authority to give up any part of Palestine. Negotiation with the enemy over the disposition of Palestine is tantamount to treason. Members of HAMAS believe that nationalism is the function of religious belief, and the defence of Moslem land is the duty of every Moslem. This view is, of course, the Arab equivalent of Gush Emunim, which sees the Land of Israel as a divine trust given by God to the Jewish people in perpetuity. Because of the extremism of HAMAS, which opposes negotiations, and because of its conflicts with Fatah and other PLO groups, it has been alleged that the Moslem group has received financial and other support from the Israeli authorities.

Islamic Jihad is a generic term, designating a number of groups whose strategies diverge but which are united by a sense of belonging to the same political and religious movement.[27] The Islamic Jihad emphasizes direct terrorist action as the best method of liberating Palestine from Zionism. Unlike HAMAS, it has developed good relations with the PLO.

The Jihad was begun by Sheikh Abd al-Aziz Odeh, an instructor at the Gaza Islamic University, and the pharmacist Fathi Shqaqi, who broke away from HAMAS. Odeh and Shqaqi were fascinated with the Iranian revolution, which encouraged them to believe that direct action could solve the Palestinian problem. They received support from Fatah, especially from Abu Jihad, who was one of its highest officials. The ideology developed by the Jihad considers present-day Arab and Islamic regimes, with the exception of Iran, as having returned to a state of Jahiliyya (ignorance and barbarism prior to Islam). The Islamic Jihad calls for their overthrow by a popular revolution, which alone will re-establish God's rights. Since Israel is the cutting edge of the West's general offensive against Islam, it is every believer's duty to struggle for its elimination. The Jihad considers dialogue with non-religious nationalists (such as certain PLO elements) as essential in the face of the Israeli occupier, which is the common enemy.

The first overt military act of the Jihad occurred in 1983, when a young Israeli settler was knifed to death by a commando group, which justified its act as having been dictated

eg - quasi - military

confusion.

by the 'Holy Jihad'. Then, on 15 October 1986, in the old city of Jerusalem, a commando of the Jihad Brigade threw grenades at new recruits of an elite unit of the Israeli Army near the Wailing Wall, killing one and injuring sixty-nine. A few days before, the brigade had assassinated an Israeli taxi driver.

Gaza in the 1980s was far more restive than the West Bank. The decade began with a series of Israeli measures, which served as a catalyst for an upsurge in violence. The first of these concerned the government imposition of a special excise tax on certain professions, which resulted in a strike on 22 November 1981 by doctors, dentists, pharmacists, veterinary surgeons, lawyers and engineers. In response, the Israeli government welded shut the doors of 1780 shops, including eighteen pharmacies, levied heavy fines on doctors and arrested protestors.

The situation was exacerbated on 1 December when civil administration was imposed on the Gaza Strip. The new civilian administrator was General Yosef Lunz – who, however, did not resign his military commission when he assumed his new post. Palestinians were thus confronted with a civilian administration whose powers, functions and relations to the still-existing military government were left undefined. The pro-Jordanian (thus 'moderate') mayor of Gaza, Rashad al-Shawwa, was uncharacteristically outspoken in his opposition: 'The civilian administration is nothing but a continuation of the conquest in civilian guise.' He added, 'Israel is worsening its attitude towards the territories in order to force people of liberal profession to leave.'[28]

When the nationalists called a strike a few days afterwards, in order to protest the imposition of value added tax in the Gaza Strip, Shawwa agreed to join in. He declared:

We reject the Israeli occupation. We reject to be enslaved by Israel or by anybody else. We are a free people. We insist on our right to self-determination on our own land and the land of our fathers and forefathers. This is the situation in Gaza today. Please do not interpret it as just opposition to the VAT. People feel that any land or house they possess will be stripped from them by the Israelis. This is how people feel in the Strip.[29]

Shawwa was ordered to end the strike in Gaza. His refusal to do so culminated in his dismissal and the disbanding of Gaza's municipal council. In August 1982 the Israeli Ministry of the Interior assumed control of Gaza's municipal structure. Gaza had no elected Arab mayor, no daily newspaper, and no right of public assembly. The people of the Strip were without any legal means of political expression.

On the eve of the *intifada* Jordan played an increased role in Gaza, attempting to fill the vacuum left after the withdrawal of Egyptian influence. According to an Israeli Radio report of 7 June 1987, 'Jordan has begun to inject funds into the Gaza Strip through former mayor Rashad al Shawwa.'[30] This allegedly included money for the education system and large sums for development plans. But the Prime Minister, Yitzak Shamir, made his position clear. 'The Gaza Strip can be subject to future peace negotiations but it must remain a part of the Land of Israel.'[31]

After Camp David and the dismantling of Israeli settlements in Sinai, there was renewed interest in Jewish settlement in Gaza. The Strip was advertised as a tropical paradise with lush beaches. Blocks of settlements were established, based on intensive agriculture and tourism. Each settlement was serviced by a new network of roads, which skirted the Palestinian camps and towns. Schools, clinics, a theatre, banks, electricity and water supply were completely separate from the indigenous population. By 1987 almost 40 per cent of Gaza's land, and most of its scarce water supply, was controlled by the 2700 Jewish colonists.[32]

Unlike the situation in the West Bank, Jewish settlements in Gaza were surrounded by barbed wire and guarded by soldiers. Many were built on sandy land and consisted of bungalow-style homes, each with a small watered garden. Most of the Gaza settlers were religious Jews, who had a strong sense of commitment. But despite the advertising campaign, even Gush Emunim zealots were reluctant to come to Gaza.

The militant reputation of the population has been a strong deterrent to Jewish settlement, along with the sweltering climate and relative distance from employment in Israel's heartland. Of course, the lack of Jewish religious identification as compared to the West Bank made it difficult to attract even zealots, who preferred the West Bank. In 1982, the Jewish Agency announced a plan to settle a hundred thousand Jews in Gaza, but this proved to be totally unrealistic. A far greater problem for the Arab population than the handful of settlers has been the seizure of land and water supplies in such a tiny, arid strip of territory.

As the twentieth anniversary of the occupation drew near, numerous reflections and appraisals were made of the previous two decades and forecasts of the future. Few were optimistic. Patrick White, a Christian brother teaching at Bethlehem University, attended a lecture by Meron Benvenisti, who predicted that nothing would come of the effort to hold an international conference on the occupied territories. Instead, Benvenisti saw a 'twilight war' of 'intercommunal strife' that would continue with 'trees, houses and stones'. But he did not foresee the intense and widespread uprising that was coming.[33]

In its June 1987 issue, the Israeli magazine *Viewpoint* interviewed the Palestinian journalist Ziyad Abu Ziyad on the attitude of the Palestinian people after twenty years of occupation. He replied, 'They are more militant and radical.' He noted specifically, 'Their mood is reflected in a rise in resistance to the occupation, which indicates a commitment to the national struggle.'

Perhaps the best summing up of the mood in the occupied territories was made by David Katab in an article published on 31 May 1987 in the Palestinian newspaper *Al-Fajr*:

Although more than 52 per cent of Palestinian land has fallen under direct Israeli control, and despite the fact that a political settlement seems very far away, Palestinians today are increasingly confident in themselves. The expansionist Israeli occupation has forced Palestinians to support their

to self-destruct
of control mechanism.

own national movement . . . . The Palestinian people have largely lost hope in salvation from the Arab world or the ideology of Pan-Arabism. The strongest sentiment among Palestinians today is towards independence of Palestinians in the occupied territories. They count only on themselves and their fellow Palestinians in the diaspora . . . . Young Palestinians make up their own minds independently of parents or community leaders . . . . These young people who have grown up under Israeli occupation take a much more radical approach to the conflict than other older Palestinians and an even more radical approach than the PLO leadership. Having grown up under the nose of the Israeli war machine, young Palestinians have come to the conclusion that might is right.

N3

During 1987, there was a rise in violence and resistance activity in the occupied territories which came more and more not from outside, but from locally organized groups. On 6 May some members of the Islamic Jihad broke out of Gaza Central Prison; their daring escape made them instant folk heroes to the youth in the occupied territories. Many young Palestinians, unaffiliated with any political group, began taking matters into their own hands, including random attacks on IDF personnel and settlers.

During the months before the *intifada*, settler vigilantism erupted again with increased fury against Arab towns and refugee camps. In June Danilla Weiss, Secretary-General of Gush Emunim, led a rampage through the West Bank town of Kalkilya in retaliation against a petrol bomb attack on Jews near the town. There were also Jewish settler riots in Nablus and Hebron, the goal of which, according to an article published on 2 June in the *Jerusalem Post*, was to put 'the screws on the local Arab population so powerfully that they would either meekly subject themselves to Israel's rule forever or get out'.

Compounding the fear of the population of the West Bank and Gaza were the many 'trial balloons' of threats to 'transfer' the Palestinians from their homes, by force of arms if necessary, to neighbouring Arab countries. As early as 26 May 1980 *Ha'aretz* carried a warning by the former chief of military intelligence, General Ahron Yariv, that there was a widely held opinion in the IDF that any future war should be exploited to expel up to eight hundred thousand Palestinians from the territories. General Yariv noted that the plans for the 'forced transfer' already existed and the means of implementation had been prepared. Ariel Sharon warned Palestinians that they 'should not forget the lessons of 1948'.[34]

In 1987 Deputy Defence Minister Michael Dekel led a group of members of the Herut party (the backbone of the Likud coalition), who proposed the transfer of the Palestinians out of the occupied territories. Also during this period, General Rehavam Ze'evi, director of a Tel Aviv museum, proposed to expel Palestinians by agreements with neighbouring Arab states, who could be persuaded to take them. Arabs in Israel might remain, but their turn would eventually come. On 10 July 1987 Ze'evi told the Israeli newspaper *Ma'ariv*, 'I was raised in the labour movement. I am a leftist. All of the views I now express are those of the labour movement.' General Ze'evi correctly pointed out that the 'transfer' idea came from the Labour party leaders, including Ben-Gurion, and that it had been put into effect during the 1948 war and since then. In a speech he noted, 'Two peoples can't live in one land. When they live in one land there is blood and fire.'[35] Of course, most of the rumblings about transfer came from the right wing, including the proposal of Yosef Shipira, a National Religious party cabinet minister, who suggested that each Palestinian willing to emigrate be given an incentive of $20,000 to leave his homeland permanently.

Often overlooked is Shamir's own participation in the transfer scare on the eve of the *intifada*. On 23 September 1987 he denied to *al-Hamishmar* that he believed in transfer. But he added, 'There are others who believe in it. Everyone's entitled to his own thoughts in Herut.' About Yosef Shipira's proposal to pay $20,000 to any Arab agreeing to leave the territories, Shamir revealed on 8 November 1987 in *Yediot Ahronot*, 'Arabs who wanted to emigrate were extended considerable aid for several years after the Six-Day War.

There was a body that took care of that. Minister Shipira was not the one who conceived the proposal. At the time things were kept quiet, as they should be.'

Shamir, of course, was confirming the 'encouragement' given to Palestinians in Gaza to emigrate (see Chapter 3). His 'trial balloon' was a warning to the Palestinians, since threats and other methods of coercion had been used to persuade Palestinians to leave Gaza in 1968. These methods had worked, since over fifty thousand had left Gaza, never to return. All of the trial balloons in 1987 left no doubt in the minds of Palestinians that the Israelis were planning a drastic reduction in the number of Arabs in the territories, along with a corresponding increase in the number of Jewish settlers.

The violent demonstrations of the Jewish settlers and the continuing hints of expulsions greatly worried Palestinians. On 3 August the former mayor of Gaza, Rashad al-Shawwa, told IDF radio about the tension that was building up: 'The Arab population in the territories is getting to feel more scared of things said by people like General Ze'evi and people like Dekel and indirectly by Sharon, and so on.' He added, quite prophetically, 'We've been trying to alert the authorities and the Israeli government that things are headed for an explosion. And we want to avoid this.'[36]

On 26 September the mayor of Bethlehem, Elias Freij, told Israeli Radio, 'I have always warned about the attitude of the settlers towards the Arabs. But now the situation has escalated into a series of acts of vengeance.' Freij mentioned the nocturnal shooting spree at the Deheisne refugee camp by settlers from Kiryat Arba as retaliation for some stones thrown by Palestinian youngsters. He added, 'The Arabs are being harassed, they are being dishonoured; above all, the terrible threat of transfer looms ominously above. We have heard many dangerous calls about transfer of Arabs from their motherland and to other countries. Who really believes in Israel's pretensions of peace?'[37]

In October that year, tensions in the occupied territories began approaching boiling point. There were widespread demonstrations in which at least a dozen people were shot, including Abu Srur, a student at Bethlehem University. There were also disturbances at the Islamic University in Gaza, which had to be closed by the administration. The Israelis made their usual claims that the demonstrations were due to PLO 'outside agitators'. But the editorial of October 18 in the Palestinian newspaper *al-Fajr* correctly noted, 'There is no room to doubt that the protests are not stirred from outside ... they are a direct result of the occupation. The truth remains that the occupation will never be accepted.'

In November, the unrest in the territories continued. There was much that heightened the population's feeling of insecurity. At an Arab heads of state summit held in Amman the issue of the West Bank and Gaza was ignored. Instead, the Iran–Iraq war attracted the attention of the Arab statesmen. On the 12th the Palestinian newspaper *al-Sa'ab* noted, 'The vague outcome reached by the summit organizers constitutes another manifestation of the state of impotence and ignominy prevailing in the Arab world.' Palestinians increased their resolve to act decisively to attain their liberation.

9
THE CHILDREN'S CRUSADE

On 13 April 1988 *an-Nahar*, a local Palestinian Arabic-language newspaper, printed a letter from Leor Kai, a thirteen-year-old Jewish boy from Tel Aviv. For four months the Palestinian *intifada* had been raging, creating a great increase in the level of tension between Arab and Jew in the Holy Land. But the Jewish youngster chose this moment to reach out to the Arabs who shared his homeland with him. Leor expressed admiration for the Palestinians and their rejection of occupation, but he wrote:

I believe violence and extremism in your ranks will not help in giving your people its independence and a state, which I support. I assure you your extremism led to extremism to the right in the ranks of our people.

Your rejection of the occupation should not attempt to hurt Israeli children and pregnant women. The solution comes through negotiations between our two peoples. You have an historical right and we also have an historical right. Therefore, we should reach a compromise that would give our Jewish people the right to an independent state after all the sufferings they have gone through.

I call, through your newspaper *an-Nahar*, on the Palestinian Liberation Organization, the legitimate representative of the Palestinian people, and on the Palestinian people and the children of Palestine to stop the violence and come to the negotiating table.

Leor ended with a request for a reply to his letter from

Palestinian youngsters of his own age. Two days later, on 15 April, *an-Nahar* published a letter from a Palestinian boy living in East Jerusalem, Salam Ismael Obeidat. Though only twelve years old, in his reply Salam gave one of the most eloquent expressions of the Palestinian rationale for the *intifada*:

> I reject the occupation because it usurped my land, freedom and my school. This is my right. I do not believe that because I am demanding my freedom and the establishment of my state that I am committed to violence and extremism. If you, Leor, were a Palestinian youth you would resist the occupation just like the children of Palestine.
>
> Be comforted that our great religion, Islam, bans us from hurting or attacking pregnant or non-pregnant women, children, old men, religious men, uprooting trees and demolishing homes, particularly homes of worship. You should know, Leor, and the rest of the Israeli children, that your soldiers are committing these forbidden acts as you see on television screens.
>
> We are not the cause of your suffering, Leor, and it is not our fault.
>
> But you are the cause of our sufferings and it is your fault. I would here ask you: Where have you been all these years, away from your historical right which you mentioned in your letter? When you came back to live next to me, what was the present you brought for me? An airplane, a tank, a gun and tear gas grenades.
>
> These are the gifts of peace for the youth called Salam, Leor.
>
> In the end, I would ask through this newspaper, *an-Nahar*, for the Jews to give up the use of force, weapons and tear gas which kill love, peace and innocent children and youths like me and you, because this will be the only way to build bridges of love and peace between our two civilized peoples and to establish a nation of peace.

It is perhaps not surprising that such a statement of the Palestinian perspective should come from a twelve-year-old.

To a large extent, the *intifada* has been a children's crusade. Many of the casualties have been children, some even younger than Salam. Israelis have claimed that the Palestinians have forced their children into the front lines, thus absolving the IDF of any blame for the casualties among the very young. But the children of the West Bank and Gaza, who are less intimidated by the Israelis than the older generation are, are often the most militant element of the population. It is they who frequently push their elders into action against the Israeli Army. Since they are the vanguard of the *intifada*, it should not be surprising that the young Palestinians are its principal victims.

The demonstrations had been set off by an incident on 8 December 1987, when four Palestinian workers were crushed to death and several others severely wounded. They were hit by a vehicle whose driver, many believed, was retaliating against the murder two days earlier of Shlomo Sekle, an Israeli Jew stabbed in the Gaza marketplace. Although there is no evidence to suggest that the Palestinians were deliberately murdered, the next day there were demonstrations in which seventeen-year-old Hatem Abu Sisi became the first martyr of the *intifada*. Later in the day, thirty thousand Palestinians took his body from Shifa Hospital to prevent the Israelis from seizing it for their usual midnight burial.

The demonstrations, which started in Jabalia refugee camp, spread like wildfire and soon involved every camp, village and town in the West Bank and Gaza. The Israelis were taken by surprise. There were criticisms in Israel that the IDF responded slowly and sent insufficient troops in the first few days of the demonstrations. But the Israeli Army chief of staff, Dan Shamron, later claimed, 'When the riots erupted in Jabalia on December 9, following the death of an inhabitant, we quickly increased the number of units there. Within three days the number of IDF forces patrolling Gaza and Judaea and Samaria increased threefold in comparison to normal times.'[1] But no matter how many troops were sent in, the *intifada* spread and intensified.

Great controversy raged in Israel on how to deal with

the disturbances in the territories. On 17 December, in an interview on Israeli television, the hawk-turned-dove, Minister without Portfolio Ezer Weizman indicated his preferred method of dealing with the situation:

I would have, for instance, removed most of the forces from Gaza, leaving only those forces necessary to guard the Jews who live there, of course; maximum exit from the region, in other words. Let them do what they want. Let them burn, let them deliver speeches, let them close down shops, let them set all the tyres in the world on fire. We should get out of there, cut contacts and stop the friction, on the one hand, and on the other, form contacts with the Egyptian and Jordanian authorities, as well as the superpowers, if possible, on how we can promote the political process. It is, after all, the absence of a political solution which results in the burning of tyres.[2]

But few Israeli officials shared Weizman's views; most felt that more, not less, repression was needed. On 21 December Israeli television quoted a senior military source: 'The IDF will send a message to the residents of Judaea and Samaria, that it will no longer permit a minority to disrupt public order.' The Army sources stated that more force would be put into the territories so that there could be a quicker reaction time to any incidents, adding ominously, 'The restraint displayed by the IDF in the past ten days was misperceived as a sign of weakness.'[3]

On the following day Defence Minister Rabin returned to Israel from an extended trip to the USA, and immediately took a tough line. He made his attitude with regard to the Palestinians clear: 'Their suffering will increase and instead of allowing them to live peacefully, as long as the political situation has not been achieved, they will suffer more and more.' He vowed: 'Every legal means – legal from an Israeli point of view – is justified to put an end to it.'[4] Although a member of the Labour party, by his merciless attitude towards the *intifada* Rabin gained great favour with the right-wing elements in the country. At times he seemed to have more in common with the Likud Prime Minister, Yitzak Shamir, than the moderate wing of the Labour party led by Shimon Perez.

Under Rabin's direction there was massive repression of the demonstrations in the occupied territories, in which hundreds of Palestinians, including many children, would be killed. Some of these Israeli atrocities were witnessed by foreign observers.

On the evening of Friday 29 January 1988 Karen White, an American journalist, was walking alone in Gaza City.[5] After seven weeks of unrest the situation was tense, but Karen was not prepared for what she saw. Right before her eyes, an Israeli soldier pulled a boy of nine or ten by his hair from a parked car. The youngster was dragged to the ground and kicked in his face and chest. Other soldiers joined in, after which the youngster was ordered to pick up pieces of orange peel from the street. A few hours later Karen noticed a group of Israeli soldiers laughing as they kicked a feeble old man in the genitals for no apparent reason. Such sights were common in the occupied territories, especially since Defence Minister Rabin had announced on 19 January that Palestinians would be confronted with 'force, power and blows' in an attempt to crush the uprising.

The next day Karen White and her friend, a British lawyer named Catriona Drew, decided to visit the office of the Gaza Bar Association which did valuable work in collecting information on human rights abuses during the *intifada*. The two women were recognized experts on Israeli human rights violations, since they had previously written an exposé on the condition of children in Israeli prisons which was included in the 1987 US State Department Human Rights Report on Israel. There were usually less violent clashes on Saturday than Friday, the Moslem Sabbath, but the women were still apprehensive as they walked along an alley which ran parallel to Omar al-Muktar Street in Gaza City.

As the two women reached an intersection faced by the Al-Omari mosque, they saw a large number of Israeli soldiers as well as a group of schoolgirls standing on the street. Two small stones were thrown which harmed no one. At the other end of the block a youth of seventeen or eighteen stood alone, facing away from the soldiers, who ran towards him from behind. When the soldiers reached the boy, they all began to club, kick, slap and punch him. In her affidavit Karen White stated: 'I did not see this boy throw any stones; the stones that landed on the intersection had been thrown from the other end of the block.' The American journalist feared for the safety of the girls as well as the teenage boy.

Soon afterwards two more jeeps arrived full of soldiers, four of whom appeared to be sharpshooters. Karen was alarmed because: 'The soldiers placed themselves in front of the schoolgirls and took aim at the group at chest and head level.' Catriona Drew notes in her statement: 'I swear that the stones that were thrown came from the opposite direction and were not thrown by any of the girls or indeed anyone on the street.' The two women put themselves in the line of fire, which forced the soldiers to back off.

As the two women were about to leave they heard screaming and shouting. The soldiers were dragging the teenage boy along the ground on his back, kicking him over his entire body, including his abdomen and genitals, punching him with their fists and pounding him with their wooden truncheons. The boy's head, face and neck were covered with blood and his nose was obviously broken.

At this point Karen saw four other soldiers aim their rifles at an eleven- or twelve-year-old girl. She followed the soldiers into an alley as they pursued the child. The American journalist found 'all four soldiers with their truncheons raised as the girl cowered against the alley wall'. A soldier grasped the girl's upper arm, causing her to whimper with pain. Karen White pulled the soldier off the girl. Another soldier appeared to be in a frenzy. Shaking violently, he began screaming, then turned and smashed the headlights and windshield of a car parked in the alley. Karen noted: 'I believe that, had I not intervened, the girl would have been seriously injured.'

When Karen got back to al-Muktar Street, the teenage boy was handcuffed to a shop door. He identified himself as Muhammed al-Jamallah. His little sister was standing next to him, screaming. Karen asked one of the soldiers for the name of his commanding officer and wrote the name down. When she told the soldier she wanted the name to use in a report to a member of the US Congress, he grabbed the paper from her and tore it to pieces with his teeth. Catriona notes that afterwards she saw the soldier 'punch Karen in the stomach and hit her with his rifle'.

Catriona argued with the Israeli commander in order to save the Palestinian teenage boy who was being brutally beaten. The officer told the women that this is 'what happens to Palestinians who throw stones'. When the women protested that the boy had done nothing, the officer replied: 'He must have done something or he wouldn't have been beaten.' When the women argued with him, the Israeli commander ordered them to leave the area. The soldier put the boy into the jeep and said they were taking him to the military hospital.

Karen then noticed a group of small children aged four to eight who appeared at the entrance to an alley. Four soldiers began screaming and ran after them. One soldier aimed his rifle at the children. When Karen yelled at the Israelis they all stopped and ran away. Karen noted: 'I wish to emphasize that at no time was their safety or the lives of the soldiers in danger. There were no demonstrations or other activities in the street to justify such excessive use of force.' With regard to the Israeli teenager who had been beaten, she stated: 'The boy was not resisting arrest but was pleading for mercy. It appeared to me that the Israeli troops were out of control.' Indeed the soldiers beat a Gaza doctor, Yusef Mahdi, who attempted to treat the boy.

Later that same day in Gaza a twenty-year-old Palestinian woman, Hanan Hassan Khamis, was waiting for her brother to come home from the market. On his way back the young man found a thirty-six-year-old neighbour lying in the street, bleeding and unconscious. The youth stopped to take the man to the hospital. Israeli soldiers approached the young man and demanded to know what he was doing in the area. The youth told them that he lived there and, like so many other Palestinians, worked in the construction industry in Israel. The soldiers looked at his hands, which were covered in cement, and said he must have been throwing stones. Six soldiers started to beat him with truncheons and the butts of their rifles.

Hanan and some other young women came along, and when she saw her brother she started to cry and shout. A soldier threw a tear gas bomb at the young women. In her affidavit Hanan stated: 'I lost consciousness. When I regained consciousness, I was told my brother had been taken to Shifa hospital.'[6]

Hanan was taken home. At midnight she heard a knock on the door. Before anyone could open the door, there were ten Israeli soldiers inside the house. They demanded to know where to find Hanan's brother. She told them that he had been beaten by other soldiers and taken to the hospital. An Israeli replied: 'No, soldiers did not beat him.' After they had left, Hanan recalled: 'I went to the hospital to visit my brother. The staff at the hospital told me that at 1 a.m. Israeli soldiers had come to the hospital and in the hospital had beaten my brother severely.* He was then taken to prison. Thus ended a typical day in Gaza in the early phase of the *intifada*. Teenagers, even children, were beaten, tortured and frequently murdered by an occupying force that was clearly on a rampage.

*   *   *

*There is a great deal of evidence that raids on hospitals were very common. On 19 December 1987 the *Guardian* reported that the police were seen removing several injured Arabs from the hospital in Gaza. A doctor stated: 'I don't mind that they beat me but if they stop me from treating people it's absolutely inhumane.' The Amnesty International Report of 1 August 1988 notes, 'Wounded Palestinians have been dragged out of hospitals against the advice of doctors and beaten before being taken to detention centres. Doctors and medical staff too have been assaulted . . . . Fewer than half the Palestinians needing hospital treatment are getting it. Many are afraid to go to hospitals for fear of being assaulted.' A Swiss medical psychologist told a UN panel, 'Since human rights are no longer respected even in hospitals, the soldiers enter the hospitals, even the operating theatres, take away and interrogate the wounded; they stop the ambulances and interrogate those inside which means that many villages and camps keep their wounded at home.'[7]

During the early months of the uprising there were continuous claims by Israeli spokesmen that the *intifada* would soon be over.[8] On 19 December 1987 Yossi Beilin, the political director of the Foreign Ministry, told an interviewer, 'I believe we are at the end of a difficult period.' On the 30th Israeli TV reported, 'Calm has been restored in the territories this week.' Several weeks later, Chief of Staff Dan Shamron claimed that there would be 'calm in two or three weeks'. He boasted, 'The main question is not when the wave of riots will die down, but what will remain in the collective memory of the inhabitants.' Shamron believed that the Palestinians had learnt a lesson and the IDF's stern measures would ensure a quick and permanent end to all thoughts of any other resistance. He was wrong.

The *intifada* went on. In an interview on 19 April 1988 the military commander of the West Bank, Amran Mitzna, once again assured the Israeli public, 'The unrest is in constant decline, which is partly the result of suppression and partly the result of solutions and means that provide answers in the long run.' On 12 May Prime Minister Shamir claimed, 'I know the situation here. I think the situation is getting better and improving.' To any American who lived through the Vietnam War, this all sounded like 'the light at the end of the tunnel' theme which was heard so often from official Washington spokesmen.

Also similar to Vietnam were the stories being told by conscience-stricken soldiers who gave honest testimony of the brutal methods being used to quell the *intifada*. On 18 December one young soldier told the newspaper *Ha'aretz* about his service in Gaza, 'I break into a cold sweat when I think that I'll have to go back to that filthy place. I'm not the kind of guy who disobeys orders or refuses to serve in the occupied territories. But I doubt whether I am emotionally capable of again seeing the terrible things I saw this time at close quarters.' In particular the young soldier was horrified by the behaviour of the border police, most of whom were Druze, an Arabic-speaking people known for their martial qualities, who had sided with the Zionists in 1948 and were much feared by the Palestinians in the West Bank and Gaza. In the article, the young soldier described how the Druze border guards interrogated Palestinians suspected of throwing stones or petrol bombs. 'I saw them really smash up thirteen- or fourteen-year-old kids a few times, and I just felt sick.' The soldier found it difficult to talk about, but he added, 'For the first time I really understand what occupation means.'

On 11 March 1988 the newspaper *Yediot Ahronot* published the testimony of Sergeant Efrayim Adam. He recalled an incident when a unit of the elite Givati Brigade burst into a mosque in Gaza during Friday prayers, 'in spite of the fact that it had been quiet there, and took out one of the worshippers'. The apprehended man, who 'offered no resistance, was placed under arrest, beaten and taken to the regimental commander's tent. There he was beaten by the regimental commander.' Sergeant Adam added, 'He was then taken to a local police station where a trumped-up charge of having struck an officer was lodged against him.' When the man was taken to prison, an Army doctor recommended that he be taken to hospital, since 'his body was blue with bruises from the beatings'. Sergeant Adam was not sure what became of the man.

This soldier made it clear that what he witnessed was not an isolated incident. 'In the course of my reserve service I saw many aberrations: the maltreatment and wanton beatings of an elderly man; and the beating of an eight-year-old boy whose teeth were broken in front of his father, for the sole reason that the soldiers thought he wanted to throw a stone.' In the early months of the *intifada* there were numerous such stories in the Israeli press as the IDF attempted to quell the uprising.

In their first explanations of the cause of the *intifada* both the Israeli government and the PLO blamed the uprising on a conspiracy initiated by the other side. On 13 December 1987 General Shay Erez, head of the West Bank civilian administration, told IDF radio that the uprising was 'inspired by forces outside the region. The PLO exerts pressure to create unrest.'[9] While on 22 December Yasser Arafat charged that 'what is now taking place is a premeditated crime planned by Yitzak Shamir and carried out by the Israeli army on the orders of Yitzak Rabin'.[10]

There is, however, no evidence to support either conspiracy theory. Both sides, along with everyone else, were surprised by the *intifada*. At the outset the IDF had only very small forces in the occupied territories and was baffled as to how to handle the demonstrations. For his part, Arafat did not even cancel his December trip from his base in Baghdad to several Middle Eastern capitals, because he did not realize the full importance of the uprising. Indeed on 18 December the *Jerusalem Post* expressed the opinion of most observers when it labelled as 'autistic nonsense' the explanation by some Israeli officials that the uprising was 'sparked by PLO terrorism'. Arafat's claim of an Israeli conspiracy to provoke the uprising was also dismissed by most serious commentators.

Arafat soon abandoned his conspiracy theory, and began claiming that the *intifada* was the culmination of unrest which began on 24 October 1986 when the Palestinians demonstrated 'as a sign of solidarity with their brothers in the Lebanese camps besieged by the Amal Shi'ite militia'. According to the PLO chief, since then 'there have been ups and downs but never a complete calm situation'.[11]

While it is true that there was considerable unrest in Gaza in the year before the uprising, there is no evidence that this was motivated by sympathy for the PLO. Indeed the principal group in Gaza during this period was the Islamic Jihad, which before the *intifada* was anti-PLO. Arafat's claims in early 1988 that the uprising had grown out of pro-PLO demonstrations can be seen as an effort to convince all concerned that the demonstrators were marching in support of the Palestine Liberation Organization and its leadership. But Arafat's explanations of the origin of the *intifada* could not silence those who saw the uprising as a movement independent of the foreign-based PLO.

After they abandoned their conspiracy theory, the comments on the *intifada* among Israeli government leaders tended to divide along political lines. Some moderates in the Labour party agreed with Foreign Minister Shimon Perez, who conceded: 'The incidents were not organized by the PLO and Jordan but were spontaneous and erupted from within.'[12] However, Defence Minister Yitzak Rabin, who represented the less conciliatory Labour party faction, claimed that the uprising was to some extent spontaneous but that the PLO 'hitched a ride on the wave of incidents and did everything they could both outside and inside the territories to encourage the continuation of these demonstrations and these disturbances'.[13] Many Likud party members took a similar position.

Ariel Sharon, the leader of the extreme hard-liners in the Likud party, continued to insist that the *intifada* was the result of a PLO conspiracy. On 13 January he told Israeli TV, 'It should be understood that this is no accidental wave of terror. It is a situation which has evolved mainly as a result of the strengthening of the PLO political arm.'[14] The Gush Emunim leader, Yisrael Harel, saw the uprising as a result of the weakening of the Shin Bet security agency.[15] He believed the Shin Bet could at least have warned of or possibly even prevented the outbreaks if its discretionary powers had not been reduced after revelations that its agents had tortured and murdered arrested Palestinians. Not surprisingly, many Gush supporters blamed the outbreaks on the restraint of the Israeli security and military forces and the supposedly over-benevolence of the occupation in general.

Putting aside the obviously politically motivated explanations from each side as to the cause of the *intifada*, the sudden outbreak must be considered a mystery of stupefying proportions. How is it possible, after twenty years of relative docility, that on 9 December 1987 the Palestinians in the occupied territories could explode with such sustained fury? At the outset, few observers could have anticipated the remarkable endurance of the Palestinian protesters. Not only Israeli officials but even commentators who were sympathetic to the Palestinians doubted that the *intifada* could last. On 16 December Ian Black of the *Guardian* wrote, 'The crucial question now is whether this week's level of attrition and sacrifice can be maintained by the Palestinians much longer.' No one at the time imagined that the *intifada* would last years rather than months.

The West Bank and Gaza had been held on average by a force of 1200 Israeli troops along with a few hundred border guards and Shin Bet agents. This was about one Israeli for every thousand Palestinians living under occupation. Palestinians accused of resistance activity were sent notices ordering them to report for questioning, which could lead to imprisonment or deportation. The occupation authorities grew accustomed to the fact that suspected Palestinians would report for questioning without the necessity of sending a troop of soldiers to apprehend them. Palestinians worked on constructing the homes of the settlers who had come to usurp their land, but there was no record of any acts of sabotage. It is no wonder that everyone was surprised by the uprising.

The outbreak of a full-scale civil revolt represents a failure by Israeli intelligence agencies similar to that which enabled surprise attacks to be launched by the Arab armies on Yom Kippur in 1973. In both cases the Israelis were over-confident. They had beaten the Arabs so easily in 1948, 1956 and especially in 1967 that it was understandable for them to discount the Arab potential of launching an undetected military offensive in 1973. The Israelis were equally over-confident about the occupied territories which they had exploited with so little effort for two decades.

But beneath the surface the Palestinians deeply resented the occupation. Over the years many grievances had built up. Land confiscation, excessive taxation, deportations, collective punishments, military courts and book banning were among the numerous irritants. The continued existence of the refugee camps (for which both Arabs and Jews are responsible) was another underlying cause of the revolt. It is no accident that the uprising had begun among the residents of the Gaza refugee camps. The young people born there knew of no other life. In Gaza they were stateless, but they considered themselves residents of towns and villages in Israel from which their parents had been expelled in 1948.

Severe as these grievances were, many observers have overlooked the greatest humiliation suffered by the people of West Bank and Gaza. Clearly occupation is never a pleasant experience, but being occupied by an alien nation with which the Palestinians had been in conflict for almost a century made the grievances suffered during the occupation seem worse.

Many peoples in Africa suffer as bad and in some cases worse political and economic deprivation than the African population living under the Pretoria apartheid system. But being dominated by whites makes the hardships of the black South Africans seem worse. Palestinians in the West Bank and Gaza had suffered under Jordanian and Egyptian rule, which frequently was far from benevolent. But these were Arab regimes which shared historical, religious, linguistic and cultural traditions with the Palestinians – unlike the Israelis who were Western, Jewish and with whom the Palestinians had never had good relations. The legacy of 1948 made the Palestinians fear that the Israelis wished to uproot them once again; indeed with the Likud settlement programme of the early 1980s it became clear that the fear that the Israelis planned eventually to annex the territories and expel their population appeared to be well founded.

Added to these long-term grievances were numerous other factors which accelerated tension in the period immediately before the uprising. Certainly the downturn in the Israeli economy after the prosperity of the 1970s hit the occupied territories very hard. It was the end of the oil boom in the Gulf States, which made thousands of educated Palestinians unemployed. Returning graduates found that in their own homelands the only employment available to them was unskilled labour in Israel's factories and construction industry, which many would not accept. It is estimated that on the eve of the *intifada* there were twelve thousand unemployed college graduates in Gaza and the West Bank. Many of them would play a key role in organizing resistance to the Israeli occupation.

But it was the very young – teenagers and even children – who formed the cadres of the uprising. This generation had learnt not to fear the Israelis, whom their elders regarded as invincible supermen. Typical is the story of the eight-year-old arrested by the Israeli soldiers for throwing stones. The soldiers asked the boy who told him to throw the stones. The eight-year-old replied, 'My brother Muhammed.' When the soldiers went to the boy's house they found that the eight-year-old's brother Muhammed was four. Occupation had taught the youth of Gaza and the West Bank to hate but not to fear. To throw stones even before the *intifada* became an honour, and to get caught and show defiance was a sign of manhood.

An incident which caught the imagination of young Palestinians and helped trigger the revolt was the hang glider attack in which a young PLO commando killed six Israeli soldiers on 26 November 1987. This deed by a daring and courageous Palestinian showed the youth of the occupied territories what could be accomplished against a vulnerable foe. According to the Israeli specialist on Arab affairs Yehuda Litani, the incident captured the imagination of young Palestinians: 'Legends abound in refugee camps, universities and high schools about the lone Palestinian hero who won a battle against the whole Israeli army.'[16]

Also around this time Ariel Sharon moved into the Moslem quarter of Jerusalem, and the guards and soldiers he brought with him created friction. This provocative move was designed to make the Palestinians understand that the right-wing Zionists planned to colonize even areas of dense Arab settlement such as East Jerusalem and the large towns of the West Bank as a prelude to the expulsion of the indigenous population. Sharon believed that Jordan was the natural homeland of the Palestinians. He was supported by former Deputy Defence Minister Michael Dekel who stated: 'The Western countries have the moral and political responsibility to handle the transfer of the Arab population of Judaea and Samaria to their country – the Hashemite Kingdom of Jordan'.[17] Such talk naturally alarmed the people living in the occupied territories.

Several other factors could be mentioned that increased tensions in the West Bank and Gaza, including Palestinian disappointment at the international outlook; to many Palestinians it seemed as if they were abandoned by everyone. Even the November 1987 Arab summit ignored the occupied territories. As one Palestinian political activist noted: 'It's hard for Arab governments to develop a strategy to deal with their top priorities. When we saw that our situation was moved to a low priority, it signalled that we'd better rely on ourselves.'[18]

The feeling of abandonment increased when in December that year Gorbachev and Reagan met in Washington, but once again the issue of the occupied territories was passed over. There were many who felt that even Yasser Arafat and the PLO were more concerned about the battle of the camps in Lebanon, which was costing so many lives and draining the energy of the PLO.

In the first weeks of the uprising in Gaza the principal role was played not by the PLO but by HAMAS, the Islamic Resistance. On the eve of the *intifada* Islamic influence in Gaza was strong – indeed, 80 per cent of the students at the university voted for HAMAS in academic elections. On 30 December 1987 the Israeli newspaper *Yediot Ahronot* reported: 'Experts predict that disappointment with the PLO's futile political and military policies was one of the main reasons that local youths (Shebab) took matters into their own hands . . . disappointment with the Palestinian secular establishment will also lead into the arms of religious preachers who will promise them a reign in heaven if they are martyred in the *Jihad* against the "Zionist occupation".'

Arafat was clearly concerned about the role of the Islamic fundamentalists in the early months of the *intifada*. Many observers saw the uprising as being directed against the foreign-based PLO. Arafat repeatedly denied claims that the Islamic Resistance had overshadowed the PLO. He told an interviewer, 'But why are all the demonstrators in the refugee camps – even the Israeli Arabs – chanting PLO slogans? Why are they waving the Palestinian flag and pictures of me? Were not the deportees officially expelled because they belong to or supported the PLO?'[19]

The IDF, following their usual policy, tried to boost the influence of the HAMAS extremists, which would support the Israeli claim that there were no Palestinian moderates with whom to negotiate. HAMAS strikes and demonstrations were rarely interfered with, while similar activities by those supporting the PLO were put down with great brutality. The Israeli media avoided giving publicity to pro-PLO leaders in the occupied territories, but sought out the leaders of

HAMAS. On 15 January 1988 the right-wing Israeli newspaper *Ma'ariv* interviewed Sheikh Ahmad Yasin, leader of HAMAS in Gaza. With regard to the future of Gaza, Sheikh Yasin stated, 'Israel must leave the area of its own volition and leave the internal problems to us. If it wants to hand the area over to somebody that body must be the United Nations so that it can station international troops here.' When asked if he would agree to be represented by Arafat and the PLO, Sheikh Yasin replied, 'It is hard to tell. If it is decided that he should conduct the negotiations we may agree to this but only on condition that he makes no concessions.'

The *intifada* revealed that Islamic fundamentalism had spread to the West Bank. Although, like Sheikh Yasin in Gaza, he does not publicly admit to membership of HAMAS, Sheikh Bassam Jarrar is generally believed to be a leader of the Islamic fundamentalists in the West Bank. The young Sheikh, who has received considerable publicity, has argued in favour of an Islamic republic to replace the state of Israel. He has rejected both a two-state solution and a democratic secular state of Jews and Arabs, which is the ultimate goal of the PLO. He believes that Jews who refuse to convert to Islam must return to the lands of their origin. Sheikh Jarrar's opposition to Zionism is total. He told an American interviewer, 'You see, Moslems believe they reach satisfactory self-realization only when they are in contact with evil. I consider my life here as a godsend. My goal is to educate people to reject the influence of Satan. I mean Israel. I am confronting evil first hand.'[20]

HAMAS considered itself part of the uprising, although it does not recognize the PLO as the sole legitimate representative of the Palestinian people and is against the convening of an international conference on the creation of a Palestinian state in the West Bank and Gaza. Some, including the Israeli journalist Yehuda Litani, have claimed that HAMAS has received covert help from Israeli intelligence, who see it as a way of dividing the Palestinian camp.[21]

But HAMAS is not the only Islamic group active in the occupied territories. The Islamic Jihad organization takes a much more pro-PLO line and has worked actively with the nationalist leadership of the *intifada*. Because of its pro-PLO stance the Islamic Jihad has been vigorously pursued by the Israeli authorities. During the *intifada* its members have been prominent in demonstrations. The American journalist John L. Anderson, who visited Gaza in February 1988, noticed how closely supporters of the Islamic Jihad worked with members of Fatah and other resistance groups. According to Anderson, because of the Jihad's involvement there was a pronounced Islamic influence to the entire resistance movement in Gaza. He notes, 'Islam was always there, commanding the lines of even the ostensibly secular.'[22] He saw resistance groups attending services in mosques, visiting the graves of martyrs for religious ceremonies and, by order of the commanders of the uprising, praying together for help in fighting their enemies. Sensing his surprise at this religious observance, one resistance leader told Anderson, 'Look, our people here are Fatah, Communists, Jihadi Islamic, but we are all Moslems.' Most demonstrations took place on Friday, the Moslem holy day, usually right after noon prayers.

Anderson's assignment in Gaza was to study the stone-throwing youths (usually referred to as the Shebab, 'the guys') who were at the forefront of the uprising. A twenty-two-year-old university student whom he calls Nayef explained to him the organization of the resistance forces at the Breij refugee camp in Gaza. According to Anderson, 'It amounted to a fairly sophisticated strategy for urban guerilla warfare without the usual weapons.' Much depended on the role of the very young.

According to the Palestinian journalist David Katab, similar methods were used by the resistance in Nablus.[23] He notes that when the alarm is sounded the local youth, aged fifteen to nineteen, divide into three teams. The first is composed of lookouts, whose job it is to spot the incoming Israeli troops from their rooftop positions. The second team is defensive; its main task is to cover the offensive team when it takes on a particular mission. The offensive team itself is made up of the quickest and most courageous. After the offensive team advances on the Israeli position and throws stones, the defensive team takes over, creating a diversion to allow the attackers to retreat. Dressed in kefiyyahs and scarves to hide their identity, the youths considered it a victory to keep the Army out of their neighbourhood. Children as young as ten or even seven play a role, since it is they who generally set car tyres ablaze. Youths of eleven to fourteen have the job of rolling stones on to the road or using sling shots to taunt Israeli soldiers. It is the college students or graduates who provide the local leadership for the uprising.

Many observers, including Anderson and Katab, have noted that the local *intifada* committees have received direction from a United National Leadership of the uprising. The group is secret but reportedly consists of representatives of Fatah, the Popular Front (Habash), the Democratic Front (Hawatmeh), the Palestine Communist Party and the Islamic Jihad. The unity achieved at the Palestinian National Council (PNC) in Algiers in April 1987 made co-operation between the Arafat, Hawatmeh and Habash factions possible. The Palestine Communist party, which only recently gained official representation in the PLO, had long supported a two-state solution, so that its adherence to the United National Leadership is not surprising. Before the *intifada* the Islamic Jihad had fought against the various PLO factions, but with the coming of the uprising they had joined against the common enemy.

Jebril's Syrian-based Popular Front General Command dissident faction did play an important role during the crucial early stage of the *intifada*, but there is no evidence to support the claim that this group was represented in the United National Leadership.[25] Nor has HAMAS been represented. Indeed, its failure to participate has weakened it – to the advantage of the rival Islamic Jihad.

The leadership of the *intifada* grew out of the establishment of local committees in the occupied territories in the early 1980s. A political activist told an Israeli journalist, 'Everyone tries to belong to an organization.'[26] He added, 'Political views are expressed in every framework, and every framework is political. A student committee is elected on a political basis. Trade unions are political, as are sports associations.' He made it clear that most of the cadres for these organizations are enlisted by one or the other of the various

PLO or religious factions. The Palestinian activist revealed, 'Look, here in Gaza forty-three thousand people have been imprisoned for various terms over twenty years of occupation. This means at least twenty thousand people who are active members of organizations. This means a great deal of power. You should know that everyone who gets out of prison does so as a member of one of these organizations.'[27] The Israelis were not unaware of the growth of this grass-roots network, and their desire to crack down on the groups in the period before December 1987 was one of the reasons for Rabin's 'iron fist policy' that helped trigger the *intifada*.

During the early months of the uprising the Israelis imposed curfews which unwittingly helped to provide an opportunity for the community organizations to take root in many towns and refugee camps. These committees provided food, milk and medicine for the besieged camps and towns. The success of these local committees was a catalyst in the establishment of the National Committee.

By the time John Anderson arrived in Gaza the PLO dominated the United National Leadership. He notes that in the Breij refugee camp 'there was a local uprising committee that followed broad guidelines suggested by the National Unified Command of the *intifada*.'[28] Relations between the PLO-dominated United National Leadership and the local committee were not always good. Arafat's attempts to dictate policy in the name of the United National Leadership was sometimes resisted. Calls for the boycotting of work in Israel, without any substitute income being provided, were ignored by people who had to support their families.

The United National Leadership issued a series of appeals. The first, which appeared on 8 January 1988, called on Palestinians to co-operate with shop closures and work stoppages, and warned of punishments 'in the not too distant future for those who did not co-operate'.[29] Beginning with number 3 on 18 January, the communiqués were signed 'Palestine Liberation Organization – Unified National Leadership of the Palestinian Uprising in the Occupied Territories'.

Most of the communiqués were disseminated in the territories via the radio. Indeed to a large extent the *intifada* was a radio revolution. The Baghdad-based Voice of the PLO broadcast not only the communiqués but also interviews with Arafat and other PLO propaganda. Beginning in January a more powerful transmitter, calling itself *Al Quds* Palestine Arab Radio, came on the air; the station greatly alarmed the Zionists. As Israeli Radio announced, 'This is the first time that the terrorists have had such a powerful radio station, which broadcasts in three wavelengths simultaneously, at their disposal.'[30] *Al Quds*, which was based in Syria, mixed revolutionary songs and pop music with political propaganda and the communiqués of the United National Leadership, the text of which was altered to suit the rejectionist line of the Jebril faction that operated the station. Although it sometimes deviated from the pro-PLO United Leadership, *Al-Quds* played an important role. Its most controversial function was to reveal the names of collaborators who were forced to confess in public the error of their ways or face retaliation.

Despite the great popularity of *Al Quds*, there is no evidence that the rejectionist Jebril faction has gained in strength during the *intifada*. This is probably due to Jebril's refusal to moderate his position and co-operate with Arafat. In an interview, Jebril told a Beirut newspaper, 'The people taking part in this uprising have met with reporters and news agencies. We note that they rarely speak of the PLO leaders because they no longer trust them because of their inclination to bargain and hesitate.'[31] Jebril added, 'We want to say to our people that armed struggle and not international conferences or running after [Egyptian President] Husni Mubarak, King Hussein or the USA is the only road to liberation. We live in an age of power and only the strong are respected in this world.'

But Jebril's claim that the people living under the occupation had rejected the PLO leadership was not correct. Certainly the Palestinians 'inside' have demanded a larger voice in directing PLO policy, which for two decades had been determined by the foreign leadership. But it is clearly false to suggest that the people in the occupied territories have rejected Arafat and the PLO as their representatives.

Nor have the West Bank and Gaza population endorsed violence and rejected negotiations, as suggested by Jebril and other extremists. Perhaps the definitive statement of Palestinian goals in the early stage of the *intifada* was the fourteen-point programme formulated on 12 January 1988. It was presented at a press conference two days later, despite the police detention of several of its authors, including the journalist Hanna Siniora.[32]

The preamble made clear that only the PLO could represent the Palestinians at negotiations, and that people from the occupied territories must be allowed to meet with the PLO leaders so that they could play a role in formulating PLO policies. The programme was presented in the name of 'all Palestinian institutions and personalities' and covered a full range of economic, political and human rights issues. Most of the demands represented a desire to end the occupation and for the Palestinians to detach themselves from the Israeli economic, political and legal system. Indeed, when Thomas Friedman of the *New York Times* asked a Palestinian lawyer to summarize the aim of the *intifada*, he replied, 'First of all it was to show the Israeli public that we are not Israelis.'[33]

Friedman believes that by not using guns, but instead throwing non-lethal stones, the Palestinians were trying to signal to the Israelis that 'they were not out to murder them, but were ready to live next door to them if they would only vacate the territories and allow a Palestinian state to emerge there'.[34] There may be some truth to this, in view of a survey conducted by Israeli academics on the eve of the *intifada*, which indicated that 54 per cent of the Palestinians in the occupied territories would accept a two-state solution.[35] Since another survey revealed that over 80 per cent of the people in the territories recognized Yasser Arafat or other mainstream PLO personalities as their leader, there is reason to hope that – with some reluctance in certain cases – an overwhelming majority of Palestinians could accept a two-state solution negotiated between the PLO and Israel.

Friedman points out that, besides wishing to convey a message of moderation to Israelis, another reason the Palestinians have avoided lethal force is their obvious fear of Israeli retaliation. He quotes Prime Minister Shamir's threat that if the demonstrators used firearms, 'There will not even be a memory of them left.'[36] Indeed, despite Arafat's claim that firearms would eventually be used, [37] the Palestinians in the occupied territories made their aversion to them obvious. Thus when Israeli soldiers dropped their weapons during a confrontation, it was standard procedure for Palestinian demonstrators to return the gun to the soldier.

Palestinians also avoided using firearms because they were concerned about the image they portrayed to the international media. On 27 March 1988 Defence Minister Rabin told *Der Spiegel* that, if the Palestinians resorted to guns, 'On television it would no longer look like a revolt of civilians against the military, but like a battle of terrorists against the military. It seems for the time being as if they have been clever enough not to shoot.'

Soon after the *intifada* began, Israeli leaders criticized the media for inciting the protests. Chief of Staff Shamron claimed: 'The media does not only convey pictures, it also unintentionally creates them. Quite a large percentage of the demonstrations started due to the presence of the media.' When speaking to a group of visiting American congressmen Shimon Perez bemoaned the fact that 'When you see on television a young boy throwing a stone and a young soldier holding a rifle, you instantly are on the side of the boy with the stone. That's a fact.' Yitzak Shamir gave his own explanation for Israel's negative image in the international media when he stated: 'Arabs and extremists have a better understanding and linkage with the media people, who are inclined to see international events from a leftist viewpoint. They get information and indoctrination from the Arabs of East Jerusalem and trust them more than they trust us.'[38] Shamir neglects to mention the enormous Zionist influence on the Western media.

The Israelis, however, took vigorous steps to prevent the media from using Palestinian sources. In January 1988 the journalist Hanni Assawi was arrested because he served as a useful link between the *intifada* and Western news correspondents. *Al-Fajr*, the main Palestinian paper, was also suppressed. Its office in Gaza was closed, on charges that the staff maintained ties to PLO-related elements. Several months later its senior reporter, Tawfiq Aber Husa, was detained by police because of his 'contacts with Israeli and foreign reporters'.[39]

There was, in fact, much sympathetic coverage of the Palestinian *intifada* in the Western media. Western European criticism of the Israeli occupation, which had long been substantial, greatly increased. The constant reports on TV of Israeli soldiers beating Palestinian civilians had a definite impact on public opinion in western Europe. Even in the Netherlands, long known as a bastion of pro-Zionist sentiment, there was a noticeable shift in public opinion. The Dutch refused to host a visiting Israeli youth delegation or a previously planned concert by Israeli performers. Some Dutch municipalities announced that they would not attend a goodwill conference scheduled to be held in Jerusalem.[40]

In Italy, which had been very strongly pro-Palestinian, the public was horrified by the stories of Israeli atrocities against unarmed civilians. Many politicians, expressing the public mood, spoke out against Israel. Indeed, three members of a visiting Italian parliamentary delegation staged a demonstration along the main road to Ramallah near the Al-Am'ari refugee camp and chained themselves to an electric pylon.[41] A small lunatic fringe in Italy expressed their outrage by poisoning Israeli fruit, in order to discourage imports grown on land stolen from the Palestinians in 1948.

Thomas Friedman of the *New York Times* offers an unconvincing explanation for the sympathetic portrayal of the Palestinians by the western European media. He suggests that the European criticism of Israeli atrocities in the West Bank and Gaza is a form of anti-Semitism. Friedman claims: 'There was a pronounced tendency in the German, French and Italian media to focus on Israel as a triumphant and ruthless occupier which seemed to be a not too subtle attempt by these countries to absolve themselves of some of their own guilt for how their own Jews were brutalized in World War II.'[42] But Friedman's pseudo-analysis is a crude attempt to justify the pro-Israel bias of American journalists, who are out of step with the media practically everywhere else in the world. He does not consider the possibility that, under pressure from the powerful Zionist lobby, the American media may be less objective than the European press, where the pro-Zionist and pro-Palestinian influences are more evenly matched.

Friedman also claims: 'The extensive focus on Israeli soldiers beating, arresting or shooting Palestinians was so obviously out of proportion to other similar and contemporaneous news stories, such as the Iraqi army's poison gas attacks on the Kurds or the Algerian army's shooting to death of more than two hundred students in one week.'[43] But atrocities of Third World people against other Third World people is never as newsworthy as atrocities or conflicts between Western nations such as Israel or South Africa and Third World people. In Africa there are massive atrocities and human rights violations of blacks against blacks, but these are rarely reported even in the back pages of Western newspapers. But if a white man is killed in Africa or if white police beat black protestors in South Africa, it is likely to be front-page news in Europe and America. Friedman's claim that Israel's human rights violations are over-reported is not true, if the coverage of South Africa is considered. Besides, it has been the Zionist lobby and their supporters in the press who have encouraged the media to set up news bureaus in Israel so that they can cover the great achievements of the Jewish state. Are these journalists to be sent home because the news from Israel is not good?

One of the most serious problems for the Israelis during the *intifada* has been whether to allow the press into the occupied territories. Former US Secretary of State Henry Kissinger recommended that the IDF bar the press and deal even more brutally with the demonstrators without the presence of witnesses. But the Israelis rejected this suggestion. On 8 March 1988, in an interview on IDF radio, Chief of Staff Dan Shamron addressed this issue:

It is impossible to seal off an area to the media . . . . There is no doubt in my mind that the media could easily mix in the traffic in this large area . . . had the media been banned from the area, I believe exaggerated rumours from the territories would have been generated . . . . There is the option – which we use – for the local unit to declare the area a closed military zone.[44]

The IDF had good reason to keep the media out of areas of the West Bank where demonstrations were taking place. On 11 March *Ha'aretz* reported the story of a reservist, Roni Matalon, who did his military service in the West Bank. About IDF atrocities he noted: 'I want to make it clear that the only ones who are punished are those who are accidentally filmed by TV crews. By the way, TV plays an important psychological role for soldiers. It provides the bulk of incriminating evidence.' Because of this, the media are often harassed by the IDF. The chief targets are Israeli newspeople, rather than foreigners.

On 10 January 1988 *Al Hamishmar* published a story by Shelly Yehmovitz, who told of her experiences while travelling in Gaza with her husband, Amir Weinberg, a photographer for *Yediot Aharonot*. About twelve miles outside Gaza City they saw a black cloud hanging over the horizon. The couple did not know what was happening. Shelly believed that it was thunder clouds, but a few moments later she saw a clearer view: 'Gaza, Khan Yunis and the refugee camps were really burning.'

The couple drove to Khan Yunis. They were stopped by an IDF officer who grabbed Amir's loaded camera and drove off towards the compound. Shelly reports: 'In the rear view mirror we could see a group of soldiers venting their rage on a local detainee. They hit him all over the body with everything they could lay their hands on. Amir photographed the scene with another camera with a telescopic lens.'

They were spotted by a senior army officer. He opened the car door and dragged Amir out, while wresting from him the camera which he threw to one of his soldiers. 'I'm going to rip you apart,' the IDF officer yelled at the Israeli photographer. Then, as Shelly recalls, 'two soldiers grabbed hold of Amir, dragging him along the road, kicking and beating him. Another soldier entered the car, took out all cameras and lenses and dumped them in an army vehicle.'

Eventually, the couple was released with the cameras – minus the incriminating film, of course. Shelly Yehmovitz draws a frightening conclusion for Israelis from her experience:

> From the moment I saw soldiers beating up the local detainee (a scene which makes everything published in other papers appear pale in comparison) and throughout Amir's beating, I thought I was dreaming. This is happening to us – in spite of having held important and senior posts in the army, in spite of being law-abiding citizens. It was happening to us. Not to them – the poor Palestinians . . . .
>
> There's no more us and them. The border has become fuzzy. Yesterday it was them, today it was me, and tomorrow it will be you – in your living room. And the Gaza Strip will only be a historical way station marking the point at which it all began.

One of the effects of the *intifada* has been an erosion of Israeli democracy. It would of course not be possible to suppress such an uprising in a brutal way without having some effect on the values and institutions of the occupying country. Some of the practices in the territories have been used by the Israeli government against its own people. There was a general crackdown of dissident groups in Israel, including the closing of the newspaper *Derech Hanitzotz*. There were restrictions on TV reporting, so that Israelis did not see the beatings or other atrocities which viewers in Europe, America and elsewhere saw vividly portrayed in their living rooms. There was also corruption of the Israeli legal system, as numerous cases of brutality against Palestinians by the Army were suppressed. The standards of Israeli courts in the occupied territories were being applied in Israel. A poll held in January 1988 clearly showed how suppression of the *intifada* had affected attitudes towards democracy in Israel. A startling 46.4 per cent believed the country was too democratic – this was an increase from the already high figure of 35.5 per cent before the *intifada*.[45]

Opinion polls conducted in 1988 also indicated that over 40 per cent of Israelis believed that their government should 'encourage' Israeli Arabs to leave the country. Such a showing greatly frightened the eight hundred thousand Arab citizens of Israel, who comprised 18 per cent of the population of the country. These people were the descendants of the 150,000 Palestinians who for a variety of reasons were allowed to remain in Israel after the founding of the State in 1948. Though technically citizens of the country, the lot of Palestinians in Israel was never very good. More than 25 per cent of all Arab families lived in overcrowded conditions, compared to 1 per cent of Jewish families. Despite this, Israeli Arabs had no access to public housing, all of which was *de facto* segregated for exclusive Jewish use. Arab local municipal councils received only a third of the budget allocations of Jewish councils the same size. There was also discrimination in education and employment. Since Arabs (except Druze) could not serve in the Army, they were excluded from the substantial benefits due to IDF veterans.

Before the *intifada* there had not been too close a contact between Palestinians in Israel with their brothers in the occupied territories. Many Israeli Arabs feared that such collaboration would lead to further repression from a government which already viewed them as a potential fifth column. But the uprising in the West Bank and Gaza emboldened Israeli Arabs, who now openly expressed their Palestinian identity. Stones and petrol bombs were thrown and the Palestinian flag was flown in many Arab villages in Israel. On 21 December 1987 Israeli Arabs organized a general strike to demonstrate solidarity with the Palestinians in the territories.

A second country-wide strike and demonstration was organized for 30 March, Land Day. This commemorated the demonstration in 1976 against the government seizure of Arab land in Israel, in which six Arab citizens were killed. Before the 1988 anniversary there was fear of widespread violence, so the Israelis mobilized massive security forces.

Although not as violent as feared, the day of 30 March did not pass without incident.

There were large demonstrations not only in Israel but also in the occupied territories, where the Palestinians wished to show support for their brothers in Israel on their national day of protest. Central Front Commander Amran Mitzna told a radio audience that evening that he attributed the large numbers of casualties – four dead and forty-five wounded – to 'firm and immediate action' on the part of the army 'in all places where there was an attempt to disturb order and act with violence'. Israeli Radio reported that IDF soldiers had only fired 'after finding themselves in real danger'.[46]

As the *intifada* progressed there was a growing Palestinianization of the Israeli Arabs. Ariel Sharon accused Israeli Arabs of joining the enemy and seeking 'to destroy us' instead of 'fighting together with us as loyal Israeli citizens'.[47] But Israeli Arabs see no conflict between their support for a Palestinian state and loyalty to Israel. Many compare their situation to that of Diaspora Jews who are faithful to their country while still feeling sympathy for Israel.

Although most Israeli Arabs support a West Bank Gaza state, few had any interest in moving to such a country if it was formed. Abdul Wahab Darawshe told an American journalist, 'My ancestors were born here more than five hundred years ago and I didn't invite Israel to capture my homeland. I did not choose Israeli citizenship. But I will not leave my homeland.'[48]

Abu Raia Sakhnia, mayor of an Arab town in Israel, agreed. 'Not a single person would leave this our land here.' He added that, out of sympathy, people in his town were sending food and medicine to the victims of the *intifada* in the occupied territories. But the people of his town wanted justice for themselves, especially economic justice. According to the mayor, 'I am a citizen of this state. I pay the same taxes as Jewish people. I want equality for the people of this state.'

During the first year of the *intifada* there was a small improvement in the economic situation of Israeli Arabs because of the strike by about 50 per cent of the workers from the occupied territories. Israeli Arabs were needed to perform the menial jobs which Israeli Jews had long since given up. In general, however, the economic impact of the *intifada* on the Israeli economy was minimal. Bank of Israel Governor Michael Bruno was probably honest when on 10 March 1988 he announced that 'so far the riots have not had an unequivocal effect on Israel's economy'.[49] Bruno noted that increased security costs had come at the expense of military training programmes and other non-essential expenses. He did note a drop in income from tourism; but overall, the Israeli economy lost only about 2 per cent of total GNP in 1988 over the previous years. These losses were largely confined to the building industry (due to loss of Arab workers), the tourist trade and the reduction in the quantity of durable goods sold in the territories (due to a boycott of Israeli products).

Apart from a rise in the cost of new apartments because of the construction slow-down, most Israelis noticed little change in their daily lives because of the *intifada*, which seemed remote. Jewish casualties were very small, so that few Israeli families were affected. There were no pictures on TV of soldiers beating Arab women and children. Newspaper reports were generally ignored and often elicited more anger against journalists than against the Israeli Army. Some Israelis took a 'they are getting what they deserve' attitude towards the Palestinians, while others succumbed to the 'our boys could never do that' syndrome.

Some Israelis, of course, were interested in a resolution of the occupation. The *intifada* saw a prodigious increase in the number of Israeli peace groups – most of which, however, were very small. Peace Now, which had exercised a great deal of influence during the Lebanon war, was not as successful during the *intifada*. Most of the more radical Israeli peace groups perceived Peace Now as being too establishment-orientated, because many of its members were affiliated with the Labour party. Also, before the *intifada* Peace Now had refrained from expressing overt support for a Palestinian state and for negotiations with the PLO.

But, despite its moderate approach, Peace Now gained little support during the *intifada*. Ironically, before the uprising many Peace Now activists had hoped for an outbreak that would demonstrate to the Israeli people that holding on to the territories was untenable. As Peace Now activist Jamet Aviad noted, 'In the beginning of the *intifada*, we thought finally we could muster Israeli public opinion to make it impossible for the government not to compromise.' But another Peace Now leader, Chaim Oron, observed that 'the uprising has driven Israeli society to a more extreme point of view'.[50]

There was in fact a hardening of attitude by most Israelis, who responded to the *intifada* with outrage since many believed that the Palestinians were being ungrateful for the many services rendered to them by Israel. The numerous Israeli peace groups remained small since their appeal was limited to secular, university-educated intellectuals who had no real support from the broad mass of the Jewish population. Merimad, the only dove-ish religious party, failed to win a single seat in the Knesset. Some of the small peace groups were formed for a specific purpose, such as the restoration of Beita, a small village devastated by the IDF in retaliation for the death of a Jewish girl.

Beita, with a population of 7500, was a typical northern West Bank town known for its olive crop and beautiful surroundings. It is a white, stony place with narrow, unpaved streets which twist and turn up terraced hills. As in most towns in the area, the people of Beita solidly support Fatah. Beita's first contribution to the uprising came on 20 January 1988 when, at 4 pm, the bus which took Beita workers to their jobs in Israel was burnt by the local population. Soon after this incident Israeli soldiers raided the town and beat up some of the local men. In the following months there was the usual stone throwing, followed by IDF retaliation in the form of more beatings and jailing of those unfortunate enough to be caught.

But on 6 April that year the town entered history. A group of teenagers from the Gush Emunim settlement of Elon Moreh went on a hike through the area, in order to show whose land it was. Accompanying the youths were two armed guards. One of them, Roman Aldubi, was such an extremist that he had been banned by the Army from entering Nablus on suspicion of having been involved in the murder of a

Palestinian child. *En route* Aldubi fired a 'warning shot' which killed a farmer, Musa Salih. The Israeli teenagers and their guards were then surrounded by the villagers of Beita, some of whom threw stones. In the ensuing melee, one more Palestinian was killed and another wounded. But little notice was taken of this because a Jew – fifteen-year-old Tirz Porat – also perished, according to a preliminary IDF report by 'a stone thrown at her by the mother of one of the slain Arabs'.[51]

In an interview on 7 April Chief of Staff Dan Shamron referred to the 'cruel and despicable murder of a girl from Elon Moreh in the village of Beita'.[52] The chief of the central command, Amram Mitzna, announced that 'so far four houses have been demolished but this is only part of our reaction'. He added: 'We have not yet apprehended the people who actually murdered the girl although it is very possible that one of the four men we have apprehended played some part in it.' Soon afterwards the Army blew up more houses and killed a man who was fleeing their round-up. But this attracted little attention. All that mattered was that a Jewish girl had been killed. Her funeral became a political circus of the Israeli right, attended by Meir Kahane, Ariel Sharon and Prime Minister Shamir, who threatened that 'the heart of the entire nation is boiling. God will avenge her blood.'[53]

The evidence soon indicated, however, that the Jewish girl had been killed not by the Palestinian villagers but by a shot fired by her guard, Roman Aldubi. This did not, unfortunately, prevent further reprisals against Beita, including the deportation of six villagers and the destruction of more houses. Army bulldozers even uprooted dozens of trees and almond groves along the road leading to Beita. All of these actions had a profound effect on the town. An American journalist who visited the place in August 1988 observed, 'Beita is now a militant little village.'[54]

One inhabitant told the journalist: 'Now we know how the Israelis treat the Palestinians, the way a wild animal treats a victim.' Scribbled on the walls of the village were extremist slogans: 'No matter how many they kill, we will remain steadfast'; 'No concessions on Haifa, Jaffa and the

Galilee'; 'Yes to martyrdom and the PLO'. Soldiers came every two or three weeks and ordered them to clean off the walls, but this did not dampen the spirit of the villagers. They told another American journalist: 'The people here believe they are a symbol of Palestine.'

Khalil al-Wazir, known as Abu Jihad, was another symbol of Palestine during the early months of the *intifada*. A close aide of Arafat, Abu Jihad was believed to be co-ordinating the resistance activities in the territories from his Tunis headquarters. Reports indicate that for several months the Israelis had been considering his assassination, despite a long-standing policy that PLO and Israeli leaders were off-limits to each other's assassination attempts. But during the *intifada* there was no closed season.

In the early morning hours of 16 April a commando team burst into Abu Jihad's Tunis home, killing him along with his chauffeur and two bodyguards. Although all the evidence pointed to Israeli responsibility, Yitzak Shamir refused to admit the involvement of his country. When asked about it on Israeli Radio, he replied: 'Why should you talk about such things? You know I have avoided talking about it.'[55] Yasser Arafat was not so reluctant to discuss the assassination. He called Abu Jihad's loss 'great and irretrievable'. As for responsibility, he had his own explanation. 'The operation was a joint one. Can anyone believe that a warship can anchor a full week without the approval of the US Fleet?'[56]

On 18 April the Israeli newspaper *Al-Hamishmar* published an analysis of the Abu Jihad assassination by Pinhas Inbari. He pointed out that the Israeli establishment preferred Palestinian commando raids to the *intifada*, where they were fighting civilians rather than guerrillas. 'It would have been best for Israel had the PLO decided to go back to terrorism thereby directing the fight against Israel from stones to Kalashnikovs.' Thus, according to Inbari, the assassination of Abu Jihad 'could be perceived as an attempt by Israel to drag the PLO back to terrorism so as to transfer the major front from the uprising in the territories to the armed PLO outside'.

The assassination led not to terrorism but to an intensification of the *intifada*. In Jerusalem the Supreme Moslem

Council declared three days of mourning and a general strike, during which hundreds of black flags were flown. In Gaza there was a new wave of Molotov cocktail attacks on the occupation troops. As the PLO chief was being buried in Damascus, mock funerals were held in several towns in the territories. A 'Day of Rage' was proclaimed to commemorate the assassination. About a dozen people were killed and scores injured throughout the occupied territories.

The Israeli atrocities committed during the *intifada* had a profound impact on American Jewish liberals, many of whom had already been concerned about the invasion of Lebanon in 1982. Although most leaders of Jewish organizations publicly supported the Lebanon invasion that was engineered by Prime Minister Begin and Defence Minister Sharon, there was a definite split in the American Jewish community. A survey conducted by the American Jewish Committee in 1982 revealed that about half of American Jews favoured a homeland for the Palestinians in the West Bank and Gaza and a halt to the expansion of Israeli settlements in order to encourage a peace agreement. About three-quarters of US Jews wanted Israel to talk to the PLO if it would recognize Israel and renounce terrorism. Only 21 per cent of US Jews wanted Israel to maintain permanent control of the West Bank.[57] However, as in every ethnic community, the moderates tended to be much less active than the extremists, who dominated most American Jewish organizations.

But under the weight of the *intifada* even the major Jewish organizations in the USA doubted the wisdom of Israel's inflexible occupation policy, which created a great deal of ill feeling in America and Europe. Morris Abrams, the conservative head of the presidents of major Jewish organizations, visited Jerusalem and announced that 'the status quo is not indefinitely acceptable to American Jews' and 'the occupation is the cause of the disturbances'. Several weeks later Abrams remarked, 'It will be increasingly difficult to maintain support for Israel if conditions do not improve.'[58]

It was becoming possible for American Jewish intellectuals to speak out. On 14 March 1988 in the *New Republic* Martin

Peretz wrote, 'I am shamed by the whole occupation or more precisely by the psychological inability of the Israeli body politic to free itself unambiguously from the false security that comes from ruling over another people.' In the same issue Charles Krauthammer noted: 'Identification with the Zionist enterprise today has become increasingly a source of anxiety and shame.'

Perhaps the strongest reaction to the *intifada* came from the liberal Jewish magazine *Tikkun*, which boldly criticized the occupation and the direction being taken by Shamir and his Likud party. In its March/April 1988 issue the editor, Michael Lerner, wrote: 'We did not survive the gas chambers and crematoria so that we could become the oppressors of Gaza.' Lerner presented arguments which were difficult to repudiate. Noting that, if the repression in the territories really was necessary, 'that in itself would be enough to discredit the occupation', he added: 'The longer the occupation exists, the more angry and radical young Palestinians become.'

But despite their opposition to the occupation, most liberal American Jews saw the atrocities being committed by the Israeli forces during the *intifada* as 'uncharacteristic of Zionism,' an ideology which they still defended as basically moral and totally different from South African apartheid. However their arguments supposedly proving the difference between South Africa's exploitation of its blacks and Israel's exploitation of the Palestinians in the occupied territories were not convincing.

The parallels between Israel and South Africa are in fact remarkably close – especially the policy of using a subject people as cheap labour while denying them any right of self-determination. Of course in many ways the plight of the Palestinians is worse, since they experienced greater brutality even before the *intifada* and because the Israelis are trying to expel them from their homeland. Even South African apartheid recognizes the right of the blacks to remain in their country, even if only as second-class citizens confined to tribal Bantustans. The claims of liberal Jews that Israel is a democracy are untenable, since it is clearly not a democracy for the Palestinians. Indeed a survey of Israelis conducted in June

1988 revealed that 49 per cent believed that the expulsion of the Palestinians was the best way to preserve democracy in the country.[59] Clearly the Israeli concept of democracy is not the same as that held in Britain or America.

Right-wing American Jewish publications did not bother to portray Israel as a democracy or apologise for the human rights violations in the occupied territories. Their greatest fear was that Israel was being far too humane towards the Palestinians, whom they portrayed as a reincarnation of the Nazis. On 22 April 1988 one of the largest-circulating American pro-Zionist publications, the *Jewish Press*, printed an editorial which suggested the fate that lay in store for the Palestinians.

> When America was created, did we return even one inch of land to the beaten Indians of the West after we occupied their land? The Indians didn't throw rocks at our settlers, they threw deadly arrows. Did this nation, ever since that takeover, even consider returning land to the Indians? Of course not! Untold thousands were killed and the remainder were put on reservations. Then our government passed law after law to make certain the Indians would not rise up against Americans any more.
>
> If Jordan is so concerned about the Palestinians, they could open their borders and the Palestinians would have their homeland overnight. But Jordan is playing another game.
>
> Hitler said it first, 'If you tell the big lie often enough – people will begin to believe you.'

Equally extreme was an article in the May 1988 issue of *Commentary* by Ruth R. Wisse, who saw the basic cause of the Arab–Israeli dispute not in the occupation but because 'the Arab world reformulated the Nazi theory of *Lebensraum* in Mediterranean terms'. Wisse believed that it was the duty of American Jews to defend Israel now that it was being criticized for the suppression of the *intifada*. Wisse attacked Martin Peretz and Charles Krauthammer of

the *New Republic* and other moderate Zionists for showing that 'identification with the enemy is the greatest task
of the Jewish intellectual'. She also blasted those Jews,
including the noted scholar Irving Howe, who had signed
an advertisement headed: 'Israel must end the Occupation'.
According to Wisse, the effect of such criticism of Israel by
American Jews 'can only be to further the Arab campaign
of distortion'. Wisse and those who thought like her were
concerned that, because of the *intifada*, the Zionist lobby's
long-standing stranglehold on American Jewish public life
was beginning to slacken. Many who had previously been
afraid were now speaking out against the occupation. But the
extreme Zionists were escalating their hysterical attacks on
Jewish liberals. On 24 May 1988 Irving Howe told the *Village
Voice*: 'The question that the Jewish liberal establishment has
to face is: Are you in favour of allowing tolerance and freedom
of speech to those with whom you disagree or not?'

Perhaps the best reply to those in the American Jewish
community who considered Jewish critics of Israel to be
traitors was written by Hal Wyner, an American Jewish correspondent in Israel for West German and Swiss newspapers.
In an October 1989 leader in the *New York Times*, Wyner
wrote: 'I do not see how I can in any way do a service to the
Jewish people by concealing or distorting the truth when it
comes to Israel. The issue is not self-hatred but self-respect.'
Wyner told the New York Jewish community: 'As difficult as
it may be to believe, most stories on the *intifada* that appear
in the Western media are characterized not by exaggeration
but by understatement.' He added: 'It is clear that as far
as Israel's image in the world is concerned, any objective
description of what is going on will be extremely damaging.
And it is not surprising that the Jews of the world react so
strongly to these reports.' The Jewish journalist listed what
was really going on in the occupied territories. 'On a regular
basis people are being shot in cold blood, randomly killed and
maimed, detained without trial and beaten and humiliated by
soldiers acting on orders.' There was a growing number in the
American Jewish community willing to listen to such candid
reportage.

An issue greatly troubling the US Jewish community was the Israeli attempt to deport Mubarak Awwad, a Palestinian advocate of non-violence who was seeking to extend his stay in Jerusalem. Awwad was a disciple of Mahatma Gandhi and his principle of non-violence; some Israelis and American Jews defended him, but most Zionists claimed that he was not a real follower of Gandhi. Overlooked in the debate was Gandhi's strong commitment to the Palestinian struggle against Zionism. The great human rights leader had written: 'Palestine belongs to the Arabs in the same way as England belongs to England and France to the French.' Of the Arab revolt in the 1930s, Gandhi commented: 'According to the accepted canons of right and wrong, nothing can be said against the Arab resistance in the face of overwhelming odds.'[60]

On 6 May 1988 a group of Israelis with American citizenship met the US Consul-General in Jerusalem in order to demand that the American Ambassador intercede with the Israeli government on behalf of Awwad. On the same day Shamir's media adviser, Avi Panzer, informed the press that Awwad had to be deported because he had 'played a major role in the recent rioting in the territories'.[61] A member of Shamir's Likud bloc told the press, 'I don't even need evidence that he is one of the leaders of the uprising. I would expel him from here as quickly as possible. It's a shame we wasted so much time.' Defence Minister Rabin joined Likud in demanding Awwad's deportation. Foreign Minister Perez was more equivocal. On 19 May he told Ha'aretz: 'We have always said we will not censor ideas, only stones and weapons.' But Perez stopped short of denouncing the deportation order, saying only that the matter should be left up to the courts.

Numerous appeals came in from all over the world for Israel to allow Awwad to remain in Jerusalem as head of the Centre for the Study of Non-Violence, so that he might help negotiate a solution to the Israeli-Palestinian impasse over the occupied territories. One of the appeals came from Coretta King, widow of Martin Luther King. But Shamir stated that any comparison between Awwad and King did 'harm to the memory of the civil rights leader'.[62]

On 5 June the Israeli Supreme Court upheld the government's decision to expel Awwad. Shimon Perez supported the verdict. Once in the USA, Awwad spoke to numerous groups about his philosophy of non-violence. He stated, 'I am a pacifist. I never carried a gun in my life. When I deal with people carrying a gun, I say "What about using another alternative?"'[63] Mubarak Awwad was one of many Palestinians deported during the *intifada*. Most appealed against their deportation order, but no one who has ever made such an appeal has ever won in an Israeli military or civilian court.

Another form of punishment used on the population in the occupied territories was administrative detention, and it became more common during the *intifada*. Under this system a prisoner may be kept up to six months, subject to renewal, without a hearing or even being told of the charges against him. During 1988 prisons holding detainees became very crowded.

'It's a concentration camp, a torrid desolate sight.' This is how the Israeli lawyer Tamar Peleg described the detention centre at Ketziot in the Negev Desert. A scorching inferno, especially in summer, Ketziot held two thousand prisoners in truly inhumane conditions. Over twenty were squeezed into one tent, with only their tiny mat for a living space. The prisoners were free to step outside the tent, but only those who had gone mad would do so in view of the sweltering heat. Detainees were allowed no personal belongings except their underwear and a copy of the Koran. Other books, a radio or even a wristwatch were forbidden. They could take a shower only once every ten to fourteen days. They received no vegetables or fruit. And two prisoners had to share the same plate.

For many, not knowing why they have been arrested is the worst punishment. The most expansive explanation most of them get is: 'We have evidence that you were active in the Palestine Liberation Organization.' Four Palestinian writers and poets held at Ketziot were told that their crime was having links with Israeli intellectuals. In order to prove the justice of the accusation, the Palestinian writers smuggled out of Ketziot an open letter addressed to Israeli intellectuals opposed to the occupation. It was published in an Israeli newspaper.[64]

Under the blistering sun of the Negev, suffering the pain inflicted by having to continually lie on the sand, we appeal to you from this extermination camp, which exterminates all that is human in Man. If Hell existed, this Negev prison would be its main gate of entry.

We live on crumbs of bread, bits of butter and jam, and tiny portions of beans and warm water. The worms, the snakes, and the scorpions share our foul beds with us. It's been over sixty days that we have not been allowed to change clothes . . . .

And although we are imprisoned in the Negev desert, and in spite of the blistering heat, we promise that the ink in our pens will not dry up. We will continue to write for the sake of justice and peace, for the sake of a smile on a child's lips; we will continue to write so that no tear falls from a child's eye for a slain brother or father; and we will always write to express our true aspirations. We will write so that we can one day see Shlomo and Ahmed playing together – rather than see Shlomo leading Ahmed to prison in the middle of the night. We are imprisoned here and you are free. As you know, the value of an author is not judged by the quantity of his work, but by his humanity.

But despite letters and protests men and boys continued to be tortured, beaten, starved and cruelly mistreated in every way possible at Ketziot. After a visit to the camp, Avi Katzman, writing in *Koteret Rashit*, perhaps best summed up the legacy of the Negev detention centre: 'Every generation leaves vestiges in the desert. What will our generation leave?'

As the *intifada* dragged on, the IDF increased its repression. On 25 July Defence Minister Rabin reported on Israeli Radio: 'The notion that there has been increased activity in the territories recently results somewhat from the nature of our response which is firmer and which I believe will help achieve calm.' The following month Rabin reported an even greater increase in repression. 'We are now pre-empting violence before it starts by closing certain areas, sometimes even large areas like the Gaza Strip.'[65]

Many international organizations concerned with human rights protested about the continuing Israeli repression. The International Committee of the Red Cross (ICRC) usually does not comment publicly about violations of human rights. However, since it has the responsibility of monitoring the Fourth Geneva Convention, which regulates occupation activities, the ICRC officially protested about Israeli atrocities in the West Bank and Gaza since 'thousands of people have been the victims of brutality and grave ill treatment at the hands of Israeli soldiers'.[66] The Red Cross noted that many Palestinian casualties had been 'young children, pregnant women and the elderly'.

A Red Cross official, Maurice Aubert, noted in his protest that the consequences of IDF atrocities 'have been observed by ICRC delegates during their visits to hospitals and detention centres. The Red Cross officials complained that the Israeli occupation had very grave consequences in humanitarian terms. Israeli officials were shocked that the ICRC had sent such an 'unprecedented' letter, which was a marked change from the usual 'subdued' tone of the organization.

The scope of the protests from many quarters, including several American groups, was more intense than in previous examples of human rights violations. Part of the reason was the extensive television coverage, which made it impossible to deny the IDF brutality. Of course, the Israelis found it difficult to sustain their usual assertions of moral superiority. For decades Zionism has been sold in Europe and America on the basis of its claim to the moral high ground, which has always been more apparent than real. But with the *intifada* the true nature of the Zionist treatment of the Palestinians has become clear.

Amnesty International was one of many agencies to condemn Israeli human rights abuses during the *intifada*. In its report issued on 17 August 1988 the organization noted that 'thousands of Palestinians have been beaten not only in the course of dispersing demonstrations or making arrests but also in order to punish and create panic'.[67] Not surprisingly, the Israeli government was not happy about the report. The Foreign Ministry expressed 'wonder and indignation', but the IDF atrocities described by Amnesty were regarded as standard Israeli procedure by almost all international observers.

Dr Samir Salamen Khalil, a paediatrician, made perhaps the most thorough study of Israeli atrocities during the first year of the *intifada*; it was based on 2400 medical reports of Palestinian hospital cases. Dr Khalil's study indicated 540 deaths during the first year of the *intifada* of which 339 were in the West Bank and 201 in Gaza. Of these, 76 per cent died from bullet wounds, 16 per cent from gas, 4.5 per cent were trampled to death and 3.5 per cent died from beatings. In the first year of the *intifada* Jewish settlers murdered sixteen Palestinians, many of whom were severely mutilated or burnt alive. Most of the casualties were very young. About 25 per cent of the dead were under sixteen and half between seventeen and twenty-five.[68]

Dr Khalil noted that many Palestinians had been killed by plastic bullets, which at close range were lethal. His findings are supported by the Swiss medical psychologist Dr Nago Humbert, who noted: 'I have opened one of these bullets and there is lead inside.'[69] The IDF defended the use of plastic bullets, and indeed in January 1989 extended their use in the occupied territories despite worldwide condemnation.

According to both Dr Khalil and Dr Humbert, the deaths from poison gas resulted when the canisters were shot into homes, hospitals and other buildings. Both gases used, CS and CN, are generally not lethal when used in the open, but are extremely dangerous to those who inhale them in confined spaces. It should be noted that about a thousand pregnant Palestinian women were forced to have abortions because of the risk to the foetus as a result of gas inhalation. It is tragically ironic, in view of the Holocaust, that the Israelis should use poison gas against civilians. And it is disturbing that the gas canisters are clearly marked 'Made in Salzburg, Pennsylvania, USA'.

*   *   *

The enormous sacrifices of the *intifada* emboldened the Palestinians to assert openly their support for the PLO as their sole legitimate representative. Thus loyalty to King Hussein, which already was very low, reached vanishing point as 1988 progressed. But Jordan had maintained ties to the West Bank despite twenty years of Israeli occupation. King Hussein continued to subsidize many West Bank institutions such as religious foundations, schools and clinics. He also continued to pay about twenty thousand former Jordanian government employees who worked for the Israeli military administration.

Between 1986 and 1988, with backing from the US government and Israel's Labour party, King Hussein floated a plan for a $1.3 billion economic rehabilitation project that was intended to 'improve the quality of life' in the occupied territories. Both the Israeli Labour party and the Reagan administration perpetuated the delusion that there was a 'Jordanian Option', by which King Hussein would agree to accept political authority in the West Bank under Israeli security supervision. For two decades Hussein had refused such a deal. But by 1988 his attitude made little difference, since the Palestinians in the occupied territories wanted no part of Jordanian rule.

Despite Jordan's financial contributions, only a handful of older-generation leaders such as the mayors of Gaza and Bethlehem remained loyal to Hussein. Most of those who benefitted from the royal largesse – government clerks, teachers, religious officials and former office holders – supported Arafat even as they accepted Jordanian dinars. The *intifada* was the decisive blow which destroyed the delusion that Hussein retained support in the occupied territories. The crowds shouted for the PLO, not for Jordanian rule. There is no mention of the King in any of the demands put forward by the leadership of the uprising.

Hussein had not welcomed the *intifada*. First, his advisers feared that the rebelliousness could spread to the large Palestinian population in Jordan. Second, there was even greater apprehension that the uprising might provide an opportunity for the Israelis to implement their long-nurtured plan to expel the West Bank population over the River Jordan thus overwhelming the Hashemite kingdom. Some Amman officials feared that Israel was purposely antagonizing the Palestinians to this end.

In view of the solid support in the occupied territories for the PLO during the *intifada*, Hussein was anxious to show that he was not standing in Arafat's way. At a press conference in May 1988 the King announced, 'I am not prepared nor will I negotiate on behalf of the PLO.' He left open the possibility of attending a peace conference in a joint Palestinian–Jordanian delegation if this was agreeable to the PLO. The King told reporters, 'We are determined to dispel any impression or idea that we are seeking to extend our control or influence with regard to the Palestinian dimension.'[70]

On 31 July 1988, in a dramatic television address, Hussein proclaimed: 'Jordan is not Palestine.' The Hashemite monarch announced his decision to 'sever administrative and judicial ties' with the West Bank in the hope that an 'independent Palestinian state will be established in the occupied Palestinian land, after it is liberated'.[71] While not officially dissolving the union of the two banks that his grandfather King Abdullah had proclaimed in 1950, Hussein effectively renounced his claim to sovereignty over the West Bank, thus removing the last obstacle in the path of the PLO's claim as sole representative of the Palestinian people.

The King implemented his policy immediately. He dissolved the Jordanian Parliament, since half its deputies were from the West Bank, and abolished the Ministry in the occupied territories, replacing it with a Bureau for Palestinian Affairs in the Foreign Ministry. The King also cancelled the five-year plan for the economic development of the West Bank and Gaza; discontinued the payment of subsidies to sixteen thousand employees of the civilian administration in the territories; and pensioned off the 5400 employees who received their wages directly from Amman. Symbolic steps were also taken, such as dropping West Bank cities from the TV weather forecast and the official Jordanian atlas.[72]

West Bank residents continued, however, to carry Jordanian passports, since Hussein did not wish to leave them stateless like the population of Gaza. The King did not rule out a confederation between Jordan and the Palestinian state, but he could clearly read the writing on the wall. After the summer of 1988 his main goal was to prevent the conflict between Israel and the Palestinians from spilling over into his realm.

The *intifada* became an issue in the Israeli elections of November 1988. During the campaign, Likud politicians castigated Labour for its 'moderate' approach to the uprising and for Foreign Minister Shimon Perez's policy of attempting to initiate 'Land for Peace' negotiations. The Labour party entered the election campaign with a rehash of the Allon Plan that was outdated after Hussein announced his renunciation of the West Bank. The Labour party was bitterly divided between hawks and doves over the issue of negotiating with the PLO.

Many in Likud claimed that, if they had been in exclusive control, the uprising would have been over in a week. Indeed these voices blamed the Labour party for causing the *intifada* in the first place, by showing weakness. With greater justice, the Labour party doves charged that the right-wing calls for annexation and expulsion were a major cause of the uprising. During the election it often seemed as if the right-wing politicians were outbidding each other in terms of who could be the most extreme.

The public mood in Israel since the *intifada* had moved to the right. Rallying behind the boys in uniform in time of crisis is a common reaction in many countries. Many Israelis accepted the right-wing argument that Israel must control all of historic Palestine or the Zionist state would eventually disappear. Although Jewish casualties in the *intifada* were extremely small, it was always possible for right-wing politicians to focus attention on the death of a single Jew while ignoring the slaughter of so many innocent Palestinian civilians. During the election campaign right-wing politicians made the struggle of the people of the occupied territories appear as an effort to exterminate the Jewish people.

Several extreme right-wing parties sprang up during the election campaign after their Kahane's Kach party was disqualified by the Israeli Supreme Court because of its overt racism. One of the new parties, Moledet (Motherhood), was founded by General Rehavam Ze'evi, whose call for 'transfer' of the Palestinians in the occupied territories to neighbouring Arab countries had contributed to the uneasiness of the Palestinians in the West Bank and Gaza in late 1987. During the election campaign Ze'evi argued that 'transfer' was a humane and practical solution that would obviate Israel's need to deal with millions of Arabs within its borders. He did not take a position against Israel's Arab citizens but merely argued for the 'voluntary transfer' of the Palestinians in the occupied territories. Ze'evi stated that Israel could be made 'unattractive' for the West Bank and Gaza Arabs. If, after annexation by Israel, they faced unemployment and shortage of land and water, 'then in a legitimate way and in accordance with the Geneva convention, we can create the necessary conditions for separation'.[73]

In May 1988 Tsomet (Land of Israel Loyalist Alliance), founded by the super-hawk former Chief of Staff Raphael (Raful) Eitan, held its first national convention, which was addressed by Prime Minister Shamir. Many in Likud welcomed Tsomet as an ally and possible coalition partner in a right-wing government. A supporter of Eitan gave an accurate portrait of him at the convention.

He's the only one who can raise us up from being a bent and bowed flock, and teach us how to kill and killing's the only way we'll ensure we stay here. Everyone's done it — the Americans killed the Indians; the Germans killed until they united their country, the British killed in the Falklands, and they weren't ashamed, they were proud to do it. It's the only way and Raful is the only one.[74]

Most observers expected the November 1988 election to decide the issue of the occupation. But it was not to be. The big surprise was the gain of the religious parties, who won 18 seats out of 120 in the Knesset. Likud and Labour formed a government, with Likud gaining slightly in influence over the 1984–8 coalition arrangement. The PLO had clearly hoped for a Labour victory, to be followed by negotiations over the territories. But although the Israeli moderates lost in November, soon afterwards the moderates would triumph in the Palestinian camp.

10
A STONE'S THROW AWAY

There was an air of expectation as 380 delegates descended on Algiers in mid-November 1988 for the nineteenth session of the Palestine National Council (PNC). It was ironic that this meeting of the PNC in Algiers was being called the *intifada* congress, since Palestinian delegate Edward Said noted, 'Algiers had just had its own brutally suppressed *intifada*, so the presence of several hundred Palestinians and at least 1200 members of the press was not welcomed by the Benjedid government.'[1]

Everyone understood that the purpose of the meeting was to agree on a Palestinian Declaration of Independence for a West Bank–Gaza state, as well as a political platform on which to conduct international negotiations. This would not be easy. The Palestinian Communists, Fatah, the Democratic Front, the Popular Front and various smaller groups all had their own agenda. PLO chairman Yasser Arafat had his task cut out for him. Many believed that the nineteenth PNC would be one of the most crucial Palestinian meetings and also one of the most controversial.

In April 1987 the eighteenth PNC too had been held in Algiers. At that meeting Arafat had welcomed back into the fold George Habash and Nayif Hawatmeh, while a delegate from the Palestinian Communist party had been elected to the PLO executive council. The union of Fatah, the Democratic Front, the Popular Front and the Communists on the eve of the *intifada* was fortuitous, even if the Syrian-backed groups led by Jebril's Popular Front-General Command had not attended the congress.

But this *intifada* unity was threatened in May 1988 when Arafat's political adviser, Bassam Abu Sharif, announced, 'We accept Resolution 242 and 338 in the context of the other UN resolutions, which do recognize the national rights of the Palestinian people.'[2] To many Palestinian factions UN Resolution 242 was anathema, since it implicitly recognized Israel. George Habash was shocked by Bassam Abu Sharif's statement because 'it frankly expresses a readiness to hold direct negotiations with the enemy and to recognize the legitimacy of the Zionist presence on the land of Palestine'.[3]

On 13 November Algerian television interviewed some of the principal delegates to the nineteenth PNC. Abu Sharif indicated, 'There is a Palestinian semi-agreement on the declaration of national independence.' But differences persisted with regard to UN Resolution 242. George Habash declared: 'We do not agree in any form to the offering of free concessions without anything in return.' He felt that acceptance of 242, with its implicit recognition of Israel, should be used as a negotiating chip. 'If we strip ourselves naked prior to the convening of the international conference, this will mean that at the international conference there will be new concessions to be offered.'[4] But Habash stopped short of threatening to walk out over this issue. He made it clear that no matter what the outcome of the conference, he planned to remain in the PLO as a leader of the 'loyal opposition'.

The factions who were not attending the PNC were unconditionally opposed to the acceptance of 242. Jebril's *Al Quds* radio station in Syria reported a statement by the Islamic Jihad: 'Sharing the homeland with the enemy violates God's orders and the formal legal opinions of Moslem scholars.'[5] There was no doubt that Jebril's Popular Front-General Command faction was equally opposed to any concessions under any circumstances.

At the PNC meeting, Arafat was torn between a conciliatory faction led by the Communists, who wanted to recognize Israel and accept the June 1967 borders, and a hard-line faction led by Habash, who advocated no compromise before an international conference. There was a heated debate. Columbia University professor Edward Said was greatly impressed by the speech of the PLO's number two man, Abu Iyad. Born Salah Khalaf in Jaffa in 1933, Abu Iyad was generally considered a hard-liner and the power behind the Black September terrorist group of the early 1970s. But at this PNC meeting he argued that 'decisions have to be made now, not only in the face of the discouraging realities of the Israeli elections, but because our people need an immediate concrete statement of goals'.[6] Abu Iyad urged the delegates to accept UN Resolution 181, which had proposed a partition of Palestine in 1947, as well as Resolution 242.

Arafat and the PLO had been considering the proclamation of a Palestinian state since the beginning of the *intifada*. But it was King Hussein's renunciation of his role in the West Bank on 31 July that year which set the stage for the birth of the new state that would have a government in exile similar to that of the Free French and other German-occupied countries in London during World War II. It was understood that Israel would not recognize the new state, but it was hoped that a government in exile would give the PLO greater status in the world community and increase its bargaining position. It was also hoped that the proclamation of a state would give comfort to those suffering under the occupation and be a tangible symbol of a success earned by their sacrifices. The passing of the political platform was more controversial.

In the end, by a majority of 253 to 46 with 10 abstentions, and with 29 delegates not voting, the PNC passed a motion accepting Resolution 242 and all other UN Resolutions pertinent to Palestinian self-determination as the basis for participation in an international conference for peace in the Middle East. As expected, George Habash announced that for the time being he would refrain from open opposition. It was agreed there would be two documents, a Palestinian Declaration of Independence and a political communiqué outlining the PLO's negotiating position for a resolution of the Palestinian question.

In the early morning of 15 November Yasser Arafat read out the Declaration of Independence to the PNC. The PLO leader announced the creation of the state of Palestine, 'with its capital in the holy Jerusalem'.[7] Independence was declared on the basis of the UN Partition Resolution of 1947. According to Edward Said, this was done 'first of all to say unequivocally that an Arab Palestine and an Israeli state should coexist in a partitioned Palestine. Self-determination should be for two peoples, not just one.' But he added that 'the principle of partition was asserted, not the territories specified in the 1947 UN resolution. All of us felt that since Israel has never declared its boundaries, we could not declare ours now.'

Like the Israeli Declaration of Independence, the Palestinian document declares that it is the right of all the exiles in the Diaspora to return to their homeland. 'The state of Palestine is the state of Palestinians wherever they may be . . . to enjoy in their collective national and cultural identity.' The declaration also pays tribute to the *intifada* and to 'the souls of our sainted martyrs'. But the thirty exiled members of the United Command popular committee of the occupied territories were conspicuous by their absence from any policy-making role at the PNC meeting. A true union between Palestinians in the Diaspora and those living under Israeli occupation was yet to be made.

Accompanying the declaration was a political communiqué which called for the convening of a peace conference on the basis of United Nations Resolution 242. Jebril's *Al Quds* radio station denounced the communiqué: 'The PLO today proceeded to commit a crime against our Palestinian people and their historic and national right to their land by declaring its recognition of UN Resolution 242.'[8] His statement added that those who recognized Resolution 242 'have made Palestine represented by a piece of the Palestinian land through which they define the whole Palestinian land'. Other rejectionist Palestinian groups joined in the condemnation of the PLO's acceptance of partition on the basis of the 1947 resolution and the acceptance of Resolution 242 with its implicit recognition of Israel, which they regarded as heresy.

But ten Arab League members, as well as Turkey, Malaysia and Indonesia, immediately recognized the new state of Palestine. Eventually, only Syria and Lebanon (occupied by Syria) among the Arab states failed to recognize the new nation. While sympathetic, most of western Europe was more hesitant. The British Foreign Office called the declaration 'premature'.

Israel denounced the Palestinian Declaration of Independence and its accompanying statement. Foreign Minister Perez warned that the West should not be fooled by talk of Palestinian moderation. Prime Minister Shamir described the PNC meeting as 'another step in the Arab terrorist organization's war against Israel's very existence and independence'. He added, 'We will react accordingly.'[9]

Shamir backed up his threat. Even as Yasser Arafat read out the Declaration in Algiers, the West Bank and Gaza were put under tight curfew. The Israelis even cut off the electricity supply and stationed reinforcements in the streets to prevent any outbreak of joy and celebration. No major incidents were reported. In some places, Palestinian flags were defiantly flown and whistles were blown, but the population of the occupied territories had decided not to give the Israelis the satisfaction of breaking up independence celebrations.

A key question was the American reaction to the PNC meeting. For over a decade, Washington had said that it would negotiate with the PLO if it renounced terrorism, recognized Israel's right to exist, and accepted UN Security Council Resolution 242 which called for respect for 'the sovereignty, territorial integrity, and political independence of every state' in the Middle East. But the initial American response to the nineteenth PNC and its Declaration was cautious. 'This is definitely a step forward, but does not go far enough,' remarked a Reagan administration official. President-elect George Bush, who would take office in a few months, was also reserved. 'I think the jury is still out. If indeed there is specific recognition of Security Council Resolution 242, that would be a very important step forward. I will have to wait until I am sure that is exactly what has taken place.'[10]

Signals from the PLO were confusing. Its representative at the UN, Zuhdi at-Tarzi, stated that his organization recognized the Jewish state. He told a Saudi newspaper, 'We admit

Israel exists and is carrying out occupation. We also admit that the occupation must end.' But George Habash had a different view. The Popular Front leader 'reiterated that the PNC statement does not recognize Israel'. He claimed that the Declaration 'recognizes Resolution 242 and even this can be debated'.[11]

But the incoming Bush administration wished to encourage the moderate elements in the PLO without alienating the American Jewish community. Like all new American presidents, Bush hoped to make progress in Middle East peace negotiations. American–Palestinian dialogue was a prerequisite. It was best, however, if the Reagan administration recognized the PLO, thus sparing his successor the outrage of the American Jewish community.

It would, however, be a tortuous journey before Washington was satisfied that Arafat had met American conditions for a US–PLO dialogue. On 7 December 1988, in Stockholm, Arafat agreed to 'an international conference to be held on the basis of UN Resolution 242 and the right of the Palestinian people to self-determination, without external interference, as provided in the UN charter'. This did not, however, satisfy the US Secretary of State, George Schultz, who refused Arafat's request for a visa to enter the USA in order to address the UN General Assembly. The UN special session was forced to convene in Geneva, where on 13 December Arafat declared that he sought a comprehensive settlement among the parties, 'including the state of Palestine, Israel and other neighbours within the framework of the international conference for peace in the Middle East as the basis of Resolution 242 and 338'. Schultz was still not happy until Arafat held a press conference the following day, when the PLO leader made another statement which mentioned that he sought a settlement based on the 1947 partition resolution.[12]

Schultz now announced that he was appointing Robert H. Pelletreau, Jr, American Ambassador to Tunisia, to open a dialogue with the PLO. Yitzak Shamir called the American discussions with the PLO a 'blunder' that would 'not help us, not help the United States, and not help the peace process'. But Habash's reaction to the American–Palestinian dialogue was very positive: 'Despite the American intention of not recognizing the Palestinian state, which was made very clearly, we welcome the move.'[13]

Abu Ilad found President Bush's remarks on the Middle East 'relatively positive and flexible'.[14] During this period other Palestinians expressed their opinions on the future development of the newly proclaimed state. Most of their comments reflected moderate, optimistic and open-minded views, including the statements of the President of the new state – Yasser Arafat.

Arafat implied that after negotiations he would accept a Palestinian state limited to the occupied territories. 'There are many states in the world smaller than Palestine,' he declared.[15] 'We can negotiate on this at the peace conference. Many compromises are conceivable.' With regard to union with King Hussein's realm, Arafat noted, 'First we want an independent state and then the people should decide whether they want a confederation with Jordan.' For economic reasons Arafat noted that 'we will demand the establishment of a corridor between the West Bank and the Gaza Strip'.

The PLO delegate to the UN, Zuhdi at-Tarzi, believed that since the port of Gaza was not adequate the new state of Palestine would have to pay Israel to use its excellent facilities at Haifa in order to export produce to Europe. Tarzi told an Israeli newspaper that the proposed new nation would live in a close economic relationship with its Jewish neighbours. 'After all the 120,000 [Palestinian labourers] crossing the green line every day will continue to do so only without reservations. They may even rent flats close to their jobs, instead of travelling home every night.'[16]

In accordance with PLO doctrine, the peace activist Mubarak Awwad saw a Palestinian state as a transition.

I am for a two-state solution. But the two-state solution does not solve the problem. Even once there is peace, even once there is a state of Palestine, negotiations still will have to take place. The farmer from Haifa, a fellow who had land and a house – he has to get money or some other form of compensation for his land. Eventually there must come a time when Israel and a Palestinian state can live in such harmony that the two states will form a real confederation. In the beginning it is most important to have a Palestinian state. But we need, even in the beginning, to create a state that lives in peace with Israel and Jordan, a state whose borders are open to economic and cultural cooperation.[17]

Awwad believed that commando attacks on Israel would not be a problem after the creation of the Palestinian state. 'When they have a state of their own, Palestinians will do a better job with those who want to continue the struggle than the Israelis can do.' But Awwad had no tolerance for the Israeli settlers living in the West Bank after a Palestinian state was formed. 'They came and stole the land. They are invaders. They came as prostitutes. In no way will I accept the settlers at all.'

Unlike Awwad and many other Palestinians, Ambassador Tarzi had a much more moderate attitude towards the settlers, whom he did not see as an insurmountable obstacle to peace.

During the days of the British rule, for instance, there were Greeks and even German villagers in the area. They were settlers who accepted the laws of the country. Some of them became citizens, while others retained their foreign nationality, subject to local laws .... The Palestinian state can include foreigners .... If they want to live there because of spiritual ties and if they do so within the framework of the laws of the state, that could solve everything.[18]

Tarzi's comments on the Jewish settlers were a hopeful sign. Equally encouraging were the observations of the Palestinian American professor, Ibrahim Abu-Lughod, a member of the Palestine National Council, who asserted that the new state would be 'democratic, secular and at peace'.[19] Abu-Lughod believed that there were many other reasons to be hopeful about the Palestinian chances of creating a viable nation. 'Today, despite exile, statelessness and subjugation, they are cohesive and socially and educationally accomplished as the best Arab community in the Middle East and compare favourably with other achieving nations.' The professor added, 'Palestinian Arabs have created institutions that organize and mobilize dispersed population, nourish the identity and promote the achievement of their political programme.' He specifically mentioned the Palestine National Council. 'Its 482 members, drawn from all corners of the world, represent all social, political and economic strata of Palestinian Arab society.'

Of course, Jerusalem remained a considerable stumbling block to a two-state solution. According to Ambassador Tarzi, 'I cannot say there is no problem. With some goodwill, we will eventually find a solution.' Tarzi added, 'If Jerusalem means so much to a Jew from Brooklyn, who has never been there, consider what it means to a Palestinian who was born there.' But Yasser Arafat made clear that he had no inclination to accept Israeli rule over the whole of Jerusalem. 'The eastern part of Jerusalem was conquered by force. Not even the United Nations has recognized the annexation of the Arab part of Jerusalem. Thus you will hardly expect me to do so.' However, Arafat did not rule out the internationalization of the Holy City. 'All this will have to be discussed at a peace conference,' he stated.

Arafat has persistently claimed that a Palestinian state was very near. 'It will happen very soon. It is already a quarter to twelve.' At other times he has asserted that a Palestinian state was 'a stone's throw away'. But on several occasions he has hinted that such unrealistic statements were intended to bolster the morale of those struggling against the occupation. When asked on Moroccan television why he claimed so often that a Palestinian state was so close, Arafat replied, 'If we assume the distance is a thousand kilometres, what would the Arabs decide to do? Would they travel the thousand kilometres in a rocket, a plane or a car, or on foot? What would be our Palestinian and Arab decision? When would the state be established?'[20]

During the first two years of the *intifada* it was widely assumed that the formation of a Palestinian state would come eventually. Typical was the Rand Corporation Report on the Palestine Question, which was issued in August 1989. It stated, 'The forces which, now unleashed – and the response evoked in Israel – have now made the ultimate emergence of a Palestinian state on the West Bank and Gaza inevitable.'[21] A report by Israel's Jaffee Centre for Strategic Studies examined Israel's options as a result of the *intifada*. The research team, headed by General Ahron Yariv and including other retired Army officers, concluded that contrary to government policy eventual establishment of a modified Palestinian state and qualified negotiations with the PLO were the measure least likely to harm Israel's interests over the long run. Despite the panel's call for a lengthy process of ten to fifteen years, in which the Jewish state would maintain its 'security arrangements' in the West Bank and Gaza, the Jaffee Centre report was seen as another indication that a Palestinian state was 'inevitable'.

In an interview, Thomas Friedman expressed his opinion that 'Israel could unilaterally offer the Palestinians a state in the West Bank and Gaza with boundaries that Israel considers proper, with the understanding that the state would be completely demilitarized and Israel itself would control all the mechanism of demilitarization.'[22] Numerous similar plans were offered at the time. But despite the overwhelming justice of the Palestinian cause on historical, legal and moral grounds, Israel's greater strength, fortified by the support of what had become the world's only super-power, was more than a match for the Palestinians, who were receiving only tepid support from the Arab world.

Since December 1987 there has been an effort by the Palestinians to break away from Israeli institutions and to set up an indigenous administrative apparatus that would eventually become the structure of an independent state. Over the years of occupation popular committees of youths, students, women and workers had been formed. Many of these committees dealt with medical and agricultural relief work. Beginning in December 1987, popular committees sprang up to handle the difficult problem of food relief during the *intifada*'s frequent periods of curfew. Neighbourhood by neighbourhood, village by village, refugee camp by refugee camp, food relief committees were formed.

Gradually, committees were created to cover every area of life, including education, security, business activity and sanitation, in addition to health and food distribution. Dr Mahdi Abdul Hadi, a Palestinian researcher, claimed that there were 45,000 local committees of various kinds in the territories. 'We are building self-sufficiency,' he stated.[23]

During the early stage of the *intifada*, 'little Palestines' were set up in isolated villages. They were run by local committees who issued their own propaganda literature, flew the Palestinian flag and plastered walls with *intifada* slogans. The Christian village of Beit Sahur was one of the most militant communities in the West Bank. Under the direction of a lecturer from Bethlehem University, students taught the villagers to raise crops on whatever small plots were available. Beit Sahur was one of the Palestinian villages which refused to pay Israeli taxes.

Call Number 10 by the United National Leadership of the popular uprising urged the population 'not to pay taxes. The accountants are responsible. They shall not deal in this matter. Our steadfast merchants should not present or fill in tax forms.'[24] But even in the early stage of the *intifada*, this tactic was not very successful. On 24 March 1988 in *Der Spiegel* Defence Minister Rabin stated, 'The tax evaders do not worry me. Nobody gets a working or business permit unless he can prove he has paid his taxes. So far we have lost 20 per cent of the income and VAT in the territories. We can live with that.'

Also during this period there was a mass resignation by Palestinian police, who were seen by the *intifada* leadership as collaborators. In March 1988, when the three hundred Arab policemen resigned, Rabin did not appear concerned. 'If Palestinian police resign,' he said, 'the Palestinians will be the only ones to suffer.' The Defence Minister summarized the situation: 'What is being done now is an attempt to undermine the commercial structures. Israel will not be affected, but Palestinians will be harmed.'

Palestinians clearly *were* harmed by the constant calls for strikes for Arabs from the occupied territories who worked in Israel. When asked how the Palestinians would make up the loss of wages from the recurring strikes, Arafat retorted, 'How will the Israelis run their economy without the Palestinian workers? To whom will they turn?'[25] but as we have seen, the Israelis suffered little economic damage. The Palestinians, however, needed to work in Israel in order to survive.

In order to pay for the *intifada*, including the cost of the strikes, additional health services, alternative schools and the boycott of Israeli goods, large sums were required from the Arab world. But sufficient resources were not forthcoming. In an interview on 16 May 1988 Arafat admitted, 'Arab support has started to arrive, but it is still below par.' Several weeks later the Arab summit in Algiers rebuffed Arafat's request for increased financial support for the uprising.

Lacking funds from the Arab world, the *intifada* leaders found it difficult to withstand the Israeli counter-measures against the Palestinian self-sufficiency campaign. In August 1988 Israel outlawed the popular committees and decreed that any Palestinian found to be a member would be arrested. Hundreds of committee members were rounded up. The tax strike was countered by collection campaigns and the confiscation of the property of those who refused to pay.

One of the Israelis' biggest weapons was an $8.5 million databank designed to keep track of all Palestinian property, family ties, political attitudes and employment records. Meron Benvenisti called the computer 'the ultimate instrument of population control'.[26] In Gaza, the Israelis put the computer to work to force Palestinians to apply for new ID cards that would be needed to enter Israel for employment. The new cards would only be issued to those who had paid all taxes and had no charges against them for resistance activity. The PLO urged Palestinians in Gaza not to apply for the new cards, but, as with the calls for strike action, the residents of the Strip needed employment in Israel in order to feed their families.

The American journalist Thomas Friedman watched Palestinian workers in Gaza line up for the new ID cards. An Israeli officer told him, 'Why are they here? Because we are basically stronger. Look, sixty thousand people from the Gaza Strip go to Israel every day. Who is going to feed them if they stay home?' The IDF officer added, 'They all come like good children. The ID card is life.'

About ninety thousand Gaza residents received the magnetic ID cards which allow them to work in Israel. This was a big defeat to the *intifada* leadership, which had demanded that the cards be returned. Over four thousand were denied ID cards, because they were considered 'security risks'. They were given instead green cards, which barred them from leaving the Gaza Strip. In February 1990 the Gaza civil administration began renewing the magnetic IDs, which expired after six months; this gave the security forces considerable control over the population. There were plans to extend the magnetic ID card programme to the West Bank.

After two years of the *intifada*, it was clear that the Palestinian effort to disengage from the Israeli economy and occupation administration had not succeeded. According to the Israeli journalist Ron Ben-Yishay, 'The formula has been tried and has so far not worked. The United National Command of the uprising knows that, since the *intifada* began, the economic dependence of the inhabitants of the territories in Israel has grown, and that despite the population's readiness to suffer, there is a limit to what can be imposed on it.'[27]

As time passed there were other disturbing trends, including the increased tendency for the Palestinians to kill other Palestinians, just as blacks were killing blacks in South Africa. In some parts of the West Bank there was soon open warfare between nationalist supporters of the PLO and those considered to be collaborators. Some of these were former members of the Village League or informers for the Shin Bet (Israeli intelligence service). There were even reports of attacks on pro-Jordanian sympathizers, who became a dwindling minority after King Hussein renounced his claim to the West Bank. It was feared that some of the several hundred killed at the hands of their fellow Palestinians were murdered as a result of personal vendettas, despite a warning by *Al Quds* radio that 'an individual may not be labelled an agent by an individual or group of individuals. It must be done by popular and nationalist committees in the territories.'[28]

Another stumbling block to a Palestinian state was the existence of the Jewish settlements. Despite PLO Ambassador Tarzi's claim that these could be accommodated in a Palestinian state, the extreme militancy of the settlers and their determination to increase their numbers clearly indicated that no reconciliation seemed possible between the settlers and the indigenous population of the occupied territories.

Indeed, according to Roni Matalon, a reserve soldier who was stationed in the West Bank, Gush Emunim played a useful role for the IDF since 'the settlers symbolically served as a kind of avenging hand that can operate where the army's hands are tied'. But the tail sometimes wags the dog. Matalon notes, 'The settlers view the army as a means of achieving their strategic objectives.' Clearly, the Gush Emunim goal was to stir up the Palestinians in order to rationalize expulsions. Matalon noted the devious methods of the settlers:

They provoke [the Palestinians] in order to heat up the situation. One example of how you can misconstrue the strategy of the settlers is the foreign press stickers they affix to their cars. A print shop in Ofra printed a great number of stickers. Like a lot of other people, I naively thought that they were simply trying to protect themselves from the stone-throwers. But what I came to understand following discussions with them was that this action was intended to create a situation in which the real media people would get stoned. And that this would heat up the situation. It's not a secret: everyone in the area knows that some of the settlers' cars have such stickers.[29]

There was no realistic possibility that the settlers could ever be removed. According to the Labour party leader, Shimon Perez, 'an understanding exists between us and the Americans that no existing settlement would be uprooted'.[30] Even in the first year of the *intifada*, the settlers made plans to expand. As noted in an article in the *Jerusalem Post* of 20

September 1988 'Leaders of Jewish settlements in the West Bank said this week that the Palestinian uprising has spurred more families to join ideologically-based settlements in the heart of the area and that the housing there is inadequate to absorb the influx of new arrivals.' Aryi Ofni, deputy head of the Samaria regional council, claimed that there was a 24 per cent increase in the number of schoolchildren in Samarian settlements in the previous year. Another settlement leader claimed there were seventy-four thousand Jews living in the West Bank and three thousand in Gaza. For the Palestinians, the problem of the settlers had been getting worse, not better, since the *intifada* began.

Not only did the settlers attempt to provoke violence in the West Bank, but they also tried to block any chance of a negotiated agreement. In March 1990 settlers threatened the Israeli government with massive demonstrations if it attempted to implement a plan for elections in the occupied territories. The Gush Emunim feared that any agreement would lead to a Palestinian state. About the proposal for a dialogue in Cairo between Israelis and Palestinians, the chairman of the council of Jewish settlers, Uri Ariel, said, 'Once you have started off down that road, it will be very difficult to get off.'[31] Another settler leader threatened that five thousand activists could demonstrate to block a peace agreement. 'We can create such a madhouse that nobody will be able to work.'

The settlers had nothing to fear. Prime Minister Shamir had no intention of negotiating a peace agreement with the Palestinians. In January 1989 Defence Minister Rabin had proposed a four-stage peace plan which called for cessation of Palestinian violence, a three- to six-month period of quiet prior to Palestinian elections; negotiations with elected Palestinian leaders and with Jordan for an interim form of autonomy; and negotiations leading to a final disposition of the territories. Rabin specifically excluded the PLO from participation in the process. At first Rabin's proposal was rejected by the leadership of the *intifada*, since it differed little, if at all, from the Camp David scheme. They specifically objected to elections before withdrawal, and insisted on the exclusive leadership of the PLO.

In April 1989 Shamir proposed his own peace plan, based on Palestinian elections leading to autonomy. This was a new approach for Shamir, who had opposed the Camp David proposals, since he claimed they would lead to a Palestinian state. Many cynically believed that Shamir made the proposal for elections in the occupied territories because he believed that the Palestinians would never accept it.

After bitter in-fighting between the Likud and Labour coalition parties, on 14 May 1989 the Israeli government formally adopted 'a new peace initiative'. The first step was to be 'free and democratic elections among the Palestinian Arab inhabitants of Judaea, Samaria and the Gaza district' for representatives to conduct negotiations. The proposal categorically opposed the creation of a Palestinian state and rejected negotiations with the PLO. The maximum concession anticipated was some form of autonomy.[32]

The left wing in the Labour party, led by Ezer Weizman, opposed the plan, since he favoured a more direct approach based on wide concessions and direct negotiations with the PLO. Shamir came under even stronger pressure from the extremists in Likud, especially David Levy and Ariel Sharon, who opposed all concessions. In order to appease the hard-liners, Shamir modified his plan to exclude Jerusalem Arabs from the Palestinian negotiating team and to include a provision for the maintenance of Israeli law in areas of Jewish settlement in the occupied territories. Shamir made it clear that he intended to concede nothing to the Palestinians.

Indeed, for month after month talks for a West Bank–Gaza election dragged on. Shamir tied the negotiations up in knots over procedural questions, especially the composition of the Palestinian delegation. The Prime Minister refused to talk to anyone affiliated with the PLO. The fiction would have to be maintained that the Palestinian delegates were speaking for themselves rather than the PLO, since Israeli law prohibited its citizens from meeting with representatives of 'terrorist organizations'. Indeed, on 31 December 1989 Shamir set off a parliamentary crisis when he dismissed Ezer Weizman from the cabinet because he had supposedly had meetings with the PLO representatives. The parliamentary crisis was ended in a compromise when Weizman was dismissed from the inner cabinet but allowed to keep his Science Ministry portfolio.

Despite Israel's refusal to deal directly with him, Arafat stated that 'the PLO once again leaned over backwards and approves the idea of a dialogue between representatives of the Israeli government and representatives of the Palestinian people in the occupied territories and Diaspora'. Commenting on the arrangements for negotiations, Labour party leader Shimon Perez stated, 'I do believe it is acceptable to the Egyptians, to the Palestinians, and I do not see why it should not be acceptable to us as well.'[33] But Prime Minister Shamir, whose Likud party was the senior coalition partner, refused to accept a slightly modified version of his own plan. Likud felt that Israel could afford to take a hard line, since events were moving in favour of the Zionists and against the Palestinians.

Principal among these changes was the liberalization in the Soviet Union and the end of its control over eastern Europe. The new regimes were likely to be less friendly to the Palestinians, and the Jewish state stood to gain substantially in diplomatic support and economic ties. Gorbachev's USSR was also far less likely to support the Arabs militarily in any future confrontation with Israel.

But the most important change in eastern Europe to benefit Israel was the increased emigration of Soviet Jews, an exodus that was expected to reach one million in the 1990s. Most of them had an unusually high level of education, which would promote Israel to a regional super-power in the near future. Prime Minister Shamir caused a sensation when he declared, 'For a big immigration we need a big and strong state.' Clearly, it is hard to imagine an Israel swollen by a million immigrants remaining within its 1967 borders.

Israel was greatly aided by American laws, which limited Soviet immigrants to fifty thousand per year; this was a tragic policy which was not in the interest of the United States. Most Soviet Jews wanted to go to the USA, where they had relatives and a chance to live in political and economic security. Had they been allowed to enter the USA they would have greatly enriched American life, in view of their high educational level and technical skills. Closing the doors of the country to them, thus forcing their exodus to Israel, meant that America would pay for their settlement in the form of increased aid to Israel. The USA would also reap the whirlwind of conflict that would come from Israel's expansion to accommodate the Soviet immigrants. In the long run, the Jewish state could become a high-tech commercial rival of the United States in the next century. Israel would then be in a position to attract American Jews to settle in the expanded state, which is the ultimate Zionist goal.

American Zionists were understandably jubilant over the exodus of Soviet Jews to Israel. The Zionist lobby had for years insisted that American trade concessions to the USSR be based on the freedom of Jews to emigrate. But that lobby had not favoured liberalizing American immigration rules to allow Soviet Jews to go to their preferred destination. Forcing Soviet Jews to go to Israel was a key goal of the Zionists. In an article in the *New York Times* on 12 February 1990 William Safire wrote that 'the prospect of a million Jews in Israel over the next decade changes all demographic assumptions'. Safire agreed with Yitzak Shamir that 'a big and strong state' was needed because of the influx; thus the annexation of the occupied territories must follow in due course. But Safire understood the Israeli Prime Minister's later disclaimers, since the American columnist noted that Shamir had backtracked because paying for the refugees would be easier if they were not seen as West Bank settlers! Safire's conclusion, that the Soviet emigration doomed all hopes for a Palestinian state, was difficult to refute.

Let's cut the pussyfooting: the freedom of Soviet Jews changes the equation. Time for 'new thinking' in the Middle East, because the question of severing Judaea and Samaria is now moot.

Palestinian Arabs who live there have a golden opportunity to achieve autonomy, perhaps canton sovereignty, by quickly taking advantage of the offer on the table to freely elect peace negotiators.

The UN won't create a state of them. The Kremlin will

not jeopardize trade status by cracking down on emigration, nor will the US absorb the exodus.

Self-government is within their grasp: for Palestinians, it's now or never.

The PLO was not blind to the devastating effect of Soviet emigration on the Zionist-Palestinian conflict. Arafat attempted to unite the Arab countries in order to put pressure on the Soviet Union to halt the stampede of Jews to Israel. But Arab protests to Gorbachev had little effect. As American Zionists knew, the Soviet leader cared more about American economic support for his country than the tepid intercessions of the Arab oil sheikhs. Palestinians began to realize that any gains they had made during the *intifada* were slipping away.

According to Edward Said, 'No matter what causes Jews to suffer elsewhere, somehow Palestinians are made to pay for it.'[34] The Palestinian–American scholar asked, 'Why did the US and Israel agree in 1989 that Soviet Jews, who once enjoyed the right to go anywhere after receiving visas, [now] be given the option of emigrating only to Israel?' Said believed that 'as a genuine Palestinian peace process grew imminent,' the Israelis pressed Washington to close its doors to Soviet immigrants, thus making them available as cannon fodder in the struggle to gain control over the occupied territories. In view of Israeli history, Said felt genuine concern for the future. 'Since the '67 war, a significant part of Israel's political establishment has advocated a "transfer" – forced eviction – of the Palestinian population from the West Bank and Gaza.' Indeed, the extremist parties which openly advocated 'transfer' would soon find their way into the Israeli ruling coalition.

Shamir's adamant refusal to accept his own proposal for elections in the occupied territories led to the break-up of the National Unity government. In March 1990 he dismissed the leader of the Labour party, Finance Minister Shimon Perez, over the peace negotiations issue. After a vote of no confidence, President Chaim Herzog gave Perez and then Shamir a chance to form a new government. Perez failed in his effort to gain the necessary majority of 61 votes in the Knesset. Shamir, who remained as caretaker Prime Minister, was then given a chance to form a cabinet.

During the interim period considerable panic and anger was caused on 11 April 1990, when 150 Jewish settlers occupied buildings in the Christian quarter of Jerusalem's Old City. Christians all over the world were outraged at the acquisition by Jews of the four-building complex called St John's Hospice. The Easter week occupation led to demonstrations and protests from many religious leaders, including Pope John Paul II, who expressed 'profound concern'. Many sacred shrines, including the Church of the Holy Sepulchre, were closed for the first time in centuries as a protest. Even the chief American Zionist lobbying group, the American Israel Public Affairs Committee (AIPAC), called the move into the Christian quarter 'insensitive and provocative'.[35]

At first the caretaker Shamir cabinet denied any involvement, but after increased scrutiny by the press and members of the Knesset, on 22 April the government issued a statement admitting that $1.8 million had been given by the Settlement Ministry for the purchase of the property. On 27 April the Israeli Supreme Court ordered all but twenty of the settlers out until a final court decision was reached on the legality of the sale of the buildings in the Christian quarter to a Jewish group. Many saw the occupation of the buildings as a danger signal of things to come.

Another disturbing incident occurred when demonstrations broke out among Palestinians in Israel and the occupied territories after the shooting by a deranged Israeli of Arab workers at Rishon Leziyyon, seven miles south of Tel Aviv. In a burst of automatic rifle fire from the former IDF soldier, seven Arab workers were killed and many more injured. An *intifada* manifesto blamed the Israeli government for the Rishon Leziyyon massacre, because of 'its extreme positions and the hatred the Israeli political system bears toward Palestinians'.[36]

In his reaction to the Rishon Leziyyon incident, Kach party leader Meir Kahane showed why he had been banned from the Knesset for his outspoken remarks, which were extreme even by Israeli standards: 'I do not weep for the seven dead Arabs any more than I would have wept over seven dead German labourers during the war with the Nazis, who were gunned down in exactly similar circumstances.' Kahane added, 'One who does not hate the enemy, the wicked, with all his soul, does not really believe that they are the enemy and that they are wicked.'[37] Most other Israeli leaders – even the parties on the extreme right – had enough decency to express regret for the murder of the innocent Arab workers.

But all Israeli leaders condemned the Palestinian demonstrations mounted as protests to the Rishon Leziyyon killings. Co-ordinator of activities in the occupied territories Samuel Goren told Israeli television: 'I would say that some elements are taking advantage of the attack, which was perpetrated by an apparently unbalanced man.' He added, 'This event is in no way connected to the political issue.' Chief of Staff Dan Shamron saw the demonstrations as an effort to renew the faltering *intifada*. He stated, 'Understandably, the population is highly motivated to act for the establishment of a Palestinian state.' But he added, 'There is no way we will allow the return of the former phenomenon of mass marches in the street.'[38] At least a dozen Palestinians were killed by the IDF during the protests against the Leziyyon massacre.

On 30 May there was a further reaction to the Rishon Leziyyon killings. A group of Palestinians landed on the Israeli coast at Nizzanim. All of the commandos were killed or captured, with no Israeli casualties. General Shamron asserted that the Palestinians 'simply aimed at killing civilians in the most densely populated areas of Israel, namely the central coastal area near Tel Aviv.'[39] Other reports disputed the claim, indicating that the Palestinians had the opportunity of killing civilians but declined to do so.

The mastermind behind the abortive landing was Abu Abbas, leader of the Palestine Liberation Front. In a lengthy interview, he revealed that he had been planning the Nizzanim operation for over two years. Abbas declared the landing to be a success: 'I believe the enemy sustained very heavy losses, especially military personnel in the southern coast.' He even claimed that ten thousand Israeli troops had been removed from Gaza to deal with the landing. The Palestine Liberation

Front leader gave himself much credit for his accomplishment: 'This in itself helped lift the siege, albeit temporarily, from the angry Gaza Strip.'

Abu Abbas apologized to Arafat 'for not informing him in advance of the operation'. The commando leader asserted that 'the PLO had no connection with the operation'. But Abbas denied that the operation had violated PLO policy: 'I know that the brother leader of the Palestinian revolution said no to terrorism and banned any operation outside Palestine territory. I agree with this. I am against any military operation outside Palestinian territory, particularly against innocent people.' He added, 'Is it possible for any Palestinian official to say no to armed struggle at a time when tens of thousands of heavily armed Israeli soldiers are firing at our people?'[40]

On 16 June the second highest official of the PLO, Abu Iyad, commented on the Nizzanim operation: 'We have never pledged to halt armed struggle against occupation inside the occupied territories.' But, the PLO official noted, 'the eleven young men who reached the beach before the Israeli Army reached them had enough time to open fire and kill as many Israeli holidaymakers as they could . . . but they did not do so.' Abu Iyad stated the PLO's attitude toward the Nizzanim landing: 'Had they killed any Israeli civilians, we would have had enough courage to condemn the operation. Anyhow, we are against killing civilians, both inside and outside Israel. We fight only the Israeli Army, which occupies our territory. This is how we understand armed struggle.'

Abu Iyad indicated that the USA was exerting strong pressure on the PLO to condemn the Nizzanim attack, despite the fact that no civilians had been killed. The PLO regretted the incident, but refused to call it 'terrorist'. It seemed unfair for the United States to accept the Israeli version of the incident without proof. But Shamir had formed a new extreme right-wing government, which favoured the expulsion of the Palestinians and insisted that the USA break off contact with the PLO. Abu Iyad commented:

The new government will launch small wars to occupy Jordan or a large part of Jordan, to deport the Palestinians from the West Bank and Gaza Strip and absorb the new Soviet immigrants . . . the *intifada* will develop in accordance with the developments in and size of Israeli violence. It is unreasonable for Palestinians to respond to Israeli bullets with stones. I believe war will start in six to eight months at most. This is the period required to absorb tens of thousands of Soviet immigrants in Israel.[41]

Abu Iyad's pessimistic analysis was not difficult to understand. Ariel Sharon was a prominent member of the new government with an eye on the Prime Minister's seat. Yitzak Rabin accurately described Sharon's position in the new cabinet: 'The government is a Sharon government under the name of a Shamir government.'[42] The new coalition also contained Rehavam Ze'evi's Moledet party, as well as Raphael Eitan's Tsomet faction. They made no secret of wanting the Palestinians expelled; indeed it was the central point of their platform.

A further ominous sign came on 21 June when President Bush announced the suspension of the US–PLO dialogue. The President acted in order to prevent congressional action that could have been more severe. Many in Congress were acting under pressure from the Zionist lobby, which wanted to use the Nizzanim landing as a reason to break off US relations with the PLO. The Israelis had been claiming that Arafat, in speeches and interviews in the Arab world, had violated his pledge to recognize Israel and renounce terrorism. But this is not true.

A US government report noted that in his remarks in Arab newspapers and on television and radio Arafat consistently recognized Israel and denounced terrorism. Commenting on the PLO's pledge in December 1988, the former assistant Secretary of State for the Near East, Alfred L. Atherton, stated, 'We found that their commitment is genuine and it has not eroded since then.' Another former high-ranking State Department official, Richard Murphy, commented on the PLO: 'After many years of trying to find the key to their status as a movement, they have decided it lies in acceptance of Israel as part of a two-state solution.' On PLO plans to undermine Israel by stages, Murphy added, 'Everyone can have his fantasies, but I think it's been consigned to Fantasyland.'[43]

Despite the opinions of State Department experts, Bush accepted the Israeli version of the Nizzanim raid. He demanded that Arafat denounce the landing as a terrorist act and discipline Abu Abbas. The President indicated, 'At any time that the PLO is prepared to take the necessary steps, we are prepared to promptly resume the dialogue.'[44] But most Palestinians saw the suspension as just one more sign of the Zionist lobby's stranglehold over a country which could always be depended upon to do Israel's bidding.

June 1990 was a disastrous month for the Palestinians. The new right-wing Israeli government offered no hope of negotiations and had proven its mastery over the Bush administration. Many saw the demonstrations in May, after the Rishon Leziyyon killings, as a last hurrah for the *intifada*. Indeed, in June, resistance activity had subsided to its lowest point since December 1987. Few were predicting that a Palestinian state was a 'stone's throw away'.

11
THE SADDAM MIRAGE

In the West Bank and Gaza Palestinians were electrified by the announcement. Saddam Hussein agreed to the evacuation of Kuwait, which he had occupied ten days earlier, if it was proceeded by 'the immediate and unconditional withdrawal of Israel from the occupied territories in Palestine'.[1] The Iraqi dictator proposed a package deal in which 'the oldest occupation' would be ended first and 'the same measures passed by the UN Security Council against Iraq would be adopted against any party that fails to oblige itself or comply with the arrangement.' In effect, Saddam was posing as the champion of the Palestinians, who were encouraged to believe that he had invaded Kuwait in order to secure a bargaining chip for the liberation of the West Bank and Gaza.

Before the 12 August announcement support for Saddam in the occupied territories was not completely solid. Palestinian teenagers taunted Israeli soldiers, 'Saddam is coming! He's on his way. Saddam is going to sweep you away.'[2] In Gaza, on the other hand, in view of financial contributions they received from the Gulf states, the Islamic fundamentalist group HAMAS denounced the Iraqi invasion. But when Saddam linked his occupation of Kuwait with the occupation of the West Bank and Gaza, he gained enormous support among Palestinians. The East Jerusalem lawyer Ziyad Abu Ziyad told an Israeli journalist, 'I think this proposal should be taken seriously because it opens the door to a comprehensive settlement for the region.' According to an Arab member of the Knesset, Abd-el Wahab Darousha, 'British Imperialism

detached Kuwait from Iraq. We support the return of this
historic right.'[3]

Israelis were shocked that Saddam Hussein received strong
backing not only in the occupied territories but from the
Palestinian citizens of their state. After 12 August Arab
crowds marched in Israel carrying banners which boldly
proclaimed, 'Saddam Hit The Americans and Israelis with
Chemical Weapons.' One Israeli Arab declared, 'Saddam is
leading the revolution of the poor, he is the Arabs' Robin
Hood.'[4] In large measure the positive response to Saddam
was motivated by the high unemployment, poor municipal
services and other injustices suffered by those living in Israel's
Arab ghettos. But most Israelis saw the Palestinian support of
Saddam as treason.

'The Arabs in Israel are crossing a red line by showing
support for an enemy who is threatening to annihilate half
of Israel with chemical weapons,' said Eliezer Tsafrir, Arab
Affairs Advisor to Prime Minister Yitzak Shamir. Even moderate Israelis were disappointed at the Palestinian attitude
toward the invasion of Kuwait. According to leftist legislator Dedi Zuckor, 'This is a major mistake, maybe a historic
mistake. We are now at least three years back.' In September
1990 Yossi Sarid of the liberal Citizens Rights Party declared,
'I no longer feel the need to meet with Palestinians . . . I didn't
expect to find them on friendly terms with such a dictator.
Maybe they haven't digested deeply the democratic rules of
the game.'[5] The following month, however, the Israelis would
inflict on the Palestinians an atrocity that would actually
increase their support for Saddam Hussein.

'Police opened fire on stone-throwing Palestinians at the Temple Mount in Jerusalem's Old City . . . The clash erupted after
the Palestinians threw stones from the Mount at thousands
of Jews worshipping below at the Wailing Wall,' read an
Associated Press bulletin on 8 October 1990. As reports came
in of the massacre of seventeen Palestinian worshippers at the
Temple Mount, the Western news media continued to claim
that the incident was caused by rock-throwing Arabs. Most
American and British newspapers carried the conclusion of

an official Israeli Temple Mount inquiry headed by former Mossad Chief Zvi Zamar, who placed the blame for the massacre squarely on the victims:

> It was evident from the rioters' actions, and certainly from the actions of the ringleaders, that there was a threat to the lives of the Border Police, the thousands of worshippers at the Western Wall and even the rioters themselves. The result was bloodshed.
>
> This was a terrible criminal act, committed by masses whipped up by the preachers using the loudspeaker, and led to the tragic chain of events . . . Temple Mount police, who were attacked by wild masses, were in danger of losing their lives.[6]

Gradually, however, there appeared a number of serious investigatory reports which showed that the official Israeli view of the massacre was untenable. One of the best was done by the journalist Michael Emery, who obtained tourist videotape which gave a revealing perspective of events. These tapes showed that, 'The Palestinians did not rain stones into the Wailing Wall until after the border police had fatally shot several Palestinians and wounded scores of others. By then the plaza had been cleared of worshippers.'[7]

In July 1991, Israeli Judge Ezra Kama ruled that at least some of the deaths at the Temple Mount were clearly unjustified and that the Border Police story that they opened fire out of fear of their lives was 'exaggerated and strange'. In particular Judge Kama criticized the use of live ammunition 'without reasonable need'.[8] However, he ruled that no charges could be brought against the police since it was not possible to determine who among them had fired the fatal shots.

The Temple Mount massacre greatly accelerated tensions between Palestinians and Israelis, particularly in Jerusalem. On 21 October 1990 an Arab stabbed three Israelis in the quiet Jerusalem neighborhood of Baka. The shooting two weeks later in the U.S.A. of Meir Kahane also increased fears, since his Israeli followers vowed retaliation. Jerusalem, which had been spared much of the violence of the *intifada*, became a battleground where neither Jew nor Arab felt safe. According to Palestinian Professor Sari Nusseibeh, whose family had lived in Jerusalem since the twelfth century, conditions in the Holy City during the autumn of 1990 were not good. He described the merger of East and West Jerusalem as artificial: 'The unity exists only as a state of force. The political wall today is far thicker than the wall that existed before 1967.'⁹

There was renewed apprehension in the occupied territories that the Israelis would use the Gulf crisis as a cover to launch a war against Jordan in which the Palestinians would be expelled from the West Bank. It was long-standing Israeli policy to expel Palestinians under cover of war. On 23 January 1979, Foreign Minister Moshe Dayan, who had been responsible for many expulsions during the 'War of Independence', warned the Palestinians that if they were rebellious, 'They would better remember and have in mind what happened with the Arab people in 1948 ... they find themselves, some of them, as refugees in Lebanon and this should serve as a lesson.'¹⁰

A hint of this was given by Israeli Housing Minister Ariel Sharon, who at the beginning of the Gulf crisis urged that 150 Palestinian leaders should be expelled from the occupied territories as retaliation for the communal violence. According to Sharon, 'The army should be ordered to eradicate: not to calm things down, soothe tensions, make the situation bearable or permit life to continue ... There should be one word, eradicate – the leadership should be deported.'¹² Of course many saw the deportation of the Palestinian leadership as the first step in the 'transfer' of the Palestinians from Israel, the West Bank and Gaza.

There was, however, enormous pressure by Washington on Israel during the Gulf crisis not to mount an attack on Iraq or Jordan. The Americans feared that any Israeli action would destroy the coalition which President Bush had assembled against Saddam Hussein. Future historians may discover how close Israel came to launching an attack on Jordan and Iraq. But forcible expulsion during a war or crisis is not the only or the most likely way the Israelis could push the Palestinians out of the last remnant of their homeland. More subtle pressure might be applied, as it was in Gaza in the late 1960s.

As we have seen, there were many threats of expulsion on the eve of the *intifada* in 1987. Such threats were again made during the uprising. Israeli leaders such as President Chaim Herzog and Defence Minister Rabin warned that if the *intifada* continued the Palestinians faced another 'tragedy', an obvious reference to 1948. According to the *Jerusalem Post* of 19 November 1989 Deputy Foreign Minister Benjamin Netanyahu told an audience at Bar Ilan University that the government had failed to exploit politically favourable situations to carry out 'large-scale' expulsions at times when 'the danger would have been relatively small'. Netanyahu mentioned the June 1989 Tiananmen Square massacre as a time when the attention of the international news media was diverted, creating an opportunity for expulsions. Netanyahu later denied making the remarks but the *Jerusalem Post* presented a tape recording of his speech.

On 9 November 1989 *Ha'aretz* carried out a survey by pollster Hanokh Smith which indicated that Israelis favouring 'transfer' had increased to 52 per cent, an all time high and up 14 per cent from his survey six months earlier. Palestinians obviously have good reason to fear mass expulsions. Rumours of 'transfer' are constantly circulating in the Arab world. On 9 January 1990 an Arab newspaper claimed that 'the PLO had a report on a plan endorsed by the US administration calling for the expulsion of half a million Palestinians from the occupied West Bank and Gaza Strip within two years'.[11] Such reports are taken seriously in the Arab countries.

In a 6 September 1990 *New York Times* leader, former Knesset member Uri Avenery warned that as a result of the Gulf crisis 'certain influential Israeli circles betray eagerness for an Israeli invasion of Jordan.' He noted that traditionally many right-wing Zionists have favoured the conquest not only of the West Bank but of the East Bank kingdom of Jordan as well. A war with Iraq and Jordan was also desired by many in Israel, noted Avenery, as a convenient opportunity to 'transfer' the West Bank Palestinians as well as to annex a slice of Jordan.

Indeed on 11 November 1990* in an interview with the Israeli newspaper, *Yerushalayim* General Revamin Ze'evi, leader of the extreme right-wing party Moledet, confirmed that during the Labour administrations of Levi Eshkol and Golda Meir in the late 1960s Palestinians were 'encouraged' to leave their homes:

> I want to reveal here for the first time that it was Eshkol who established a department in the Mossad and Golda inherited it from him. They called it – it no longer exists – the Transfer Department. At that time years ago, they paid 30,000 Arabs to move to other countries.

Ze'evi's revelation made it clear that the exodus from Gaza was the result of an Israeli policy that had special priority (in Israel important assignments are given to Mossad). Ze'evi mentions only those Palestinians who were paid to leave. Not surprisingly he neglects to mention the physical coercion that was used to force out many more Arabs from Gaza in the late 1960s. Using a combination of financial incentive and physical coercion along with a mass influx of Jewish settlers it would not be difficult for the Israelis to create a panic that could empty the occupied territories of most of its Arab population in a few years. The disappointment of Palestinians hopes during the Gulf crisis helped create the atmosphere for such an eventual but subtle mass expulsion.

On 15 January, the United States and its allies launched Operation Desert Storm. Against such an air bombardment, Iraq was all but defenceless. Saddam's only weapon was the grossly outdated SCUD missile which he used against Israel in the vain hope that drawing the Jewish state into the war would break up the coalition against Iraq. Armed only with conventional warheads and not chemical weapons, the SCUDs would take the life of only one Israeli, but would provide enormous propaganda benefit to the

---

*Four days before the first edition of this book, with its revelations about Palestinians who were coerced into leaving Gaza after the 1967 war, was published. (See Chapter 3.)

Jewish state, able to pose as the innocent victim of an Arab onslaught.

But the sight of Israelis scurrying to shelters during SCUD attacks gave the Palestinians cause for encouragement. When asked by an American journalist what he thought of the missile attacks, a Palestinian shopkeeper replied, 'We were happy. A little scared but mainly happy.' Support for Saddam increased enormously among the Palestinians. According to West Bank Professor Hanan Ashrawi, the Palestinians saw the Iraqi leader as 'an almost mythical figure from Arab culture and history.'[13]

The Israelis used the war as rationale for a crackdown on the Palestinian leadership in the occupied territories. Dr Sari Nusseibeh was arrested on charges of sending information to Iraq on the accuracy of SCUD missiles. Nussibeh was held in 'administrative detention' for six months under the British emergency regulations, which dated from before 1948 but were still used to imprison West Bank Palestinian activists. No evidence was presented that he helped Iraq; few doubted that he was arrested simply as a warning to the Palestinians in the occupied territory.

Another warning to the Palestinians was the appointment of General Ze'evi as Minister Without Portfolio in Shamir's cabinet. Placing in his cabinet the leader of the Moledet party, who advocated the 'transfer' of Palestinians out of Israel, West Bank and Gaza, made it clear that Shamir was using Israel's enhanced position and the disunity and weakness of the Arabs to take a much harder line. It was also a signal that any civil disobedience or other resistance by the Palestinians during the Gulf crisis or after would be dealt with severely. The Palestinians understood the warning. There was no widespread unrest in the territories up to the expulsion of Iraqi forces from Kuwait in late February 1991.

At first the Palestinians refused to believe the news of defeat. 'Every Palestinian knows that Saddam will emerge victorious. You see, he's got a secret weapon,' Abdul Majeed Shahnin told an American journalist.[14] But the extent of the Iraqi disaster soon became so obvious that the Palestinians could no longer hide the catastrophe from themselves. 'It's very difficult for Palestinians to admit that they were sold out,' said Mohammed Kamel, a merchant from Jerusalem's Old City. 'We are depressed and desperate because we have no friends or allies. This is the story of our lives.' In their frustration, some Palestinians criticized the Iraqi dictator. 'I stopped praying for Saddam because he turned out to be just another lying and cheating Arab leader who doesn't give a damn about us,' declared a Gaza resident.

The Gulf crisis was one more defeat for the Palestinians, who had already suffered more than their share of calamities. Even before 2 August 1991 the Palestinian cause was not faring well. The steam was running out of the *intifada* and the waves of Soviet immigrants were dashing hopes for a Palestinian homeland. During the Gulf crisis the occupied territories lost the substantial financial assistance of Kuwait and Saudi Arabia, as well as the money sent by Palestinians working in the Gulf. Even worse was the replacement of many Palestinians who worked in Israel by Soviet Jews. By early 1991, the occupied territories were an economic disaster area. According to the head of American Near East Refugee Aid, Peter Gubser, 'Conditions in the West Bank are as bad or worse than I have seen them, probably worse even than the aftermath of the 1967 war.'[15]

From the point of view of international diplomacy, the position of the Palestinians was just as bleak. Although the Arab masses had not supported the war against Saddam, since they feared American imperialism more than they feared Iraq, several Arab governments had joined President Bush's coalition. Many in America and Europe called for the resignation of Yasser Arafat for his presumed error of failing to denounce the Iraqi President. But the PLO chairman had no choice. The people of the occupied territories had placed their trust in Saddam. If Arafat had spoken against the Iraqi leader, the Palestinians in the West Bank and Gaza would have turned to the Islamic fundamentalists and other extremists who proclaimed Saddam as a saviour.

Professor Hanan Ashrawi of Beir Zeit University emerged as the most eloquent spokesperson for the Palestine cause.

She summarized accurately the position of her people in the wake of the Gulf disaster:

> Since 1988, the PLO has accepted the notion of a two-state solution, of Israel's right to exist as a nation state. The problem is that Israel won't acknowledge ours ... In August Iraq invaded Kuwait and promised the Palestinians, who had lost hope, the faint possibility of liberation. Many knew it would not work. But if they dreamed of an Arab liberator on a white horse, if, in their despair, in the absence of any semblance of a peace process, they clung to this reed, can you really blame them?[16]

In their desperation, the Palestinians were willing to grasp at any straw, even the ill-fated Soviet plotters who in August 1991 attempted to restore their country to its repressive past. Some inhabitants of the West Bank and Gaza hoped that if Gorbachev fell, they might regain Soviet support. After the anti-democratic coup failed, a prominent Gaza lawyer, Fraih Abu Middain, echoed a common Palestinian sentiment: 'The Soviet people must revolt again in order to be a superpower to complete with the United States.'[17] The Palestinians in the occupied territories had considerable nostalgia for the good old days when Soviet support for their cause helped to balance America's unconditional aid to Israel.

When the Soviet coup failed, once again, the Israelis made the most of the PLO miscalculation. Ariel Sharon blasted the Palestinians for the hopes they placed in the anti-democratic forces in the USSR – while neglecting to mention his own opposition to the democratic force in Israel. In August 1991 the Shamir government celebrated the PLO's renewed unpopularity by building more Jewish settlements in the Hebron area.

According to US Secretary of State James Baker, Jewish settlements in the occupied territories were the chief stumbling block to an Arab–Israeli peace agreement. But despite their refusal to make concessions on the issue of Jewish settlements in the occupied territories, the Israelis demanded a $10 billion 'loan guarantee' (de facto gift) from Congress to pay for the absorption of Soviet immigrants. In the summer of 1991 it seemed unlikely that the Bush Administration would be able to link the new demand for $10 billion (which is in addition to the usual $3 billion a year in aid to Israel) to an agreement by Shamir to limit West Bank settlements. Indeed Thome Dine of AIPAC and the chief of the Zionist lobby in Washington vowed 'linking the absorption guarantee to settlements on the peace process is something we will fight with all our being. "Despite a poll showing that that a clear majority of the American public opposed additional aid to Israel without a halt to settlement activity, it appeared probable that once again the Zionist lobby would prevail.

Many American Zionists believed that President Bush and Secretary of State Baker were diabolical enemies of Israel for daring to hint that America might decline to increase aid to the Jewis state. Extreme Zionists looked to Vice President Dan Quayle as their saviour, particularly in view of President Bush's poor health. Thus an editorial in the largest American Jewish religious newspaper actually claimed: 'Today Israelis are crying out because of the rough treatment Bush and Baker are according them. God will hearken to their cry and he may sent along Quayle.'[18] Clearly the incredibly well-organized Zionist lobby in America is Shamir's greatest asset in his drive to annex all of Eretz Yisrael.

But just as a Palestinian state is not inevitable, the total absorption of the occupied territories into Israel is also not certain. Clearly the process of annexation can be delayed until events in our fast-moving world create an opportunity for the Palestinians. Though the odds are against them, there are some hopeful signs for the people in the occupied territories.

Most important is the increased sense, created by the *intifada*, of Palestinian identity. The process of building a national consciousness has been going on for nearly a century; clearly it has received a giant boost from the uprising. But will the Palestinians become a nation without a homeland like the gypsies, the Armenians and, before 1948, the Jews? If so, history has shown that a nation can survive almost indefinitely without a country of its own. Even if they are completely expelled from historic Palestine, it is unlikely that after the great sacrifices of the *intifada* the Palestinians will disappear as a people. This is something for the Israeli leadership to consider. The annexation of the West Bank and Gaza by the Israelis, even with the expulsion of the indigenous population, will not end the problem. Israel may then face really serious terrorism and strife with its Arab neighbours. Perhaps the Israelis will come to realize that in the long run it is better to solve the problem by finding a way to satisfy Palestinian national aspirations.

Should the Palestinians accept the autonomy offered by Shamir? On 1 July 1990, Israeli TV indicated the provisions of the Israeli Prime Minister's offer to the Palestinians:

> Management by the Palestinians of the judicial system, authority in the spheres of agriculture, industry, trade and tourism; and Palestinian responsibility for finances, including tax collection in the territories, as well as for education, including the universities ... a strong police force to be operated by the Palestinians themselves, as well as the running of prisons.[19]

Might it be possible to use autonomy as a step towards the creation of a Palestinian entity? Many right-wing Israelis fear such a development, which is why they are opposed to autonomy. A Palestinian self-governing council might be a vehicle with which to fight for land and water rights and for a curtailment of Jewish settlements. But it is unlikely that a Palestinian West Bank council would be allowed sufficient latitude to challenge the occupation authorities. When nationalist West Bank mayors opposed the Israelis in the 1970s they were soon removed from office. The Israelis would surely dissolve any Palestinian council which demanded fundamentally important rights.

Some Palestinians whisper about the possibility of a PLO state composed of Jordan and the portion of the West Bank not yet settled by Jews. But such a scheme would be difficult to sell to the Israelis and many Arab governments, not to mention PLO hardliners. Most Palestinians are not yet ready for such an arrangement, but they may find it the only option once a large part of the West Bank is settled by Jews.

The key to Palestinian success is the prevention of an influx of Jewish settlers. The dilemma is that any violence directed against the settlements could be used as a pretext by the Israelis for mass expulsions. So far the Palestinians have used non-lethal force against the IDF, which has replied with lethal force. If demonstrations against settlements took place along with the bombing of construction equipment, the pictures of Gush Emunim fanatics shooting at Palestinian civilians could be excellent propaganda and could create pressure against the continuation of the settlements. Harassing the settlements without killing Jews is the best tactic remaining to the *intifada*.

In the final analysis, however, Palestinian success depends on increased support from the Arab world. Despite a valiant effort, Palestinians cannot win by themselves. If the pace of Soviet emigration continues to increase, the Arab countries may come to realize that Israel is becoming a regional superpower that threatens to dominate the whole area. After the Soviet emigrants are absorbed it will be time to attract American Jews to Israel, which will complete the Zionist enterprise. A higher standard of living will, however, be needed to attract affluent American Jews. This might be achieved by 'high-tech' industries or by Israeli control of the Arab oil fields.

Israel is perfecting a system for protection against nuclear armed ballistic missiles before the Arabs even have nuclear weapons, and Israel's technical lead over the Arabs is likely to increase in the next century. But the united opposition of the Arab world might still be a formidable obstacle to Israel. The US may be willing to protect Arab oil from Iraq, but would it be reliable against Israeli penetration? The Arab realization that Hebron and Nablus are the first lines of defence for Riyad and Abu Dhabi offers the best chance for the victory of the Palestinians.

A Guide to Sources

The United Nations Archives in New York, which operates under a twenty-year access rule, is a major source of information for the early phase of the occupation. There are important records for the more recent period, including many interviews, in the files of the UN Commission on the Occupied Territories which are kept in the United Nations Library. The Jimmy Carter Presidential Center in Atlanta, Georgia, contains documents on the Camp David negotiation's and the role of the Zionist lobby in the formulation of Carter's Middle East policy.

Anyone interested in the Israeli occupation cannot do without the BBC *Summary of World Broadcasts* and the Foreign Broadcast Information Service *Daily Reports* issued by the US government. These two contain over 100,000 pages of documentation on this subject for the period since 1967. I have supplemented these sources with Palestinian, British and American newspapers. Of particular importance is the Israeli press, which frequently contains candid articles.

There are several multi-volume document collections covering the years of the occupation. The most comprehensive of these is the *International Documents on Palestine* which was published annually by the Palestine Institute for the years up to 1981. Most of the document collections published in Israel include material from Israeli-only sources. The United Nations has published much useful material, especially the pamphlets of its division on Palestine Rights.

The bibliography on the occupation is vast, reflecting the wide interest in the subject. Many of the works, however, are based solely on newspaper articles or quotes from a familiar group of recurring interviewees. Among the best-researched books are Alain Gresh, *The PLO: The Struggle Within*, Mark Heller, *A Palestinian State: Implications for Israel*, Donald Neff, *Warriors for Jerusalem*, Ari Plascov, *The Palestinian Refugees in Jordan*, Joel Migdal, *Palestinian Society and Politics* and William Quandt, *Camp David, Peacemaking and Politics*.

10

Abbreviations

Abbreviations for Archival Sources, Document Collections and Reports:

AIO — *Arabs Under Israeli Occupation* (Annual)

BBC — British Broadcasting Corporation, *Summary of World Broadcasts*

DIPC — *Documents on the Israeli-Palestinian Conflict 1967–1983*

FBIS — United States Foreign Broadcast Information Service, *Daily Report*

GA/OR — *United Nations General Assembly: Official Record*

IDP — *International Documents on Palestine*

IFR — *Israel's Foreign Relations 1947–1974*

JCL — Jimmy Carter Presidential Library (Atlanta, Georgia)

JPS — *Journal of Palestine Studies* (Document and Source Material sections)

KR — *Karp Report*

MER — *Middle East Record*

MERIP — *Middle East Research and Information Project*

RWBJ — *Resistance of the Western Banks of the Jordan*

UNA — United Nations Archives (New York)

UND — Unpublished documents, committee reports and interviews, UN Library (New York)

UNDPR — United Nations Division for Palestinian Rights

WBDP — *West Bank Data Base Project*

NOTES

Prologue

1. Michael Palumbo, *The Palestinian Catastrophe* (London: Quartet Books, 1989).
2. Mark A. Heller, *A Palestinian State: Implications for Israel* (Cambridge, Mass: Harvard University Press, 1983), p. 28.

1. *The Six-Day War*

1. On the Independence Eve anniversary celebration, see *Jerusalem Post*, 6 August 1976; Ian Lustick, *For the Land and the Lord* (New York: Council on Foreign Relations, 1988), pp. 34–36; David Schnall, *Beyond the Green Line* (New York: Praeger & Co., 1984), pp. 38–9; *Ha'aretz*, 4 April 1986.
2. David Hirst, *The Gun and the Olive Branch* (London: Faber & Faber, 1984), p. 216.
3. IDP (1967), doc. 19.
4. Lustick, *op. cit.* pp. 29–34; Shlomo Aveneri, *The Making of Modern Zionism* (New York: Basic Books, 1981), pp. 187–8.
5. Schnall, *op. cit.* p. 19.
6. Lustick, *op. cit.* p. 36.
7. *Ha'aretz*, 4 April 1986.
8. UNA, DAGI/2.2.5.2.0, box 39.
9. Schnall, *op. cit.* p. 39.
10. Palumbo, *op. cit.* p. 15.

11. Taysir Jbara, *The Palestinian Leader Hajj Amin Al-Husayni* (Princeton, NJ: Kington Press Inc., 1985), p. 189; Tom Segev, *1949: The First Israelis* (New York: Basic Books, 1986), p. 20.
12. GA/OR, 6th session supplement, no. 16A, p. 1.
13. GA/OR, 5th session supplement, no. 19, p. 13.
14. Ari Plascov, *The Palestinian Refugees in Jordan 1948–1957* (London: Frank Cass & Co., 1981), p. 46.
15. GA/OR, 7th session supplement, no. 13, p. 48.
16. GA/OR, 6th session supplement, no. 16, p. 5.
17. Joel S. Migdal, *Palestinian Society and Politics* (Princeton, NJ: Princeton University Press, 1980), p. 57; Plascov, *op. cit.* p. 66.
18. Plascov, *op. cit.* p. 36.
19. Migdal, *op. cit.* p. 39; Don Peretz, *The West Bank, History, Politics, Society* (London: Westview Press, 1986), p. 33.
20. Plascov, *op. cit.* p. 37.
21. Migdal, *op. cit.* p. 181.
22. Raymonda Tawil, *My Home, My Prison* (London: Zed Books, 1983), p. 60.
23. Clinton Bailey, *Jordan's Palestine Challenge* (Boulder, Colo: Westview Press, 1984), p. 8.
24. Tawil, *op. cit.* p. 63.
25. GA/OR, 9th session supplement, no. 17, p. 13.
26. Paul Cossali & Clive Robson, *Stateless in Gaza* (London: Zed Books, 1986), p. 12.
27. Alan Hart, *Arafat: Terrorist or Peacemaker* (London: Sidgwick & Jackson, 1986), p. 95. According to a 1959 UNRWA report, the refugee diet was 1500 calories per day, consisting of flour, rice, sugar, pulses and fats, with small supplements for babies, pregnant women and sick children. GA/OR, 14th session supplement, no. 14, p. 3.
28. Cossali & Robson, *op. cit.* p. 13.
29. *Ibid.* p. 12.
30. Hart, *op. cit.* p. 96. Egyptian control of the refugees was severe. 'Travel outside the area is restricted. Applications must be approved by the Military Governor and

in only a few instances has permission been granted.'
GA/OR, 7th session supplement, no. 13, p. 48.
31. Hirst, *op. cit.* p. 198.
32. Cossali & Robson, *op. cit.* pp. 17–8.
33. GA/OR, 11th session supplement, no. 14A, pp. 3–4.
34. Hart, *op. cit.* p. 117.
35. Cossali & Robson, *op. cit.* p. 16.
36. GA/OR, 12th session supplement, no. 14, p. 47.
37. Cossali & Robson, *op. cit.* p. 22.
38. Hart, *op. cit.* p. 171. In another interview, Khaled Hassan spoke of the aim of the early PLO: 'We wanted to create a climate and the atmosphere of the spirit of struggle in the Arab nation, so that they can have the will of fighting and I am sorry to say that we failed.' Helen Cobban, *The Palestine Liberation Organisation* (Cambridge University Press, 1984), p. 33.
39. Tawil, *op. cit.* p. 84.
40. Donald Neff, *Warriors for Jerusalem* (Brattleboro, Vt: Amana Books, 1988), p. 50.
41. Yoram Perri, *Between Battles and Ballots* (Cambridge University Press, 1983), pp. 58–9.
42. Charles de Gaulle, *Memoirs of Hope* (New York: Simon & Schuster, 1971), p. 265.
43. Ezer Weizman, *On Eagles Wings* (London: Weidenfeld & Nicholson, 1976), p. 45.
44. Neff, *op. cit.* p. 45.
45. Hart, *op. cit.* p. 234; Neff, *op. cit.* p. 33.
46. Hirst, *op. cit.* p. 211.
47. On 1 June 1967 Ahmed Shuqayri addressed an audience in Amman: 'We do not want to throw the Jews into the sea. We are against Israel as a state not against the Jews as Jews. Palestinian Jews can stay in Palestine and the same applies to Jews from other countries.' IDP (1967), doc. 334; see also doc. 432.
48. Moshe Dayan, *Story of my Life* (New York: Warner Books, 1976), p. 404.
49. Cossali & Robson, *op. cit.* p. 84.
50. Dayan, *Story of My Life, op. cit.* p. 446.
51. Neff, *op. cit.* p. 284.

52. BBC:ME/2494/A12. A similar report was broadcast a few days later. 'A Foreign Ministry spokesman has denied as unfounded the fabricated reports regarding the expulsion of the Arab population from the Western Bank. The spokesman stressed that there was no pressure on Arab citizens in the area under the military government to leave their place of residence.' BBC:ME/2495/A20.
53. UND:S/8158.
54. P. Dodd & H. Barakat, *River Without Bridges* (Beirut: Institute for Palestine Studies, 1968), p. 40. See also Palumbo, *op. cit.* pp. 47–57.
55. UND:A/AC145/RT71, p. 15.
56. *Ibid*
57. Hirst, *op. cit.* p. 227.
58. *Ibid.* p. 225. A petition by the people of the Latroun area to the UN states: 'The occupation forces ordered us to evacuate our homes and villages in the early hours of the morning, without allowing us even a few minutes to supply ourselves with provisions for the road if only for small children'. IDP (1968), doc. 375.
59. Hirst, *op. cit.* p. 225.
60. A UN report of September 1967 notes that the Latroun villagers were not permitted to return. UND:A/6497, IDP (1968), doc. 375.
61. BBC:ME/2494/A19.
62. BBC:ME/2493/A12.
63. BBC:ME/2493/A9.
64. UNA:DAGI/2.5, box 6.
65. BBC:ME/2508/A7. See also Fred J. Khouri, *The Arab–Israeli Dilemma* (Syracuse, NY: Syracuse University Press, 1985), pp. 149–161.
66. UNA:DAGI/2.5, box 6.
67. *New York Times*, 8 August 1967.
68. UNA:DAGI/2.5, box 6.
69. BBC:ME/2548/A6.
70. UNA:DAGI/2.5, box 6.
71. UND:A/6797.
72. BBC:ME/2553/A1; ME/2548/A7; ME/2551/A2. An appeal to the Israelis by the UN Secretary-General, asking

that 'in view of humanitarian considerations' they reconsider their refusal to extend the deadline, had no effect. See letter of 24 August 1967. UNA:DAGI/2.5, box 6.
73. BBC:ME/2555/A3.
74. Dayan, *Story of My Life, op. cit.* p. 481.
75. UND:A/6713.
76. MER (1968), p. 445.
77. FBIS V, 9 August 1968, H1.
78. Neff, *op. cit.* p. 298.
79. MER, p. 276; IDP (1967), doc. 92.
80. DI-PC, p. 17.
81. Neff, *op. cit.* p. 328.
82. DI-PC, p. 213.
83. Sydney D. Bailey, *The Making of Resolution 242* (Boston, Mass: Martinus Nijhoff, 1985), p. 155.
84. UND: S/8247.
85. DI-PC, p. 138.

2. *Jerusalem the Golden*

1. Dayan, *Story of My Life, op. cit.* p. 464.
2. Meron Benvenisti, *Jerusalem* (Minneapolis: University of Minnesota, 1976), pp. 108–9.
3. Dayan, *Story of My Life, op. cit.* p. 465.
4. BBC:ME/2505/A5.
5. RWBJ, doc. 2; Benvenisti, *op. cit.* pp. 284–5.
6. RWBJ, doc. 26; Benvenisti, *op. cit.* pp. 290–1.
7. IDP (1967), doc. 124. See also docs. 123, 140.
8. IDP (1968), doc. 340. Jerusalem Arabs also protested the 'Legal and Administrative Regulations Act of 1968' which mandated that every professional man licensed under Jordanian law must obtain a new Israeli license. Some 5000 businessmen, professionals and artisans were affected by this regulation. IDP (1969), doc. 382.
9. IDP (1968), docs. 278, 301, 345; BBC:ME/2749/A13; FBIS, 15 July 1968, v, H7; 31 August 1970, H9; Benvenisti, *op. cit.* pp. 233–55; David Smith, *Prisoners of God* (London: Quartet Books, 1988), pp. 71–6; Rafik Halabi, *The West Bank Story* (New York: Harcourt Brace

Jovanovich, 1985), p. 42.

10. BBC:ME/2506/A6.
11. Geoffrey Aronson, *Creating Facts* (Washington DC: Institute for Palestine Studies, 1987), p. 21.
12. Dayan, *Story of My Life, op. cit.* p. 463.
13. Dayan expressed a desire not to have 'control over the population but over topography'. MER 1967, p. 278.
14. *Maariv*, 30 April 1968.
15. IDP, 1968, doc. 159.
16. Aronson, *op. cit.* p. 15.
17. IDP, 1976, doc. 163.
18. Gershon R. Kieval, *Party Politics in Israel and the Occupied Territories* (Westport, Conn: Greenwood Press, 1983), p. 9.
19. FBIS, 1 July 1970, v, H1.
20. Uri Avenery, *My Friend, the Enemy* (Westport, Conn: Lawrence Hill & Co., 1986), p. 84.
21. Sheila Ryan, 'Plans to regularize the occupation', *Occupation Israel Over Palestine*, Naseer Aruri (ed), (London: Zed Books, 1984), p. 352.
22. *Maariv*, 6 November 1968.
23. Kieval, *op. cit.* p. 75.
24. *Maariv*, 2 February 1973.
25. Dayan, *Story of My Life, op. cit.* pp. 479–80; MER 1967, p. 284.
26. Jan Metzger, *This is Our Land* (London: Zed Books, 1983), p. 89.
27. FBIS, 20 November 1968, v, H2; *Jerusalem Post*, 19 November 1968.
28. Metzger, *op. cit.* pp. 92–3.
29. Aronson, *op. cit.* p. 26.
30. Hirst, *op. cit.* p. 244.
31. Metzger, *op. cit.* p. 106.
32. *Ibid.* p. 116.
33. *Ibid.* p. 96.
34. MER (1967), p. 283; RWBS, pp. 65–6; Munir Fasheh, 'Impact on education' in Aruri, *op. cit.* p. 301.
35. UNA:DAG1/2.5, box 9, 'Treatment of population' file.
36. Dayan, *Story of My Life, op. cit.* p. 482.

37. Hirst, *op. cit.* pp. 249–50; Metzger, *op. cit.* p. 69.
38. IDP (1969), doc. 436; Hirst, *op. cit.* p. 249.
39. Metzger, *op. cit.* pp. 70–1; Hirst, *op. cit.* p. 248.
40. National Lawyers' Guild, *Treatment of Palestinians in Israeli Occupied West Bank and Gaza* (New York: National Lawyers' Guild, 1978), p. 116.
41. Tawil, *op. cit.* p. 157.
42. Thomas Friedman, *From Beirut to Jerusalem* (New York: Farrar, Strauss & Giroux, 1989), p. 260; Halabi, *op. cit.* p. 144; MER (1968), p. 462.
43. BBC:ME/2747/A2.
44. Friedman, *op. cit.* p. 261.
45. BBC:ME/2501/A15.
46. MER (1967), p. 288.
47. BBC:ME/2748/A5.
48. BBC:ME/4754/A12. In January 1977 Rabin stated in a speech: 'There is a challenge here for all in the settlement movement who want to renew, expand and establish defensible borders for the State of Israel'. Anne Mosley Lesch, 'Israeli settlements in the occupied territories 1967–1977', JPS (Autumn 1977), p. 34.
49. WBDP, p. 52; JPS (Autumn 1977), p. 26.

3. *The Gaza Exodus*

1. UNA:DAG 1/2.5, box 9, 'Treatment of population' file. A.L. Geaney report of 13 January 1968.
2. *Ibid.* Geaney report of 4 January 1968.
3. *Ibid.* Geaney report of 13 January 1968. This was common practice during Israeli raids on villages and refugee camps; Hirst, *op. cit.* pp. 249–50.
4. UNA:DAG 1/2.5, box 9, 'Treatment of population' file. A.L. Geaney report of 13 January 1968.
5. *Ibid.* Geaney report of 4 January 1968. Statement by mukhtars, 17 January 1968.
6. UNA:DAG 1/2.5, box 9, 'Jabalia' file, 13 July 1968. Statement by two mukhtars.
7. *Ibid.* Petition of 12 July 1968.
8. *Ibid.* Statement of two mukhtars, 13 July 1968.

9. *Ibid.* Petition of Legal Consul, 20 July 1968.
10. UND: S/1117.
11. UNA:DAG 1/2.5, box 9, 'Jabalia' file. Michelmore to Bunche, 29 July 1968.
12. Cossali & Robson, *op. cit.* p. 128.
13. FBIS, 29 July 1968, v, DI.
14. UNA:DAG 1/2.5, box 9, 'Jabalia' file. Correspondence of 29 July 1968.
15. FBIS, 5 August 1968, v, H8.
16. UNA:DAG 1/2.5, box 9, 'Jabalia' file. Letter of 25 July 1968.
17. UND:S/8700. At his meeting with the Gaza mukhtars on 25 July Dayan made it clear that the Israelis had no intention of leaving Gaza. He told them: 'the present situation will last a long time'. FBIS 28 July 1968, v, H3.
18. FBIS, 5 August 1968, v, H9.
19. Sara Roy, *The Gaza Strip Survey* (Jerusalem: West Bank Data Project, 1986), p. 6.
20. *New York Times*, 6 July, 11 August 1967.
21. *Ha'aretz*, 25 August 1968.
22. 'Families that had never had contact with the PLO, families that perhaps had been victims of terror themselves'. Ariel Sharon, *Warrior* (New York: Simon & Schuster, 1989), p. 259.
23. BBC:ME/3592/A4.
24. Sara Roy, 'Gaza Strip: critical effects of the occupation' in *Arab Studies Quarterly* (Winter 1988), p. 73.
25. Cossali & Robson, *op. cit.* p. 129.
26. UNA:DAG 1/2.5, box 9, 'Treatment of population' file.
27. FBIS, 24 July 1968, v, H5.
28. Cossali & Robson, *op. cit.* p. 129.
29. Sharon, *op. cit.* p. 250; Bard E. O'Niel *Armed Struggle in Palestine* (Boulder, Colo: Westminster Press, 1978), p. 92.
30. BBC:ME/3587/A7; ME/3583/A18; O'Niel, *op. cit.* p. 93.
31. BBC:ME/3614/A3; O'Niel, *op. cit.* pp. 94–5.
32. BBC:ME/3721/A8; ME/3705/A6; ME/3645/A4; O'Niel, *op. cit.* p. 96.
33. Cossali & Robson, *op. cit.* pp. 127–8; Sharon, *op. cit.* pp. 252–4.

34. UND:A/8383.
35. IDP (1971), doc. 216.
36. IDP (1971), doc. 411; O'Niel, *op. cit.* p. 95.
37. Sharon, *op. cit.* p. 260; IDP 1971, doc. 217.
38. Roy, *op. cit.* p. 68.

4. The Emergence of the PLO

1. BBC:ME/4749, report of 7 November 1974.
2. Hirst, *op. cit.* p. 334; Kurt Waldheim, *In the Eye of the Storm* (Bethesda, Md: Adler & Adler, 1985), pp. 193–4.
3. IDP (1974), doc. 9.
4. Hart, *op. cit.* p. 409.
5. IDP (1974), doc. 10.
6. BBC:ME/4757/A3, report of 16 November 1974.
7. Tawil, *op. cit.* p. 186.
8. AIO 1974, pp. 13–14; BBC:ME/4758/A3; ME/4759/A2; ME/4750/A3; ME/4762/A6.
9. BBC:ME/4761/A3.
10. FBIS, 2 June 1972, v, D2.
11. BBC:ME/4088/A3.
12. MER 1969–70, pp. 220–2.
13. IDP (1972), doc. 187; Bailey, *op. cit.* p. 63.
14. Shaul Mishal, *The PLO Under Arafat; Between Gun and Olive Branch* (New Haven: Yale University Press, 1986), p. 102. The mayor of Nablus, Hatem Abu Gazaheh, stated: 'Anything Arab is better than Israel.' James Lund, *Hussein of Jordan* (New York: William Morrow, 1989), p. 152.
15. IDP (1972), doc. 59.
16. JPS, vol. 1, no. 3 (Spring 1972), doc. 10.
17. IDP (1972), doc. 177.
18. Aronson, *op. cit.* p. 48; John Metzger and Maartin Orth, *This Land is Ours* (London: Zed Books, 1983), pp. 155–6.
19. Alain Gresh, *The PLO: The Struggle Within* (London: Zed Books, 1988), p. 88.
20. JPS, vol. 3, no. 1 (Autumn 1973), doc. 1.

21. IDP (1973), doc. 264.
22. Tawil, *op. cit.* p. 180.
23. Aronson, *op. cit.* p. 52; Emile Sahliyeh, *In Search of Leadership* (Washington DC: Brookings Institute, 1988), pp. 57–8.
24. FBIS, 8 June 1972, v, H1.
25. Aronson, *op. cit.* p. 52.
26. BBC:ME/4747/A3. Report of 6 November 1974.
27. UND:A/AC 145/RT59, p. 48.
28. Felicia Langer, *With My Own Eyes* (London: Itaca Press, 1975), p. 160.
29. UND:A/AC 145/RT59, p. 48.
30. Langer, *op. cit.* pp. 161–2.
31. Metzger and Orth, *op. cit.* p. 164.
32. Gresh, *op. cit.* p. 17.
33. Hart, *op. cit.* p. 275.
34. Gresh, *op. cit.* p. 48.
35. Abu Iyad, *op. cit.* p. 139.
36. JPS, vol. 3, no. 1 (Autumn 1973), doc. 4, p. 197.
37. Gresh, *op. cit.* p. 142.
38. *Ibid.* p. 164.
39. *Ibid.*
40. IDP (1974), p. 419.
41. BBC:ME/4601/A8. Report of 16 May 1974.
42. 'Time passed with agonizing slowness and as the 6 pm deadline approached when the terrorists warned they would blow up the building with themselves and the children, the government gave permission for our soldiers to break into the school.' Dayan, Story of My Life, *op. cit.* p. 716. Dayan fails to mention the Israeli promise to free the prisoners.
43. BBC:ME/4003/A6. Report of 16 May 1974.
44. BBC:ME/4603/A5. Report of 16 May 1974.
45. Avenery, *op. cit.* p. 62; Hirst, *op. cit.* pp. 299–300.
46. 'According to Israel Defence Forces figures, the total number of civilians killed or wounded in terrorist attacks in Israel and the occupied territories since 1967 is less than the annual average of traffic casualties.' Heller, *op. cit.* p. 140.

47. Hart, *op. cit.* p. 17.
48. Friedman, *op.cit.* pp. 408–9.
49. IDP (1974), doc. 217.
50. IDP (1974), doc. 336.
51. DIPC, p. 151.
52. BBC:ME/4622/A2; IDP (1974), doc. 246; Gresh, *op. cit.* p. 168.
53. Yehoshafat Harkabi, *Arab Strategies and Israel's Response* (New York: The Free Press, 1977), p. 38.
54. Iyad, *op. cit.* p. 14.
55. IDP (1974), doc. 249. For the PFLP statement announcing its withdrawal from the PLO Executive Committee on 26 September 1974, see DIPC, pp. 160–5.
56. MERIP report no. 32, November 1974.
57. *New Outlook*, February/March 1976.
58. Avenery, *op. cit.* pp. 43–4; Gresh, *op. cit.* p. 200.
59. IDP (1975), doc. 261.
60. IDP (1975), doc. 316.
61. BBC:ME/5135/A3; ME/5136/A5.
62. UND:A/AC 145 RT82, p. 4.
63. *Ibid.* p. 10.
64. Metzger and Orth, pp. 170–1.
65. UND:A/AC 145/RT71, p. 10.
66. Aronson, *op. cit.* p. 56. The PNC reserves 188 seats for Palestinians from the occupied territories, but this number is not counted in the quorum. Sami Mussalam, *The PLO: The Palestine Liberation Organization* (Brattleboro, Vt: Amana Books, 1988), p. 18.
67. DP-IC, p. 183.
68. Hart, *op. cit.* p. 381.

5. Camp David

1. BBC:ME/5517/A2.
2. Eitan Haber, *Menachem Begin* (New York: Delacourt Press, 1970), p. 287.
3. *Ibid.* p. 288.
4. BBC:ME/5517/A3.

5. Jimmy Carter, *Keeping Faith: Memoirs of a President* (New York: Bantam Books, 1982), p. 288.
6. IDP (1977), doc. 99.
7. Samuel Katz, *Battleground: Fact and Fantasy in Palestine* (New York: Bantam Books, 1973), p. 205.
8. *Ibid.* p. 224.
9. Aronson, *op. cit.* p. 69.
10. Moshe Dayan, *Breakthrough: a Personal Account of the Egyptian–Israeli Peace Negotiations* (New York: Alfred Knopf, 1981), p. 1.
11. AFP 1977–80, doc. 259.
12. JCL:WHCF/CO-35, 12 June 1978. Report by Robert Goldman of the Ford Foundation.
13. William Quandt, *Camp David: Peacemaking and Politics* (Washington DC: The Brookings Institution Press, 1986), p. 46.
14. AFP 1977–80, doc. 260.
15. AFP 1977–80, doc. 261.
16. JCL:WHCF/CO-36.
17. JCL:WHCF/CO-34.
18. JCL:Press/71.
19. IFP, vol. 4, p. 51.
20. Quandt, *op. cit.* p. 83.
21. JCL:WHCF/CO-34.
22. AFP 1977–80, doc. 270.
23. BBC:ME/5631/A6.
24. JCL:WHCF/CO-34.
25. Ezer Weizman, *Battle for Peace* (New York: Bantam Books, 1981), p. 287.
26. AFP 1977–80, doc. 271.
27. Aronson, *op. cit.* p. 78.
28. Ismail Fahmy, *Negotiations for Peace in the Middle East* (Baltimore, Mass: John Hopkins University Press, 1983), p. 240.
29. BBC:ME/5664/A13.
30. AFP 1977–80, doc. 274.
31. Aronson, *op. cit.* p. 174.
32. Martin Gilbert, *The Arab–Israeli Conflict* (London: Weidenfeld & Nicholson, 1974), p. 11.

33. AFP 1977–80, doc. 282. In a speech the following week, Begin noted: 'The world must know that any agreement we may sign will not include the term "self-determination" or a "Palestinian state" . . . The Arabs of Eretz Yisrael will gain self-rule – something they had not gained under the Turkish–British regime.' FBIS, 6 January 1978, v, N3.
34. Weizman, *op. cit.* p. 136.
35. Quandt, *op. cit.* pp. 247–54; Cyrus Vance, *Hard Choices* (New York: Simon & Schuster, 1988), p. 245.
36. JCL: Moses, box 4. Press conference 358.
37. AFP 1977–80, doc. 293.
38. JCL: Rafshoon File. Document declassified at my request.
39. BBC:ME/5920/A12.
40. FBIS, 19 September 1978, v, N15.
41. Zbigniew Brzezinski, *Power and Principle* (New York: Farrar, Strauss & Giroux, 1983), p. 258.
42. FBIS, 19 September 1978, v, N22.
43. FBIS, 1 November 1978, v, N2.
44. *Ibid.* N10.
45. BBC:ME/6040/A1.
46. JCL: Moses, box 11. Letter of 2 August.
47. JCL: Moses, box 11. Letter of 3 August.
48. JCL: WHCF/CO-36.
49. BBC:ME/6944/A4–7.
50. BBC:ME/6945/A1.
51. AFP 1982, doc. 318.
52. *New York Times*, 3 September 1982.

6. *The Village League*

1. FBIS, 14 August 1981, v, I1; Hirst, *op. cit.* p. 377; Aronson, *op. cit.* pp 245–7.
2. FBIS, 17 August 1981, part v, I1.
3. Sharon, *op. cit.* pp. 551, 553.
4. FBIS, 26 August 1981, v, I4.
5. Aronson, *op. cit.* pp. 238, 253.
6. BBC:ME/6988/A6.
7. Aronson, *op. cit.* p. 254.
8. BBC:ME/6869/A8.

9. *Commentary*, May 1981.
10. FBIS, 23 October 1981, part v, I6.
11. BBC:ME/6872/A11; FBIS, 2 November 1981, v, I9.
12. BBC:ME/6881/A4.
13. BBC:ME/6884/A7: AIO 1981 pp. 81–2; Aronson, *op. cit.* p. 260.
14. UND:A/AC 145/RT343, p. 2.
15. Aruri, *op. cit.* p. 378.
16. BBC:ME/6988/A9.
17. AIO (1981), pp. 75–7; Hirst, *op. cit.* p. 390.
18. AIO (1981), p. 78.
19. Aronson, *op. cit.* p. 249.
20. AIO (1981), pp. 79–80; Aruri, *op. cit.* p. 250.
21. *Al Hamrishar*, 11 January 1982.
22. AIO (1981), pp. 80–1.
23. FBIS, 25 November 1981, v, I6; BBC:ME/6890/A5.
24. UND:A/AC 145/RT342, p. 4.
25. BBC:ME/6988/A9.
26. BBC:ME/6894/A7.
27. BBC:ME/7144/A5; ME/7198/A12.
28. BBC:ME/6977/A2.
29. UND:A/AC 145/RT338/Add. 1, p. 2.
30. BBC:ME/6990/A9.
31. BBC:ME/6977. Because of Village League activity the Jordanians promised to reduce their development, which Mustafa Dudin claimed would be replaced by Israeli funds. FBIS, 15 March 1982, v, I2.
32. *Ha'aretz*, 15 March 1982.
33. *Ha'aretz*, 9 July 1982; Hirst, *op. cit.* p. 403.
34. FBIS, 21 June 1982, v, I9.
35. FBIS, 16 June 1982, v, I6.
36. *Yediot Ahronot*, 18 June 1982. In a later speech, Sharon claimed that he had 'already felt the change in the atmosphere and that he believed we would be able to reach the point where a dialogue with the Palestinian Arabs would become a normal process.' BBC:ME/7116/A5.
37. Aruri, *op. cit.* pp. 386–7.
38. BBC:ME/7196/A6.
39. *Ha'aretz*, 7 February 1988.

7. *The Settlements*

1. *US News and World Report*, 4 April 1988. 'Fifty years ago our opponents argued about Jaffa. Today, they argue with us about [the West Bank Settlement] Alfei Menashe. In another fifty years they will argue with us about Amman [capital of Jordan]. That's the way it is.' Levinger interview in David Grossman, *The Yellow Wind* (New York: Farrar, Strauss & Giroux, 1988), p. 49.

2. David Smith, *Prisoners of God* (London: Quartet Books, 1988), p. 43. 'You can compromise about unimportant things, but you can't divide your Bible and you can't divide your holy earth. To compromise our home, a home that belongs not only to us but also to God, is abnormal! Even if they wanted to compromise, we can't.' Levinger interview in Walter Reich, *A Stranger in My House* (New York: Holt, Rinehart & Winston, 1984), pp. 16–17.

3. *Jewish Week*, 22 July 1988.

4. Lustick, *op. cit.* p. 121.

5. Reich, *op. cit.* p. 18.

6. David J. Schnall, *Beyond the Green Line* (New York: Praeger, 1984), p. 24. 'The Jewish national renaissance is more important than democracy. Democracy can no more vote away Zionism or settlement than it can decide that people should stop breathing.' Levinger interview in Smith, *op. cit.* p. 43.

7. Lustick, *op. cit.* p. 120.

8. John and Janet Wallach, *Still Small Voices* (New York: Harcourt Brace Jovanovich, 1989), p. 28.

9. *Ibid.* p. 37.

10. Halabi, *op. cit.* p. 215. For the Gush programme, see DIPC, pp. 134–6.

11. Tzvi Yehuda Kook, 'Zionism in biblical prophecy' in Yosef Tirosh (ed), *Religious Zionism* (Jerusalem: World Zionist Organization, 1975).

12. Lily Weissbrod, 'Gush Emmunim ideology: from religious doctrine to political action', *Middle Eastern Studies*, 18 (July 1982), p. 296.

13. Rosemary & Herman J. Reuther, *The Wrath of Jonah*

(New York: Harper & Row, 1989), p. 179.
14. Lustick, *op. cit.* p. 95.
15. *Ibid.* p. 124.
16. Amos Oz, *In the Land of Israel* (New York: Random House, 1984), p. 61.
17. Yeoshafat Harkabi, *Israel's Fateful Hour* (New York: Harper & Row, 1988), p. 149.
18. Lustick, *op. cit.* p. 76.
19. Harkabi, *op. cit.* p. 153.
20. David K. Shipler, *Arab and Jew* (New York: Viking Penguin, 1986), p. 236.
21. Lustick, *op. cit.* p. 134. From the very earliest days of Jewish settlement in Palestine, right up to the 1948 war, there were Zionist plans to evacuate the local Arab population by peaceful means if possible, by force if necessary. See Palumbo, *op. cit.*
22. Lustick, *op. cit.* p. 135.
23. *Ibid.* p. 106.
24. Oz, *op. cit.* p. 59.
25. Harold Fisch, *The Zionist Revolution* (New York: St Martin's Press, 1978), pp. 151–7.
26. Lustick, *op. cit.* p. 187.
27. Menachem Begin, *The Revolt* (New York: Nash Publishers, 1979), p. xxiii.
28. Lustick, *op. cit.* p. 37.
29. Sharon, *op. cit.* pp. 356–7.
30. BBC:ME/6146/A7.
31. Aronson, *op. cit.* p. 236.
32. UND: A/34/605-S/13582.
33. WBDP, p. 52.
34. *Ibid.*
35. Lustick, *op. cit.* p. 48; Aronson, *op. cit.* pp. 108–11; Halabi, *op. cit.* pp. 217–22.
36. WBDP, p. 31.
37. IDP (1979), no. 227.
38. WBDP, p. 30.
39. Smith, *op. cit.* p. 77.
40. WBDP, p. 32.
41. WBDP, p. 35.

42. Smith, *op. cit.* p. 165; Aronson, *op. cit.* pp. 88–90.
43. Smith, *op. cit.* p. 107.
44. UNDPR: 'Israeli policy on the West Bank water resources', pp. 10–11; David Kahan, *Agriculture and Water Resources in the West Bank and Gaza 1967–87* (Boulder, Colo: Westview Press, 1987), p. 113; Aruri, *op. cit.* p. 127.
45. Meron Benvenisti 1987 report, (Boulder, Colo: Westview Press, 1987), p. 52.
46. WBDP, p. 60.
47. Wallach, *op. cit.* p. 198.
48. *Jerusalem Post*, 20 August 1980.
49. Smith, *op. cit.* p. 81.
50. *Ibid.* p. 81.
51. UND:A/35/425.
52. *New York Times*, 2 June 1987.
53. Smith, *op. cit.* p. 92.
54. *New York Times*, 1 May 1988.
55. WBDP, p. 17.
56. Dehter, p. iii. See also Benvenisti, 1987 report, *op. cit.* Smith, *op. cit.* pp. 125–6.
57. Aryeh Shalev, *The West Bank Line of Defense* (New York: Praeger, 1985), p. 59.
58. WBDP, p. 41.
59. Harkabi, *op. cit.* p. 120.
60. Grossman, *op. cit.* p. 209.
61. Schnall, *op. cit.* p. 144.
62. Smith, *op. cit.* p. 60.
63. KR, p. 59.
64. UND:A/32/P.V.47 (26 October 1977), pp. 46–8.
65. UNPRC, p. 8.
66. IDP (1981), doc. 19.
67. Grace Haskell, *Journey to Jerusalem* (New York: Macmillan, 1981), p. 42.
68. Michael Romann, *Jewish Kiryat Arba Versus Arab Hebron* (Jerusalem: West Bank Project, 1980), p. 10.
69. Halabi, *op. cit.* p. 149.
70. UND:A/AC 145/RT274, p. 5.
71. BBC:ME/5332/A10.
72. Halabi, *op. cit.* p. 152.

73. Romann, *op. cit.* p. 8; Halabi, *op. cit.* p. 153.
74. Halabi, *op. cit.* p. 157.
75. Smith, *op. cit.* p. 49; Wallach, *op. cit.* p. 30.
76. Halabi, *op. cit.* pp. 158–9.
77. BBC:ME/6412/A10.
78. BBC:ME/6412/A11.
79. Smith, *op. cit.* p. 81.
80. *Ha'aretz*, 27 March 1981.
81. Romann, *op. cit.* p. 49.
82. *Ibid.* p. 50.
83. Smith, *op. cit.* p. 161.
84. *Ibid.* p. 163.
85. *Ibid.* p. 57.
86. Shipler, *op. cit.* pp. 99–102.
87. KR, p. 12.
88. KR, p. 45.
89. KR, p. 46.
90. Smith, *op. cit.* p. 182.
91. Edward Witten, 'Attitudes of Israeli Economic Forces' in *Israeli Settlements in Occupied Territory* (Washington DC: Arab League, 1985), p. 210.
92. Amos Oz, *In the Land of Israel* (New York: Random House, 1984), p. 122.
93. WBDP, p. 64.

8. The Steadfast

1. UND:A/AC 145/RT446, p. 25.
2. Raja Shedieh, *Occupier's Law* (Washington DC: Institute of Palestine Studies, 1988), p. 228.
3. UND, A/AC/145/RT446, p. 21.
4. *Ibid.* p. 4.
5. UND:A/AC 145/RT441, p. 8.
6. *Ibid.* p. 5.
7. UND:A/AC 145/RT444, p. 9.
8. UND:A/AC 145/RT446, pp. 2–3.
9. FBIS-MEA, 31 January 1986, I4.
10. Shehdieh, *op.cit.* p. viii.
11. Schnall, *op. cit.* p. 128.

12. Binur, *op. cit.* p. 185.
13. UND:A/AC 145/RT441, p. 12.
14. *Ibid.* p. 13.
15. FBIS-NES-87-175, p. 16.
16. Binur, *op. cit.* p. 35.
17. *The Link*, vol. 19. no. 2 (May/June 1986).
18. Report cited in Shehdieh, *op. cit.* p. 150.
19. JPS (Winter 1989), p. 173; Shehdieh, *op. cit.* pp. 226–7.
20. Jamal K. Nasser (ed), *Intifada* (New York: Praeger, 1990), p. 46.
21. Bank of Israel Research Department, *Economic Development in Judea–Samaria and the Gaza District* (Jerusalem: Bank of Israel, 1986), p. 23; Nasser, *op. cit.* p. 74.
22. UND:A/AC 145/RT451, p. 2.
23. Nasser, *op. cit.* p. 74.
24. *Ibid.* p. 80.
25. UND:A/AC 145/RT453, pp. 6–14.
26. *Middle East Report*, January 1989; Nasser, *op. cit.* p. 176.
27. *Middle East Report*, January 1989.
28. FBIS, 2 December 1981, v, 16.
29. *Ha'aretz*, 13 December 1981.
30. FBIS, 7 June 1987, v
31. *Jerusalem Post*, 26 June 1987; Nasser, *op. cit.* p. 22.
32. Nasser, *op. cit.* p. 22.
33. Patrick White, *Let Us Be Free* (Clifton, New Jersey: Kingston Press, 1989), p. 52.
34. *Middle East International*, March/April 1989, p. 22.
35. FBIS, 31 August 1987, v, L3.
36. FBIS-NES-87-189.
37. Felicia Langer, *An Age of Stone* (London: Quartet Books, 1988), p. 162.

9. The Children's Crusade

1. *Yediot Ahronot*, 15 January 1988.
2. FBIS-NES-87-243.
3. BBC:ME/0033/1.
4. BBC:ME/0033/A.

5. For the statement of Karin White and Catriona Drew, see Case 2C in 'Israel and the occupied territories: excessive force', Amnesty International, London (August 1988); Anne Mooney (ed), *Children of the Stones* (issue paper 20), Arab-American Anti-Discrimination Committee, Washington DC (1989), pp. 38–46.

6. Mooney (ed), *op. cit.* p. 19.

7. UNA:A/AC 145/RT491.

8. FBIS-NES-87-092, p. 15; *Ibid.*, 87–251, p. 22; *Yediot Ahronot*, 25 December 1987, 15 January 1988; BBC: ME/0031/A6.

9. FBIS-NES-87-241, p. 27.

10. FBIS-NES-87-247, p. 4. On 13 December 1987 Arafat stated that the killing of four Gaza workers which touched off the *intifada* was 'a premeditated Israeli attack intended as a beginning for the ongoing massacre.' BBC:ME/0026/A12.

11. *Le Monde*, 15 January 1988. On 10 May 1988, the Voice of Palestine radio interviewed Arafat, who claimed 'the waves of the uprising began on 24 October 1986, when we asked our people in the occupied territories to act and demonstrate in support of their besieged brothers. Demonstrations erupted but never stopped after that.' FBIS-87-096, p. 96.

12. *Hadashot*, 5 February 1988.

13. FBIS-NES-87-247, p. 22.

14. FBIS-NES-88-011.

15. *Present Tense*, June 1988.

16. *New York Times*, 15 December 1987.

17. *New York Times*, 31 July 1987.

18. JPS (Spring 1988), p. 42.

19. *Le Monde*, 16 January 1988.

20. Wallach, *op. cit.* p. 170.

21. *Jerusalem Post*, 8 September 1988.

22. *Harpers*, July 1988.

23. JPS (Spring 1988), pp. 16–18.

24. *Hadashot*, 12 February 1988; Ehud Ya'ari in *Atlantic Monthly* (June 1988); JPS (Spring 1988).

25. *Hadashot*, 17 February 1988.

26. *Ibid.*
27. *Ibid.*
28. *Harpers*, July 1988.
29. Zachary Lockmann (ed), *Intifada* (Boston Mass: South End Press, 1989), Communique no. 1, pp. 328–9.
30. FBIS-NES-88-001, 4 January 1988.
31. *Safir*, 8 February 1988.
32. For the fourteen-point programme, see Don Peretz, *Intifada* (Boulder, Colo: Westview Press, 1990), Appendix 3. On Siniora's detention, see *Guardian*, 19 January 1988; Wallach, *op. cit.* p. 171, and his interview with *Yediot Ahronot* (Leshabat supplement), 15 January 1988.
33. Friedman, *op. cit.* p. 378.
34. *Ibid.* p. 387.
35. *Jerusalem Post*, 25 December 1987; see also the survey in *Middle East Journal* (Winter 1988).
36. Friedman, *op. cit.* p. 384.
37. 'We will use firearms when the time is ripe'. FBIS-NES-88-026, 5 February 1988. 'The time for weapons is not yet come . . . another stage comes but I will not talk about it.' FBIS-NES-88, pp. 5–6, 10 May 1988.
38. *Yediot Ahronot*, 15 January 1988; FBIS-NES-88-011; *Jerusalem Post*, 12 May 1988.
39. *Hadashot*, 2 March 1988.
40. *Jerusalem Post*, 24 February 1988.
41. FBIS-NES-88-042, p. 34.
42. Friedman, *op. cit.* p. 435.
43. *Ibid.* p. 431.
44. BBC:ME/0097/A9.
45. *Yediot Ahronot*, 22 March 1988.
46. BBC:ME/0115/i.
47. Peretz, *op. cit.* p. 146. In his book, Sharon does not mention any discrimination against Israeli Arabs but claims, 'Arab citizens pay a disproportional share of taxes. Many Arab builders by and large are allowed to ignore the codes that govern everyone else. Minor fees (television and radio for example) are not enforced on Arab homes as they are on Jewish homes.' Sharon, *op. cit.* p. 544.

48. *New York Times*, 18 June 1989.
49. FBIS-NES-88-050, p. 46.
50. *New York Times*, 29 May 1988.
51. FBIS-NES-88-068, p. 21.
52. FBIS-NES-067, p. 25.
53. *New York Times*, 9 April 1988;
54. *New York Times*, 23 August 1988; Zachary Lockmann, *op. cit.* pp. 81–96.
55. BBC:ME/0132/A6.
56. FBIS-NES-88-096, p. 3.
57. Paul Findlay, *They Dared to Speak Out* (Westport, Conn: Lawrence Hill & Co., 1985), p. 265.
58. *Nation*, 12 December 1988; JPS (June 1988), p. 102.
59. Peretz, *op. cit.* pp. 137–8.
60. Mahatma Gandhi, *My Non-Violence* (New Delhi: 1943), p. 70.
61. FBIS-NES-88-089, p. 29.
62. FBIS-NES-88-102, p. 18.
63. *New York Times*, 15 June 1988.
64. *Hadashot*, 9 June 1988. On Ketziot, see also *Koteret Rashit*, 20 April 1988; *Al-Hamishmar*, 29 March 1988; *New York Times*, 3 June 1988.
65. *New York Times*, 18 August 1988; FBIS-NES-88-142, p. 28.
66. *Jerusalem Post*, 22 February 1988.
67. FBIS-NES-88-159, p. 22.
68. UND:A/AC 145/RT501, p. 1.
69. UND:A/AC 145/RT491, p. 4.
70. *New York Times*, 9 May 1988.
71. FBIS-NES-88-147, p. 39.
72. Ze'ev Schiff & Ehud Ya'ari, *Intifada* (New York: Simon & Schuster, 1989), p. 271.
73. Peretz, *op. cit.* p. 137.
74. *Jerusalem Post*, 7 May 1988.

10. A Stone's Throw Away

1. *The Nation*, 22 December 1988.
2. JPS (Autumn 1988), p. 274.

3. FBIS-NES-88-155, p. 6.
4. BBC:ME/0309/A2.
5. BBC:ME/0310/i.
6. *The Nation*, 22 December 1988.
7. Peretz, *op. cit.* Appendix 6, pp. 211–14.
8. BBC:ME/0311/A6.
9. BBC:ME/0310/i.
10. *New York Times*, 16 November 1988.
11. FBIS-NES-88-233, p. 6.
12. *New York Times*, 15 December 1988.
13. FBIS-NES-88-241, p. 4.
14. FBIS-NES-88-244, p. 33.
15. *Der Spiegel*, 26 December 1988.
16. *Ha'aretz*, 20 December 1988.
17. *Tikkun*, March/April 1988.
18. *Ha'aretz*, 20 December 1988.
19. *New York Times*, 19 April 1988.
20. FBIS-NES-90-059, p. 2.
21. JPS (Winter 1990), p. 162.
22. *Jewish World*, 18 August 1989.
23. *New York Times*, 15 May 1988.
24. BBC:ME/0099/A13.
25. *Le Monde*, 15 January 1988.
26. Friedman, *op. cit.* p. 413.
27. *Ha'aretz*, 21 February 1990.
28. FBIS-NES-048, p. 4.
29. *Ha'aretz*, 11 March 1988.
30. BBC:ME/0125/A8.
31. *Jewish Week*, 9 March 1990.
32. Peretz, *op. cit.* p. 153.
33. *New York Times*, 24 February 1990.
34. *New York Times*, 6 March 1990.
35. *New York Times*, 29 April 1990.
36. FBIS-NES-90-098, p. 15.
37. *Jewish Press*, 9 June 1990.
38. FBIS-NES-90-098, pp. 16–17.
39. FBIS-NES-90-105, p. 20.
40. FBIS-NES-90-107, p. 5.
41. FBIS-NES-90-117, p. 1.

42. *New York Times Magazine*, 8 July 1990.
43. *Jewish Week*, 4 May 1990.
44. *New York Times*, 21 June 1990.

The Saddam Mirage

1. FBIS-NES-90-156
2. 12 August 1990.
3. FBIS-NES-90-160; *Jewish Week*, 24 August 1990.
4. *Jewish Week*, 28 September 1990.
5. *New York Times*, 2 September 1990; *Jewish Week*, 28 September 1990.
6. *New York Times* 27 October 1990.
7. *Village Voice*, 13 November 1990.
8. *New York Times*, 19 July 1991.
9. Jewish Week, 20 November 1990.
10. BBC:ME/6025/A2.
11. FBIS-NES-90-008.
12. FBIS-NES-90-153.
13. *New Republic*, 11 February 1991.
14. *Time*, 11 March 1991.
15. *New York Times Magazine*, 21 July 1991.
16. *Ibid*.
17. *New York Times*, 23 August 1991.
18. *Jewish Press*, 10 May 1991.
19. Fbis-Nes-90-127.

INDEX

337

INDEX

guerrilla attacks and Israeli response to, 33, 103
and Palestinian state, 112–3, 114–5, 119, 120
Fisch, Harold, 177
Fourth Geneva Convention and civilians, 38, 74, 85, 180, 191–4, 266
France, and Israeli plans, 1956, 34
Freij, Mayor Elias, 127, 139, 145, 224
Friedman, Thomas, 119, 247, 248, 250, 282, 284
Front for the Palestinian Popular Struggle, 122

Gahal bloc, 45
Gahelet group, 15, 17
Galili, Yisrael, 38, 47, 49
Gandhi, Mahatma, 263
Gavish, Major General Yeshayahu, 93
Gaza city, 26, 31, 35, 61, 62, 90, 136
Gaza Strip, 8-9, 26–7, 49, 51, 58, 61, 65, 128, 132, 142, 151, 157, 212, 269, 294
  annexation question, 89, 90
  economic situation, 26, 27, 31–2, 61, 67–8, 70, 90, 98
  Egyptian occupation, 18, 26, 27, 32
  enforced emigration, 36–7, 84–89, 96, 224
  intifadah in, 10, 228–4, 243, 284-5
  Israeli occupation, 10, 11, 29-31, 35, 36, 48, 73, 81, 82–99
  Palestinian resistance forces in, 86, 90
  refugees, 27-30, 35–6
  terrorism in, 1970-71, 91–7, 151
  university, 215–17
  unrest in, 219–20, 222, 225, 236, 239, 241
Gazit, General Shlomo, 77
Geaney, A.L., 82, 83, 84
Geneva Conference, 1973, 132, 133, 136, 137–38
Gershon, Dr Ben-Zion, and daughter, 194
Giap, Vo Nguyen, 90
Glass, Leslie, 51
Golan Heights, 17, 48, 51, 61, 65, 78, 79, 133
Gorbachev, Mikhail, 241, 289, 291
Goren, Samuel, 293
Goren, Chief Rabb Shlomo, 55, 135
Grand Mufti of Jerusalem, 19, 20, 24, 26
Great Britain, 18, 20, 26, 34, 58
  mandate period, 18-19, 27, 55, 56, 157, 182
Greater Israel concept, *see* Eretz Yisrael
'Greater Syria' concept, 20

Gromyko, Andrei, 136
Gross, Aahron, 197
Gubser, Peter, 304
guerrilla warfare, 90, 91, 103
  see also terrorist activity
Gur, General Mordecai, 87
Gush Emunim, 11, 17, 63, 163, 170, 172–77 *passim*, 179, 181, 185, 190, 192–197 *passim*, 200, 202–3

  expansionist vision of, 177–78, 201, 218, 221, 222, 237, 257, 286, 287
Gushing, Nils-Goran, 44, 46

Habash, George, 91, 103, 108, 114, 115, 119–22 *passim*, 128, 244, 273, 270, 275, 277, 279

Hadassah House, Hebron, 7, 194–5, 196, 197
Hadya, Rabbi O., 173
Haetzni, Elijahim, 174, 177
Halabi, Rafik, 195, 196
HAMAS, Islamic Resistance Movement, 218-19, 241, 242–3, 245, 297
Hamdi, Gaza refugee, 29
Hammami, Said, 123–4
Haram esh-Sharif, 53–6 *passim*, 125
Harel, Yisrael, 237
Harkabi, General Yehoshafat, 121, 189
Hassan, Khaled al-, 33
Haushofer, Karl, 130
Hawatmeh, Nayif, 107, 116–17, 118, 119–20, 244, 273
health services, 192–4
Hebron, 6-7, 16, 17, 22, 24, 27, 37, 101, 129, 131, 156–60 *passim*, 163, 164, 167, 168, 170–1, 172, 192, 201, 222
  Jewish settlements in 38, 77–8, 193–4
  1929 massacre in, 18
  1976 and 1980s unrest in, 125, 126, 193–4, 197–199
Herut party, 223
Herzog, President Chaim, 292, 301
Hess, Rabbi Yisrael, 174
Histradut, 65, 204
Holev, Amos, 34
Horowitz, Yigal, 144
Howe, Irving, 262
human rights violations, 75–6, 80, 210–12, 230, 266–68
Humbert, Dr Nago, 268
Husa, Tawfiq Aber, 249
Hussein, King, 21, 25, 26, 27, 33, 49, 50, 54, 60, 97, 99, 152, 156, 158, 159, 179, 209
  federation plan, 103–5

339

INDEX

INDEX

INDEX